From Colonization to Democracy

From Colonization
to Democracy

*A New Historical Geography
of South Africa*

Alan Lester

I.B. Tauris *Publishers*
LONDON • NEW YORK

For my parents, Brian and Patricia Lester

Paperback edition published in 1998 by I.B. Tauris & Co Ltd
Victoria House, Bloomsbury Square, London WC1B 4DZ
175 Fifth Avenue, New York NY 10010

In the United States and Canada distributed by St. Martin's Press
175 Fifth Avenue, New York NY 10010

First published in 1996 by Tauris Academic Studies
an imprint of I.B. Tauris & Co Ltd

ISBN 1 86064 176 8

A full CIP record for this book is available from the British Library
A full CIP record for this book is available from the Library of Congress

Library of Congress catalog card: available

Typeset in Monotype Ehrhardt by Ewan Smith, London
Printed and bound in Great Britain by WBC Ltd, Bridgend

Contents

Figures

vi

Foreword

Rapid change creates problems as well as opportunities for scholars specializing in particular parts of the world. The opportunities are fairly obvious, including the ability to monitor developments from a position of advantage with respect to background knowledge and sources of data, and the challenge of interpreting events for both popular and academic audiences. The problems begin with establishing priorities, at a time when so much needs to be done. Looking into the future, trying to plot the trajectory of change, is enticing but hazardous, today's predictions easily being overtaken by the unexpected. Describing the present risks gives the permanence of print to the possibly transient features of a state of flux. Going back into the past may appear a little unworldly, rather like a retreat from the demands of both present and future.

However, the need for historical geography is never more urgent than in times of change. It is a truism to say that the present is a product of the past, but it is all too easy for those caught up in the excitement of transition to overlook the importance of those years that built up to the crucial moment. Apartheid was never a rigid, inflexible strategy, and the adaptations (or 'reforms') provoked by internal contradictions and new circumstances were part of what contributed to the project's eventual demise. Furthermore, the extent to which the inherited human geography acts as a constraint on the creation of a new society needs to be grasped, not least by those advocating or expecting dramatic transformations on the ground. For example, the built form of the apartheid city, with its racial group areas, highly differentiated housing stock and uneven service infrastructure, will take decades to overlay, just as the distinctive urban forms guided by egalitarianism under Soviet and Eastern European socialism will not rapidly come to resemble the cities of capitalism.

Alan Lester's book is therefore timely. While there are other volumes, by both geographers and historians, which provide background relevant to understanding the present period of change, this book offers a unique blend of insights from a disciplinary interface. There can, of course, be no claim to a definitive account. The past may be as fiercely contested as the present, especially in circumstances where the voices of the majority have been effectively silenced. It is not simply that a particular, partial and sanitized version of history has been written and disseminated by people of European origin. It is also that for some time South African historiography has involved conflict between the two major European intellectual traditions of liberalism and Marxism. Growing understanding of the interplay of race and class has posed challenges for both schools, stimulating refinements with a theoretical significance beyond the specifics of South Africa itself. More recently the diversity of perspectives has been broadened further by the insights of postcolonialism, with its stress on culture in the context of the construction, representation and politics of identity. Much of the originality of Alan Lester's account is to be found in his recognition of the significance of postcolonial perspectives, in the ground between what he sees as the converging positions of liberals and Marxists.

Having had the opportunity to read the first draft of Alan Lester's manuscript some time ago, I am pleased to see the final version in print. Not being his kind of regional specialist, and relying very much on the work of others in my own attempt to understand South Africa, I know how useful this book will be to those in a number of disciplines seeking background in critical historical geography. In his Introduction, Alan Lester suggests that the central geographical and psychological project of segregation and apartheid was 'simultaneously to incorporate the materiality of Africa while excluding its human essence'. Such a cleavage was exemplified by the migrant labour system, whereby an attempt was made to incorporate the physical capacity to labour without its human embodiment in the form of individual aspirations and rights. This account is a step towards the incorporation of a broader and more African human experience in the contested terrain of South African historical geography.

David M. Smith
Queen Mary and Westfield College
University of London

Introduction

The ambitious purpose of this book is to provide an explanation for the evolution of contemporary South African society and its spatial configuration. This explanation cannot be attempted without tracing the course of social and ideological formation and adaptation in South Africa over at least the last three and a half centuries, and it can only be considered if the intersections between the disciplines of history, economics, political science, anthropology, sociology and geography provide the particular focus of the study. However, within the discourse of each of these disciplines, as well as between them, there are conflicting interpretations, not just of events and medium-term processes, but of the structural conditions underlying and shaping the course of South Africa's social development.

The different conceptions ultimately boil down to varying perceptions of the motivations of the actors involved in social change, and of the way societies in general operate. This introduction is devoted largely to an analysis of what, from the 1960s to the 1980s, were two particularly divergent scholarly tendencies (although the delineating characteristics of the two schools have blurred more recently). An analysis of the traditional cleavage of interpretation between Marxists (or 'radicals', a wider term) and liberals should not only allow the author's own interpretative tendencies to become clear early on, but should also help to clarify the contribution of current research into cultural representations of the 'other' and the politics of difference. To some extent, this contemporary research has been driven by the need to 'fill the gap' between orthodox Marxist and liberal accounts like those reviewed here. A genealogy of Marxist and liberal accounts of South Africa, then, allows a greater appreciation of the relevance of postmodern work.

The central issue, around which academic conflict between liberals and Marxists revolved, is that of the relationship between capitalism as a mode of production and apartheid's racial structures. 'Given that South African economic development was profoundly structured by racial labour policies, moulded by ideology and a violent racially

I

repressive socio-political environment, it is not surprising that the interplay between political and economic forces has received a great deal of academic attention' (Nattrass, 1991: 654).

Behind this 'academic attention' though, lay a more nuanced debate over the markers of social identity and the forms of self-conception which divide the individuals comprising society into groups. The lines delineating these groups are fluid, but in specific circumstances the polarization between social units, over certain issues, is discernible. Where Marxists have tended to find the crucial basis for social group formation in social relationships ultimately derived from the capitalist mode of production – in narrow terms, class – liberals have sought more diffuse parameters of group identity, based largely on ideological constructs – ethnicity, religion, nationality and culture. In recent years, proponents of both schools have recognized areas of weakness in their own accounts and interpretations which can be strengthened using insights borrowed from the other academic tendency.

Radicals traditionally focused on 'the enormous expansion which has taken place in the allegedly dysfunctional system, the continuity of the system of racial domination in the midst of economic expansion and the extensive involvement of property owners in the system of racial domination' (Johnston, cited Nattrass, 1991: 666). The underlying interpretation was that the state has supported economic growth and the interests of capitalists, primarily through two forms of apartheid intervention: labour domination and proletarianization of the black peasantry (Bundy, 1972). Racism has therefore been seen as 'rational' in the sense that it is an ideology which has legitimated the economic exploitation of black labour. South Africa has not the kind of capitalist economy in which the forces of demand and supply prevail, but a 'labour repressive economy' (Trapido, 1971), in which the accumulation of a white class, or white classes, is made possible by political machinery which represses blacks (Fisher et al., 1978).

The radical account is not confined to politico-economic relations between whites and blacks. O'Meara (1983) extended a class analysis into the field of intra-white politics with his study of Afrikaner nationalism. Its revival in the 1930s was, for him, not so much the (re)generation of an ideology, but an expression of emerging conflict between capitals. In common with Marxist accounts of wider South African politics, 'If a system could be shown to be functional to capitalism, then it was assumed that it must have arisen for those purposes' (Nattrass, 1991: 667).

Probably the clearest manifestation of capital's social-structuring role came with the mineral discoveries of the late nineteenth century. Legassick (1980) pointed out how the scale and purpose of racial relations, developed with industrialization at Kimberley, were quite a departure from South Africa's previous racial structures. Migrant labour flows to the mines and confinement of workers in compounds allowed the acquisition and control of a large, cheap African labour force, and facilitated its separation from the small white working class. Capitalism had not just adapted to the pre-existing racial order, it had created a new one. Later, deep-level gold mining on the Witwatersrand required vast amounts of ultra-cheap labour to make any profit out of low-grade ore, particularly when the gold price was fixed. The economic importance of mining necessitated political structures supplying African labour from the reserves for temporary work in the mines.

Despite a lack of consensus within the radical 'camp' (see Magubane, 1989), during the 1970s in particular, a number of radical analysts were collaborating on, or, less evidently, mutually supporting similar interpretations of South Africa's historical development, hinging on the changing imperatives of capital.

One of the seminal works of the genre was a paper by Wolpe (1972) who argued that cheap African labour was reproduced, in the early stages of industrialization, by the pre-capitalist mode of production practised in the reserves. Industrialization itself paradoxically undermined this source of cheap labour as traditional communal and kinship modes of redistribution in the reserves broke down with the penetration of capitalist relations. For Wolpe, apartheid was quintessentially an attempt to maintain the pre-capitalist reserve economies and, therefore, cheap labour through more effective coercion and domination. 'Since the establishment of the Union in 1910 ... the state has been utilized at all times to secure and develop the capitalist mode of production' (Wolpe, 1972: 429). Apartheid was a state-led drive to maintain the rate of surplus value and accumulation in the face of a disintegrating pre-capitalist reserve economy, spurred on by the fact that disintegration was simultaneously feeding African urbanization and, therefore, political unrest. It was this threat in particular which brought the state's political power to bear alongside capital's economic power, in a mutual thrust to maintain and intensify segregation in the industrial era.

The flaws of such a reductionist account are now recognized by Wolpe himself, whose brand of Marxism is today more flexible (Wolpe, 1988). Apart from containing a romanticized view of African pre-capitalist economic relations, the 1972 account by-passes the integral role of the Afrikaner nationalist movement and its political successes within the white electorate, in the formulation of apartheid. In fact, it was a whole welter of complex political and social considerations, which convinced enough of the white electorate to vote for the

Nationalist Party (NP) for its policies to be implemented after 1948, and which convinced the Afrikaner nationalist leaders that the laws forming apartheid were the best option for South Africa's future.

The role of Africans in the industrial economy was, however, highly significant in dictating their political position. 'The measures [the state] undertook to mobilize and control labour virtually precluded the possibility of extending political rights to Africans as a way of establishing some degree of legitimacy for the state' (Stadler, 1987: 34). But the relationship between capital and the state is not timeless, nor has the government's theory on the political treatment of Africans been constant. Historical specificity has been recognized as an imperative in more recent Marxist accounts. Hence Wolpe (1988: 8):

> The contention is that the formation of structures and relations is always the outcome of struggles between contending ... classes and that this outcome is Janus-faced, being always simultaneously functional and contradictory. Which pole of the relationship will be dominant depends on the historically specific conditions of the social formation ... the 'fit' or contradiction between capitalism and racism may be eroded or expanded within particular social and economic spheres and the outcome may be a shift towards increased functionality or sharpened contradiction resulting in either case in significantly altered conditions of struggle.

Yet these shifts towards functionality or contradiction are not precipitated by class struggles alone. Dynamism within the overall mode of production must be explained with reference to extra-class political and social developments. Interpretations must involve concepts of political constituency, nationalism, ethnicity and racism, as well as class, and allow a greater role for human agents' interaction with social structures.

Wolpe's identification of the need for historical specificity though, is part of a more general Marxian move away from structuralist assumptions that functionality is synonymous with purpose in political and economic relations. Marks and Rathbone (1982) place emphasis on local and empirical history, with theorization secondary. This gives rise to a 'more nuanced and empirically detailed materialist interpretation of South African social history' (Nattrass, 1991: 673). But such approaches are still scantily extended to post-1945 developments.

With the introduction of greater 'historical contingency' (Wolpe, 1988) into Marxian accounts, the gap between the liberal and Marxist interpretations of old narrowed. But even some modern Marxist accounts face the limitation of an ambiguous definition of class in the South African context. If class is deterministically taken to be defined by an economic relationship within the mode of production, then social group identity in South Africa has not been primarily based on class. If the ideologies on which liberals always focused – ethnicity, racism, etc. – are incorporated within one's definition of class, then class more accurately defines social group formation. But is such a usage of the word 'class' still Marxist or even Marxian? Have 'Marxists' in effect ceased to become Marxists by adapting definitions of class to South African conditions? Attempts have been made to trace ideologies back to a material root, so that, for instance, the ideology of racism, which cleaves South African society, can be represented as a superstructure, developed to legitimate the material relations which form the sub-structure of society (see Marks and Trapido, 1987b). But such accounts too often fell into the related traps of determinism and conspiracy theory.

The writers of an early Marxist account (Simons and Simons, 1969) would, according to Kuper (1971), argue that 'white and black workers perform the same function in the process of production, but that various factors obscure or inhibit or distort their perception of common interests and of the reality of class struggle' (Kuper, 1971: 281). Such factors include: racial and cultural diversities and national/racial cleavages; white workers' ability to be absorbed in the ruling elite; the effects of labour migration and discrimination on Africans; reactions of African and Coloured leaders to discriminatory policies, and the rabid racialism of white workers. Although these are words placed in the mouths of Marxists by a critic of theirs, admissions of a class approach's limitations must be made by any analyst, and far from being mere hindrances to a class-based conception of society, they mean, in Simons and Simons' own words, that 'the binary model of standard Marxist theory did not fit South Africa's multiple structure of colour, class and cultural groups' (Simons and Simons, 1983 edn: 210).

The problem encountered by Simons and Simons remained for some time.

> Marxists, like Marx himself, have had considerable difficulty in accom-modating ethnicity or other communal solidarities to the mainstream of their thought ... if ethnicity or communal identities cannot be causally reduced to, or derived from, the mode of production or class or the division of labour ... then Marxism's claims as an explanatory theory of society have to be scaled down. (Welsh, 1987: 189)

Marxian accounts have persuaded liberals that uneven capitalist accumulation and development can exacerbate conceptions of ethnicity and tension, but they have not shown how they are responsible for the initial formulation of group identity. 'Europeans expressed revulsion at Khoikhoi customs, language, dress and physical appearance' (Welsh,

1987: 191) well before South Africa's age of industrial capitalism. The additional linguistic moral connotations of 'light' and 'dark', 'white' and 'black', gave emphasis to these negative racial attitudes (Welsh, 1987). This survey of South African historical social formation argues that incorporations of groups into colonial society after the turn of the eighteenth century occurred in the light of a racial stratification first developed under the Dutch East India Company at the Cape. To suppose that 'racial categorisation was imposed by late nineteenth-century colonisation under conditions of industrial capitalism grossly underestimates continuity from the social structure of the early Cape colony' (Welsh, 1987: 193). The nineteenth-century industrialists who agitated for the precursors to modern forms of racial labour regulation 'were, after all, whites before they were capitalists and hence themselves embodiments of "ancient and venerable prejudices"' (Welsh, 1987: 197, quoting Marx's *Communist Manifesto*).

The ideological imperatives of a racially-conceived society continue, at times, to take precedence over materialism. For the nineteenth-century industrialist, the two were largely compatible, but 'whites continued to endorse apartheid in the 1987 election despite nearly three years of severe economic malaise and widespread recognition among the electorate that this situation was substantially due to apartheid' (Giliomee and Schlemmer, 1989). Materialism alone does not suffice as the motive force in South African social formation, and capital alone has not been the shaper of state racial policy. That policy has meandered, pushed one way and pulled another by white con-stituencies, defined ethnically as well as by class; by the process of political electioneering only indirectly related to class, and by the political as well as economic effect of black, rather than working-class, resistance. Group identity, I would suggest, has been forged as much by psychological conceptions of difference, based on appearance, custom and differential access to power (see below pp. 33–4), as by articulation with the mode of production. The group interaction com-prising South Africa's social development then, extends beyond the scope of deterministic material accounts.

Contrary to radical thinking, classic liberal accounts, such as that of De Kiewiet (1957) held that racial structures, far from enabling economically rational labour exploitation, actually precluded its most efficient use. De Kiewiet emphasized the retention of African labour on farms, when it would have been more productive in the growing urban manufacturing sector; its constrained mobility, and the fact that its market value was not recognized in its wages. If capitalist market forces alone had dictated its use, racial and social integration would have been facilitated. Apartheid was therefore not a boon to economic efficiency.

According to such early liberal authors, pre-existing social relations determined South Africa's racial order, rather than the relations forged during the industrial period (De Kiewiet, 1957; Macmillan, 1930). But 'we cannot explain the exclusion of the workforce from political rights [in the late twentieth century] as a consequence of such pre-existing social and political structures' (Stadler, 1987: 35) alone. For instance, the reversal of the Cape franchise in South Africa's industrial era represented a discontinuity, undermining a previously more favourable black political position, rather than a continuation of pre-industrial historical progression.

Most liberals today would recognize that South Africa's industrialization was highly significant in adapting and transforming racial structures, much along the lines drawn by radicals. Nevertheless, one can temper the more sweeping statements in favour of continuity. While 'it was the mining industry and particularly gold mining which rapidly and profoundly transformed the social and political structures of colonial South Africa' (Stadler, 1987), the migrant-labour and influx-control patterns that the industry established were still superimposed on a pre-existing social stratification based on race and manifested spatially in the mosaic of African polities and 'white space'. A realization of the really significant influence that mining capital had over the state in the formative period of South Africa's industrial society, should be blended with an appreciation of historical inertia.

This account suggests that the imperatives of modernizing and progressive capital for economic stability, greater skills in the workplace and expanding domestic markets, have been a strong force behind recent reforms leading to the abandonment of apartheid. Indeed, 'it should be evident that the main axis of social change since the 1980s has been the replacement of the political and ideological mechanisms of apartheid with market relations' (Lupton, 1992: 95). But this is not to say that Marxists have been correct all along in finding the motivation for government action in the interests of capital alone. For the government, the economy was important more for the preservation of its racially defined and multi-class, white political constituency's living standards, than for the maintenance of a narrower, capitalist class's accumulation (see Chapter 8 on relations between the South African state and society).

This is also not to say that the deterministically liberal O'Dowd thesis is correct. O'Dowd (1974, 1978) saw capital growth in itself as overcoming apartheid through racial economic integration. Blumer puts the argument thus: 'social mobility upsets the established structure of status positions ... weakening established systems of authority and breaking down established systems of social control' (Blumer, 1965:

226). Such social mobility is a necessary component of the development of integrative capitalism. However, this view fails to square with the fact that it was the prospect of continued poor economic growth which pushed the government towards the abandonment of legal racial structures, not the presence of current economic growth. Additionally, capitalists alone did not have the power, even if they had the motivation, to remove apartheid.

Just as Marxists have had to incorporate liberal emphases on ideology and other non-material motivations in their work, liberals have realized the explanatory value of class differentiation, particularly within white politics. Influence over the state can be seen as the prize contested through the twentieth century by classes within white society. At a generalized level, white farmers and workers, including miners, have sought to retain African influx controls and job colour bars, while industrialists and mineowners have, with varying degrees of energy, sought to undermine them. General elections have ensured that, at certain times, the state has disproportionately served the interests of one or more of these classes. While it was not always capital that had the ear of government, class differentiation can help define which group did.

Conceptions of identity

The traditional debate between Marxists and liberals over the course of South African social development hinges fundamentally on the parameters of self-conception. If individuals define their identity primarily according to their economic relationships within the mode of production, then they will form groups based on class, and history will be shaped by the interaction between classes. If, as most Marxists themselves would agree, the parameters of identity are more diffuse and ambiguous, the principles of group formation may shift more easily over time, and social behaviour be comprised of a more complex web of interactions. An analysis of South Africa restricted to class relationships is not satisfactory since

> that conceptualization is disproportionately the propensity of educated elites. The participants, especially those at the lower levels, also entertain other ideas, some of which are at odds with this conceptualization of the conflict ... the conflict cannot be reduced to what some of its more organized and articulate participants think it is about. (Horowitz, 1991: 31)

Simons and Simons' (1969) Marxist account postulated two main possibilities for white worker mobilization. The first was organization along class lines with African and Coloured members of the working class, to attain higher living standards in relation to capitalist classes and, if possible, seize the state from them. The second was to join the capitalist class in a racial alliance against blacks. This option entailed an attachment to the white state, to attain privilege based on race rather than a furtherance of the class struggle. The white mineworkers' strike of 1922 demonstrated that these workers had emphatically opted for racial superiority rather than class solidarity. Thus Simons and Simons were forced to recognize that in South Africa, society was primarily organized along racial lines, with class divisions being secondary.

For Schlemmer, Stack and Berkow (1991), it is not race as such which defines the dominant cleavages, but culture. Questionnaires revealed that white concerns 'are precisely those associated with the maintenance of a "European lifestyle" in a pervasive cultural, not necessarily racial sense. It is about standards, daily security, privacy and control over the influences to which children are exposed' (Schlemmer et al., 1991: 172). Historically, 'whites have been a sub-society in Africa, living by most of the rules and standards of a modernising Europe' (Schlemmer et al., 1991: 171). Coetzee, in White Writing (1988), exposes traits in white literary activity which indicate a similar conclusion.

While, on a global scale, Hobsbawm identifies the mid-nineteenth century as formative in capitalism's shaping of world society, as representing 'the florescence of a classical, competitive, entrepreneurial regime of capital accumulation and social regulation' (Hobsbawm, quoted in Soja, 1989: 27) in South Africa, the same period saw the unstable interaction between divergent cultures and physically different groups in, and beyond the north-eastern frontier of, the Cape Colony. While penetrative imperial capitalism may have been shaping social interaction on a global scale, the attempts of colonial administrators to stabilize relationships between divergent racial and cultural groups overshadowed interactions between classes in South Africa's social body. When, later in the nineteenth century, capital began to exert its socially forming influence in South Africa, African incorporation in the colonial capitalist economy was already circumscribed by race. Even with the growth of a modern capitalist economy, which to some extent penetrates across most of South Africa, race and culture, rather than class, have been the most significant markers of social status and identity, and the dominant basis of South Africa's social structure.

Recent 'postcolonial' work has emphasized the extent to which cultural identities, of both colonizer and colonized, were moulded across the globe by the process of colonization itself. At this point, a brief introduction to some of this diffuse body of work's insights on colonial 'contact' will serve. Further insights will be elaborated at appropriate points in the text.

Said (1978, 1993) has attempted to demonstrate how Western identities were shaped by imperialism. Overseas involvement was not simply an adjunct to Western politics, economics and culture; it was actually partially constitutive of British and French (and now American) identity. An imperial outlook ontologically premised on the right to intervene, in order to shape the wider world, partly defined self-conception within these countries. But identities within the colonized portions of the world – both of settlers and indigenous peoples – were also, simultaneously, forged through the process of colonization and resistance to it.

Conceptions of space were a vital part of this multifaceted and often contradictory colonizing 'project':

> One important concern of postcolonialism, though by no means the only one, is an attempt to bring into focus the dispossession that the West visited upon colonial societies through a series of intrinsically *spatial strategies*. ... As Said makes very clear, it is impossible to conceive of colonialism or imperialism 'without important philosophical and imaginative processes at work in the production as well as the acquisition, subordination and settlement of space'. (Gregory, 1994: 218, quoting Said, 1989: 218 – original emphasis)

By conceptually colonizing the foreign landscape – by mentally construing the possibilities of its future uses and by renaming its features in European terms – even early white settlers overseas were presupposing and prefiguring the conquest of those landscapes and of their inhabitants. Further, by fitting indigenous peoples into their view of a world order and into their categories within which things exist, colonizers were already dispossessing those peoples of their accustomed independence:

> The incorporation of non-European 'man' into the table, the taxonomy and the grid [the frameworks of European classification] effectively prised non-European people away from the land which they inhabited, and once they had been *textually* removed from the landscape, it was easier to do so physically [and morally] as well. (Gregory, 1994: 30)

In South Africa, as elsewhere, colonial interaction, violence and dispossession, was tremendously important in the shaping of cultural, and therefore political, identity. However, even with the rejection of class and the elevation of cultural identity as the fundamental basis of South African social organization, a wider materialist motivation can still be ascribed to social formation along cultural, racial or ethnic lines:

Ethno-nationalism usually wins when it competes with class mobilization. However, this empirical observation in the ethnic relations literature always derives from a case of a threatened working class or a downwardly mobile petty bourgeoisie that compensates for denied aspirations with symbolic status. It has yet to be proven anywhere that a BMW-owning bureaucratic bourgeoisie with swimming pools and servants readily sacrifices the good life for psychologically gratifying ethnic affinities. Racial sovereignty proves durable only as long as it can deliver. A bureaucratic oligarchy can be expected to drop its 'albatross' when racialism becomes dysfunctional. (Adam, 1990: 236)

For most whites, identification with the economically and politically dominant racial group has proved more 'functional' than identification along the lines of cross-racial class. For Africans, a different prospect has been held out. The 1980s saw increasing class divisions within African society as apartheid's constraints on upward economic and social mobility began to be removed. In a post-apartheid South Africa, urban 'insiders' may well come to share more characteristics and aspirations with the white urban bourgeoisie than with rural 'outsider' Africans. Within the cities, increasing polarities between the African bourgeoisie and the African working class are to be expected as the levelling devices of apartheid recede into the past. The general perception in the modern literature, then, is that class divisions may be encroaching more on racial ones as the prime cleavages of identity in South African society, but such a hypothesis can only be proffered tentatively in the face of present, ingrained realities of racial stratification.

Convergence of interpretation

Neo-Marxist and liberal interpretations of South African society were more readily apparent as distinct tendencies in the 1970s and 1980s than they are today. Each tendency has, to an extent, undergone a progressive modification, absorbing the lessons proffered by emphases of the other. While 'rival theories ... can't be compared against an objective scale ... they are simply incommensurable, with the result that their exponents may be said to be living and working in different worlds' (Kuhn, 1970: 134–5), there has been a convergence of interpretations to the extent that, in the South African context, these 'worlds' overlap, even though each retains an additional discrete portion.

In the early 1970s, both schools lacked a historical grounding in the relationship between white supremacy and economy: liberals had glossed over it while radicals 'tended to argue from theory or from scraps of historical evidence and did no original historical research' (Saunders, 1988b: 23). Now analysts from both tendencies would broadly agree that segregationist policies aided the growth of white farming and mining sectors in the early phases of industrialization by supplying cheap and immobile labour, and that these white sectors were divided after 1910, with mineowners seeking to retain the reserves for migrants and agricultural capital largely pressing for the disintegration of the reserves so as to corral African labour on white farms. The racial system which gave mineowners reserves, it is also generally conceded, imposed the counteracting cost of a job colour bar on this same 'fraction' of capital.

Radicals would, by and large, accept that the evolution of the racial system in South Africa, while functional in many respects for white capitals, did not necessarily progress purposefully for their gratification, but for more complex reasons. Even the government of the day's interest in economic growth could not be confined to a response to the imperatives of capital *per se*.

Interpretations of the migrant labour system have also served to undermine the perception that capital's imperatives alone shape social formation. Labour migrated on a fairly large scale well before diamond discoveries gave organized, modern capital a formative role (see Harries, 1982). Migration 'was to some extent a deliberate form of African resistance to full proletarianization' (Saunders, 1988b: 25). Even some mineowners resented the expense of training migrants, and the disruption to supplies which was threatened by unsettled labour.

For both radicals and liberals, 'segregation is now seen not simply as something imposed from above, the product of what white capital, white labour or a white government wanted, but as shaped significantly by what happened on the ground' (Saunders, 1988b: 29). The emphasis of modern radicals on unintended consequences, rather than Machiavellian functionality, forms 'a point of contact between the latest Marxist empirical scholarship and liberal historiography' (Elphick, 1987: 168; see also Harries, 1982). With radicals interweaving in their accounts the Marxist 'story' of capital accumulation with parallel stories of the state, of moral, ethnic and religious communities, of natural environmental processes and of the individual, the common ground between the two schools has been consolidated. Over the last few years, writing in a post-apartheid context has allowed further refinements. With less of an imperative to state their anti-apartheid credentials, more analysts have moved away from totalizing accounts based on the dualism between white oppressors and black oppressed (see for instance, Robinson, 1996). Most analysts should now agree that 'what is needed is a dynamic approach that reifies neither ethnicity, race, nor class, but recognizes the situational salience of each' (Welsh, 1987: 202). Spivak, discussing the wider role of the human subject in history, argues much the same thing:

> That which seems to operate as a subject may be part of an immense discontinuous network ... of strands that may be termed politics, ideology, economics, history, sexuality, language and so on. (Each of these strands, if they are isolated, can also be seen as woven of many strands.) Different knottings and configurations of these strands, determined by heterogeneous determinations which are themselves dependent upon myriad circumstances, produce the effect of an operating subject. (Spivak, 1988: 341)

Gregory elaborates: 'In other words, the subject is constituted at the intersection of multiple and competing discourses' (Gregory, 1994: 188). Such a conception moves us closer to Said's favoured outcome for the analyst: 'the task for the critical scholar is not to separate one struggle from another, but to connect them, despite the contrast between the overpowering materiality [on the one hand] and the apparent other-worldly refinements [of ideological meaning on the other]' (Said, 1995: 3).

Some recent postcolonial work can be interpreted as playing such an integrative role between established Marxism and liberalism. Said's original, provocative study of Orientalism (Said, 1978) pointed out that scholars (both Marxist and liberal) had failed to realize the importance of the general dynamics of colonialism and imperialism in the formation of identity. By beginning to fill this gap in theoretical accounts of South African social formation, we can go some way towards bridging Marxist material and liberal ideological concerns. Postcolonial insights enable the identification of an alternative mechanism to that of Marxist materialism by which domination is achieved. That is, through the exercise of power through culture. For Young, 'colonial discourse analysis ... does more than make visible something which had previously been absent: it also challenges central categories and assumptions of mainstream Marxism' (1990: 174). This challenge admits the liberal emphasis on ideology, but represents ideology as but one, more apparent, and even crude, manifestation of much deeper cultural and psychological traits. Thus, according to Comaroff and Comaroff (1991: 15):

> The essence of colonization inheres less in political overrule than in seizing and transforming 'others' by the very act of conceptualizing, inscribing and interacting with them on terms not of their choosing; in making them into pliant objects and silenced subjects of our scripts and

scenarios; in assuming the capacity to represent them, the active verb itself conflating politics and poetics.

However, it must not be forgotten that the 'natives' in an early colonial situation were similarly 'possessing' (that is, incorporating within their pre-established scheme of things) the Europeans (Gregory, 1994). What shifted the balance of possession over time was increasing European force – the naked power to coerce. Following early 'contact situations', the colonies were only possessed, as Said puts it in the case of 'the Orient', 'because [they] *could* be – that is, submitted to being *made* [colonial]' (Said, 1978: 6 – original emphasis). It was because European settlers became more materially powerful that they were able to construct, on their own terms, an image of their colonies (an image that was, of course, also shaped by the nature of resistance). In proposing such an overarching scheme, postcolonialism retains its faith in a grand narrative – an adherence rejected by the postmodernist movement to which postcolonialism is related (see Said, 1995) – but it is 'important not to allow this to obscure the heterogeneity and uncertainty of the process ... colonialism took characteristic, even hegemonic forms, but ... Colonial projects were shaped by the diverse and dependent settings in which and through which they worked' (Gregory, 1994: 169).

Certainly as the balance of power shifted in favour of settlers within the British African colonies of the nineteenth century, and as African domination became easier, so African status in white eyes diminished (Curtin, 1964). Domination bred contempt. While Africans had remained outside the arena of direct white control, like other subsequently colonized peoples, a romantic impression of their pastoral, idyllic existence could still be contemplated alongside more derogatory prevailing notions (see the next chapter). But, ironically, the essence of this pastoral innocence was corrupted in the European conception once the African was brought within the expanding white cultural and economic ambit, that is, once 'he' was dispossessed. By remaining independent, the African can still be accorded dignity, but by serving the material needs of whites, that dignity is lost and the African is degraded in white eyes – see Wade (1993) for an account of the transition in English-speaking South African writing. This, perhaps, was the central geographical and psychological project of segregation and apartheid – simultaneously to incorporate the materiality of Africa while excluding its human essence. Such, anyway, is the interpretive backdrop to the following narrative of South Africa's social group formation.

I

The Foundation of
a Society

Introduction

In 1652 a settlement was established by Dutch officials at the Cape of southern Africa. The society which developed from this settlement, extending into the interior of the country, was an offshoot from the era of European discovery, description and mercantilist expansion overseas. Just as this era profoundly shaped current global relations, so its South African branch catalysed social developments that presaged modern South Africa.

The period between 1652 and the late eighteenth century has been seen as formative for South African social development in two main respects. On the one hand, white ideologies supportive of racial exclusivity and economic relations founded upon racial stratification developed; on the other hand, and more contentiously, a nascent sense of Afrikaner nationalism has been held to have emerged on the early colony's frontier. It is argued here (with important qualifications) that the material and attitudinal relations between people of different pigmentation in the early colony as a whole, and not just on the frontier, were indeed portentous, but that the emergence of a distinct Afrikaans identity must be placed later in South Africa's history. Before these issues are addressed in more detail, it is helpful if one is familiar with an outline history of early white settlement in South Africa.

A brief history of the early colony

Officials of the Dutch East India Company (Vereenigde Nederlandsche Ge-Octroyeerde Oost Indische Compagnie, or VOC) established a small settlement at the Cape in 1652 to provide refreshment and supplies to scurvy-ridden ships on their voyages around the southern tip of Africa *en route* to the Far East. The subsequent performance of the station was not spectacular. It made a loss throughout the 143 years of its existence (Ross, 1989). The VOC had a range of partial monopolies on trade, preventing personal transactions, particularly in meat, between colonists and visiting ships, and between colonists and the indigenous peoples of the Cape. But VOC officials were usually corrupt to the extent that they used their own positions to conduct just such a personal trade. These activities were to sow some of the seeds of future conflict with settlers, and they culminated in the dismissal of one governor, Willem Adriaan Van der Stel, in 1706.

The indigenous peoples, from whom the VOC intended to keep the colonists apart, are usually described as existing in two distinct categories – Khoikhoi (called Hottentots by the settlers) and San (called Bushmen). But for the white settlers, Khoikhoi and San were less easily differentiated than is commonly thought. While Khoikhoi were generally pastoralists with a strong sense of wider group identity and San were hunter-gatherers who operated in small bands, throughout the period introduced here conquered Khoikhoi, who became dispossessed of their livestock, would often fall back on hunting with San, and to an extent the groups merged (see Elphick and Malherbe, 1989; Crais, 1992). They were also of the same genetic stock, the Khoikhoi having emerged as a stronger physical type due to a milk-based diet following their adoption of pastoralism. White settlers, despite stereotyping the physical characteristics of the two peoples, often confused them. Hereafter, the word 'Khoisan' is therefore used to refer to both peoples when describing developments which affected them both similarly in the eighteenth and early nineteenth centuries.

The Cape was originally envisaged as being a self-contained settlement – a vision which turned out to be unrealistic since it lacked both the capital and, despite a significant slave presence, the labour, to develop agriculture intensively (Guelke, 1989). From 1657 the VOC allowed white farmers (freeburghers) to cultivate and trade on their own behalf while respecting the company's restrictions. The freeburghers were to concentrate on the less labour- and capital-intensive activities of livestock rearing and trading rather than wheat cultivation. In 1679 freeburghers, provided with slaves by the Company (many of whom were subsequently returned due to their continuing resistance), were allowed by the VOC to disperse and farm beyond the Cape Flats surrounding the station. By 1700 the core western Cape farmers were increasing the production of wine, wheat and livestock, and investing their surpluses in slaves and more land (Guelke, 1989), while 'trekboers', despite the presence of indigenous peoples (see below), were continuing to occupy grazing land further to the east. The settlers' individual economic success bolstered an emerging identity different from that of the VOC's employees (Katzen, 1982), but it was an identity distinguished by their permanent residence at the Cape, rather than by the kind of ethnic bonding between Afrikaans speakers that took place later in the nineteenth century.

Initially, relations between the small Dutch presence at the Cape and local Khoisan clans had been fairly amicable. Over the preceding century and a half, Khoisan had fought and killed Portuguese sailors who had stopped off at the Cape for supplies, when those sailors had attempted to take off Khoisan children or enforce unequal terms of trade in cattle, but the Dutch had been given express instructions to remain on friendly, if distant, terms with them. They even offered ceremonial sticks as rewards to co-operative Khoisan 'captains'. The first governor, Van Riebeeck, then, was able to secure some cattle (though, he feared, not enough) through negotiation with the indigenous peoples. However, the increasing European presence manifested by the freeburghers, and their drive to occupy Khoisan land and expropriate Khoisan cattle in greater numbers, brought more unequal relations. Direct conflict over the local resources of production resulted in power struggles which, ultimately, given European military technology, could only be resolved in the settlers' favour. Khoisan resistance was spirited and fierce enough to delay, but not to preclude, further larger-scale European conquest through the eighteenth century.

As land at the Cape became scarce and arable farming costs rose, white settlement was pushed inland, ostensibly under Company supervision, and dispossessed Khoisan moved north and east. It tended to be the less wealthy and the unattached settlers who pushed furthest inland, either off their own backs or in the service of others, but the basis of the white society emerging at the furthest limits of the colony was laid by subsistence farming families, with livestock but little capital, renting their new farms from the VOC. By the end of the seventeenth century the most extreme area of white settlement was about eighty kilometres inland from Cape Town. During the eighteenth century though, it shifted a further 800 kilometres east (Christopher, 1984).

Relatively dense Xhosa settlement was, meanwhile, well established along the southeast coast of southern Africa. While Bantu-speaking peoples, of which the various semi-autonomous Xhosa chiefdoms were a part, had been settled in what is now inland South Africa for over 1,500 years, the white vanguard only met the settled outlying Xhosa chiefdoms in around 1770, to form the Cape Colony's eastern frontier (Fig. 1). Already turbulent due to the arrival of dispossessed Khoisan from the colony and a power struggle within the Xhosa body politic (Crais, 1992 and Peires, 1981), the region was to remain chronically unstable for over a century. The frontier between white settler and Xhosa was never fixed in space or absolute in nature, and it was not

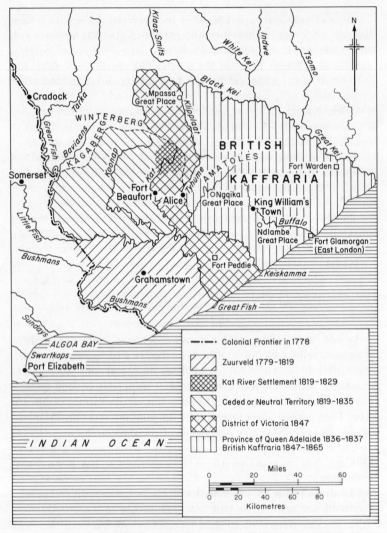

Figure 1 The eastern Cape frontier
(reproduced from R. Lubke, ed., *Field Guide to the Eastern Cape*,
Department of Botany, Rhodes University, 1988)

only a frontier between different cultures and 'modes of production'
(Marks and Atmore, 1980a), but an ecological frontier. The Xhosa had
been restrained from moving much further west by insufficient rainfall
for their mixed pastoral and arable economy. The formation of the
eastern Cape frontier, however, ultimately meant the closing of options

for those indigenous Cape Khoikhoi and San clans which had been involved, since the late seventeenth century, in guerrilla warfare with settlers over grazing lands, and which had not moved out of colonial reach to the Orange River in the north. The meeting of white and Xhosa settlement set the seal on their final subjection and dispossession within the colony.

A British force took the Cape in 1795 and kept it until the Batavian Republic was established in the Netherlands. In 1803 it was handed back to the Dutch by the Treaty of Amiens, only to be repossessed by the British in 1806, with the expectation of an ordered and prosperous colony. But the eastern frontier zone was only really incorporated into the Cape colonial system from the turn of the nineteenth century, with a deliberate extension of British rule. In a less tangible way the beginnings of industrial capitalism, rather than the previously limited mercantile capitalism in nineteenth-century Europe, helped narrow the gulf between the externally trading Cape and the remote interior (Legassick, 1989).

Social structures and racial conceptions in the Cape

In the early western Cape Colony, a coincidence of status and pigmentation was reinforced by VOC policy. Inter-racial marriages, which would have blurred the coinciding lines of colour and status, were prohibited, there were restrictions on black ownership of land and the Company appointed only white officials. But racial relations confirmed status even outside the province of Company intervention. Many of the attitudes behind a racial conception of social hierarchy were already present in Europe, and the fact that slavery was practised not just at the Cape, but in many of the VOC's territories, has a particular significance.

The development of white settler attitudes towards the indigenous peoples of southern Africa took place, as we saw in the introduction, within a wider context of colonial 'contact' which has been the focus for much recent theorizing, but it also displayed features which arose out of the particular conditions of the Cape region. In general, European contact with the peoples of the New World created a challenge for established thinking. The process of conceptually constructing these peoples as 'others' arose, from the earliest days of exploration, out of this challenge. Cohen (1980) shows how a French impression of the inferiority of Africans stemmed not just from the practice of slavery (see below), but from the initial attempt to set Africans, as a novel phenomenon, in the grand scheme of things. Their perceived technological inferiority and relative powerlessness enabled them to be positioned lower in this scheme than whites. Curtin (1964) traces a similar process of prejudicial stereotyping by the British. Originating with travellers in West Africa, conceptions of Africans were more extensively applied with further, subsequent travel:

> The European travellers [of the eighteenth century] wrote to please their audience as well as to inform. Religious beliefs were of no interest: they were mere 'pagan error'. But spectacular festivals, human sacrifice, judicial ordeals and polygamy were 'curiosities', and were therefore recounted at length. Thus the reporting often stressed precisely those aspects of African life that were most repellent to the West and tended to submerge the indications of a common humanity. (Curtin, 1964: 23)

The implications of such views for colonial psychology are explored at greater length below, but subsequent travellers and administrators, influenced by what they had read, sought and found largely confirmatory data in their own travels, furthering the process of the creation of an almost entirely alien, African other. Late eighteenth-century utopian planners of West African colonies, like Wadstrom and Smeathman, for example, 'followed the unconscious assumption of popular culture that a lack of civilization meant a lack of culture. African society therefore lay there, a *tabula rasa* ready and waiting for the utopian inscription' (Curtin, 1964: 115). Similar assumptions came to be made by later settlers as well.

The belief that African society was a blank page waiting to be written on by Europeans extended further, to characterize images of the landscape itself. Carter (1987) suggests that, in the colonization of Australia, 'the very act of naming was a way of bringing the landscape ... within the compass of European rationality that made it at once familiar to its colonizers and alien to its native inhabitants ... language was an instrument of *physical* colonization' (Gregory, 1994: 171–2). Coetzee (1988) argues the same point within the context of southern Africa's colonization (see below). 'Possession of the country depended, to some extent, on civilizing the landscape, bringing it into orderly being' (Carter, 1987: 59; see Crais (1992) for the symbolism of the European farmhouse in the landscape of the eastern Cape).

Such a possession obviously had its counterpart in the dispossession of the indigenous inhabitants. For a new meaning to be substituted, older meanings had to be challenged and, over time, gradually (but only ever partially) erased. Thus, still speaking in general terms,

> for the native, the history of colonial servitude is inaugurated by loss of the locality [both an initial conceptual *and* a subsequent physical loss] to the outsider; its geographical identity must thereafter be searched for

and somehow restored. Because of the presence of the colonising outsider, the land is recoverable at first only through the imagination. (Said, 1993: 271)

However, despite the validity of such insights into European conceptions of the colonized and appropriation of the signs and symbols of space, we must not fall into the trap of perceiving an essential passivity on the part of the colonized. Africans, for instance, were not a pliant raw material to be moulded into European conceptions. Through their resistance to colonization, they influenced the dynamic shaping of European concepts of them as different types of 'others'.

With this in mind, we can turn to the *particular* course of conceptual formation in the Cape. Although some of the reports of eighteenth-century European travellers in Africa, and the earlier journals of shipwrecked sailors making their way across the eastern side of southern Africa, were positive, emphasizing African attributes of hospitality and equanimity, even early white contact with indigenous peoples was set against a background of nascent European prejudice. Sailors who had seen Khoikhoi at the Cape were particularly disgusted by their habit of eating raw the intestines of animals and then smearing themselves with their malodorous grease. By the seventeenth century the 'Hottentot' (Khoikhoi) was already becoming a figure representing degradation in European literature (Thompson, 1985: 72). This perception represented 'frustration at the Khoikhoi failure to fulfil anthropological and economic expectations. From their first contact with the Cape, as Coetzee [1988] documents, Europeans criticised the "Hottentots" incessantly for their idleness and sloth – that is, their failure (refusal) to respond to opportunity (demand) to work for material reward' (Pratt, 1992: 44). In fact, 'the moment when the travel-writer condemns the Hottentot for doing nothing marks the moment when the Hottentot brings him face to face (if he will only recognize it) with the limits of his own conceptual framework' (Coetzee, 1988: 32).

Nevertheless, European conceptions of the Khoisan were not fixed. Pratt's analysis of late eighteenth- and early nineteenth-century European travel writing on the Cape illustrates a shifting, dynamic conception (Pratt, 1992). Peter Kolb's 1719 account identifies within Khoisan society the same 'universal' traits that would be expected of European society: religion, government, laws, customs, ceremonies, the 'art' of war, professions and so on. But, by the end of the eighteenth century, as, commensurate with the shifting balance of power between colonizer and colonized, 'modern racist categories emerged, as European interventionism became increasingly militant, and as Khoikhoi society was broken up and indentured by colonists, Kolb's humanist stance disappeared as a discursive possibility. The "Hottentots" ceased to be described, or even describable, by Europeans in terms of categories like government, professions or genius' (Pratt, 1992: 45).

Like the Xhosa later on, the Khoisan were at first posited by European Romantics as possessors of the ideal traits that Europeans lacked (savage dignity, humility and communal selflessness). But such a conception remained widespread only as long as their possession of the landscape was not contested by European settlers. Once they were in conflict with Europeans, as we shall see below, both Khoisan and Xhosa, while still being conceived as that which Europeans were not, lost the attributes to which Europeans aspired and took on instead those which they wished to reject.

Later accounts describe the Khoisan, by now dispossessed, as 'governed by caprice' (Linnaeus, 1759) – products of nature just like the other flora and fauna being described, catalogued and dominated by the increasingly imperial European eye. While Kolb held Europeans to be superior, he did not equate such superiority with the need to dominate and dispossess in the same way as nineteenth-century colonial discourse did. Even in later eighteenth-century accounts (Sparrman, 1783 and Paterson, 1789, cited in Pratt, 1992), the imperative of observing flora and fauna obscures the fact that the land is inhabited by societies. 'The activity of describing geography and identifying flora and fauna structures an asocial narrative in which the human presence ... is absolutely marginal ... as embodied in the naturalist, European authority and legitimacy are uncontested, a vision undoubtedly appealing to European readers' (Pratt, 1992: 52–3) and, one might add, perhaps even more so, to European settlers.

John Barrow, writing as a British official in 1798, after the take-over of the Cape, although not supporting domination, prefigures the colonization of the lands that he describes more overtly:

> In Barrow's account, more so than in those of his predecessors, the eye scanning prospects in a spatial sense knows itself to be looking at prospects in the temporal sense – possibilities of a Eurocolonial future coded as resources to be developed, surpluses to be traded, towns to be built. Such prospects are what make information relevant in a description. They make a plain 'fine' or make it noteworthy that a peak is 'granitic' or a valley 'well-wooded'. The visual descriptions presuppose – naturalize – a transformative project embodied in the Europeans. (Pratt, 1992: 61)

Meanwhile, of course, these same landscapes, which provided the arena for colonial designs, were 'lived as intensely humanised, saturated with local history and meaning'. They were spaces in which 'plants, creatures and geographical formations have names, uses, symbolic functions, histories, places in indigenous knowledge formations' (Pratt, 1992: 61).

While the identification of the cultural appropriation of landscape, which preceded physical colonization, is a recent phenomenon, the role of slavery in consolidating European notions of superiority over Africans in the Cape has been the subject of longer debate. Snowden (1983), in an account of colour prejudice in the ancient world, could find no discernible racism within the Greek and Roman polities. He links this with the fact that conquered foes of a variety of complexions were customarily kept as slaves. With later European expansion over-seas though, colonization produced evident status distinctions between colonial rulers who were white and subject peoples who were black. Accompanying European colonization was a racially exclusive trade in slaves. With nearly all slaves black and nearly all masters white, racist ideologies, it is argued, developed as legitimation. Although there were no overt signs of racial prejudice within the ancient societies studied by Snowden, they were nevertheless inclined, like subsequent genera-tions within Europe, to believe in monstrous tales from North Africa about the inhabitants further south. But, despite this qualification to Snowden's general argument, the institution of racially premised slavery was still enormously influential in consolidating white racial conceptions within the colonial Cape.

The majority of the white settlers' slaves (65 per cent) were brought from Madagascar, but others came from Delagoa Bay and the East African coast up to Zanzibar, carried by Portuguese and Islamic traders (Armstrong and Worden, 1989). The lack of a common language among the colony's slaves contributed to the creation of Afrikaans as a standard medium of communication. The importation of slaves was at its peak in the 1690s (Katzen, 1982), and thereafter, while slave imports continued throughout the eighteenth century, Cape-born slaves became more numerous.

There were slaves belonging to the VOC and those belonging to private individuals, the latter being more numerous. Many did not fit the common perception of a slave but were skilled artisans, although among owners they were stereotyped according to their area of origin. For most of the colonial period before the early nineteenth century, the population of slaves at the Cape, numbering some 17,000 by 1795, was greater than that of Europeans (Boucher, cited in Armstrong and Worden, 1989). Shell (1989) has attempted to explain the fact that a smaller white population was able to perpetuate slavery in southern Africa by referring to the custom of treating slaves as junior members of a patriarchal family. But the facts that slaves of diverse backgrounds were widely dispersed throughout the colony and therefore unable to communicate, and that punishments for insubordination could be extremely harsh, also helped preclude frequent revolt (for recent contributions to the debates over the practices and implications of slavery at the Cape, see Eldredge and Morton, 1994; Shell, 1994; and Worden and Crais, 1994).

Despite Cape slavery being unusual in some respects, it was significant for future social relations in that all slaves and most labourers were black, while landowners and employers were white (Worden, 1994). The white settlers' fear of violence from rebellious slaves was a salient factor in shaping white attitudes towards Africans (Katzen, 1982), but even freed slaves continued to be subject to discriminatory legislation in the late eighteenth century; for instance, being required to carry lanterns or face arrest (Worden, 1994). Slavery cemented a racial conception of class relations for over 170 years. 'By the late eighteenth century race and class had overlapped for so long ... [that] to many Europeans this social structure appeared to be natural or God-given' (Elphick and Giliomee, 1989b: 544). More specifically, the system of slavery introduced at the Cape was portentous in that it generated the first implementation of passes for 'non-white' racial groups. From the 1760s slaves and Khoisan were obliged to carry passes signed by their employers to prove that they were not runaways (Worden, 1994: 67).

However, there were spatial differences in social structures, even in early colonial society at the Cape. Cape Town society differed from that of its hinterland largely by virtue of its external links through international trade. Despite the preservation of racial distinction by the 'orthodox' elite, there was a relatively fluid intermixing of racial and status groups here, which was rare in the surrounding districts. External ties precipitated seasonal economic fluctuations which made more casual wage labour an alternative to the continual upkeep of slaves. The rate of manumission of slaves was therefore highest here. Inter-racial sexual relationships were also more common due to the presence of a garrison and the periodic influx of sailors from visiting ships. Apart from its economic links to the outside world, Cape Town was more closely attuned to the external flow of ideas. 'Cape Town was the sluice through which passed all the colony's contacts with the outside world' (Ross, 1989: 270). These contacts included the importation of western European ideological currents. Later burgher revolts against the VOC were to carry the rhetoric of Enlightenment thinking from Europe, and there was a negative correlation between the coherent expression of such ideas and the distance of their implementers from Cape Town.

While social structures in Cape Town itself were relatively fluid, the southwestern Cape environs of the settlement were marked by a more rigid set of relations. This was a settled, arable, slave-owning area, engendering stability and a more ordered social fix. Aspects of European culture were adopted by blacks but they were not included in the white church or society. Prestige was tied to land and land was in the hands of whites by dint of conquest.

Khoisan dispossession

As far as many historians are concerned, the most notable feature of South African social systems has been their marshalling of the 'non-white' population into a labouring role for white employers. These material relations have been seen as lying at the heart of the later systems of segregation and apartheid. Slavery represents an earlier and more universal form of such a system, but the first 'non-white' labouring force developed purely on southern African soil was composed of dispossessed Khoisan. The independent clans of Khoikhoi and San which had inhabited the Cape before European arrival were reduced by 1800 to a servile labouring class under the control of whites, mostly farmers. Khoisan dispossession was traditionally traced back largely to a devastating smallpox epidemic of 1713, but in fact the process began early on in their interaction with white settlers (Wilson and Thompson, 1982). This outcome and the mechanisms which brought it about are held to have ramifications for the later relationship between race and class in South Africa.

The subjection of Khoikhoi to the political authority of whites at the Cape was resisted from as early as 1659 (Worden, 1994). Mutual cattle-raiding resulted by the 1670s in the loss of independent Khoikhoi means of subsistence in the Cape Peninsula. Further north and east, Khoisan continued striving to eject white settler farmers from accustomed grazing land, through a series of raids, particularly in the 1730s, and there was a major 'rebellion' in 1799, once nominal colonial authority had been established. But ultimately the Khoikhoi were in a weak position due to the form of their pastoralist society (Elphick and Malherbe, 1989). The prestige of chiefs was dependent upon their ownership of livestock. Once this had been lost to VOC-backed expeditions securing supplies for the station or on punitive raids, they also lost their ability to rally effective resistance. If, on the other hand, they kept their cattle, their mobility as fighters was restricted.

Once independent Khoikhoi political authority had been broken through conquest, individual Khoi were more accessible to white farmers, now moving further into the interior, who demanded their skills of rearing and herding livestock. In return, in the early stages of colonial development, the farmer could offer a refuge to the family of the labourer from San attacks, filling the vacuum left by the collapse of Khoikhoi chiefly authority. Thus the dispossessed pastoral inhabitants of the western Cape were incorporated into the white agricultural economy, the terms of their incorporation being subservience to white authority and a labouring function. Such conditions were obviously facilitated, indeed encouraged, by pre-existing white racial attitudes. 'No one before the turn of the nineteenth century considered it the duty of government to end labour bondage and allow freedom of ownership and movement' for people who were not white (Elphick and Malherbe, 1989: 52). White society's view of the Khoikhoi became so entrenched that the missionary John Philip wrote: 'under the most favourable circumstances the great body of the Hottentots cannot be in any other condition than that of labourers for centuries to come. Individuals among the Hottentots ... may, in 30 or 40 years, rise to possess little farms' (quoted in Elphick and Malherbe, 1989: 46).

By 1800 most of the Khoikhoi of the interior were landless, largely immobile and dependent. After their incorporation as servants, only two institutional options remained as alternatives for some. These were service in the Cape Regiment which employed Khoikhoi soldiers under white leadership from 1793, and life on a mission established by a European, which involved significant concessions to European cultural mores (Elphick and Malherbe, 1989), with no necessary social recognition by Europeans to accompany such concessions.

The involvement of black people in the growing economy of South Africa was set along the lines established in this period. Black workers were to be primarily labourers and were to be subservient to white bosses. To this extent the incorporation of the Khoikhoi set the mould for the marshalling of the more powerful Bantu-speaking tribes into the white economy once their resistance was broken during the nineteenth century. A coincidence of race and (pre-industrial) class had already been formed by the end of the eighteenth century.

Social relations on the frontier

In the South African version of the Turner thesis, the frontier between colony and Xhosa has been credited with a special role in presaging the later social relations of South Africa as a whole. F.J. Turner had argued (in *The Frontier in American History*, 1920) that salient features of American national character were derived from the strategies adopted for survival on the nineteenth-century western frontier. Macmillan (1929) and MacCrone (1937) in turn, identified South Africa's own frontier as the crucible for the emergence of the mentality of racial segregation, and later, apartheid. In this conception, the

Calvinist pastoral trekboer (who, despite the name, usually settled permanently once a farm was established) dominated, with family, slaves and Khoikhoi labour subject to his control. Whites entered the eastern area with preconceptions of their superior Christian status over the 'treacherous and violent' blacks of the frontier region. The Xhosa were, if anything, perceived as being even further removed from the white moral community than were the Khoikhoi, and the hardships of competition for cattle and grazing with those of a different pigmentation solidified racial distinctions (see Legassick, 1980).

While there is an element of truth to this account, it is a simplification of the complicated pattern of relations on the frontier. The white patriarchal family was merely the norm, not universal on the frontier. Guelke (1989) has shown that a significant portion of frontier colonial society was composed of a 'plural' community of, generally poorer, white men and Khoikhoi wives. The offspring of such unions were known as Bastaards, and later, a polity of this origin, the Griqua, played out a significant role on the northern frontier (Legassick, 1989). Even the racially discrete social norm of the 'orthodox' frontier community was not new in southern Africa, but derived from that established in the slave-owning districts of the southwest. The development of the white frontier community's racial attitudes was also more complex.

The Khoisan of the eastern frontier region experienced dispossession later than those of the west, and, initially, with less onerous implications. During the period of the 'open' frontier of 1770–95, when the outermost limits of Xhosa settlement had only recently been encountered by colonists, white population densities were low, with farmsteads at intervals of at least one hour's ride (Christopher, 1984). Khoikhoi were thus able to move relatively freely between farms to work, and their employer's coercion to remain was not always effective. There was an element of symbiosis between white farmer and black worker and no concrete fix of race and status. Not all whites were masters and not all non-whites servants, and relations between white and black were not so much master–slave but more patron–client (Legassick, 1980).

However, racial attitudes were indeed hardened and solidified because of material struggles between white settlers and Xhosa on the frontier. The series of wars which became so important in eastern frontier life were triggered by disputes over occupation of land and mutual raiding of cattle. Antagonism along racial lines was exacerbated by the maltreatment of Khoisan and Xhosa servants, the incursions of Xhosa into 'colonial' territory (especially following drought), and the absence of overwhelming force on either side to impose order. White

administrators, when negotiating with Xhosa leaders, failed to understand the nature of Xhosa fragmentation into mutually independent
chiefdoms. Even though the precedence of certain chiefs was recognized by various Xhosa groupings, this did not mean that these chiefs
could impose a negotiated arrangement on them. Similarly, within the
white settler population, officials could not control the actions of
widely dispersed individuals (Wilson, 1982a), and mutual distrust on
the part of larger groups was continually heightened by the violent
acts of small parties (Giliomee, 1989a).

But it would be misleading to represent racial relations on the
eastern frontier as a permanently volatile blend of mistrust and antagonism periodically bursting into warfare through the late eighteenth
and early nineteenth centuries. For many whites on the frontier, Xhosa
were trading partners and labourers before they were foes. Xhosa and
trekboer were also aware of shared attitudes – especially towards cattle-
raiding as an opportunity for both to build up stock and power. The
permeability of the frontier in the late eighteenth century facilitated a
spectrum of relations between both groups with conflict lying only at
one extreme.

By 1812 though, Xhosa had been expelled from the eastern limits
of the colony, and with the infilling of white settlement, the Khoikhoi,
despite frequent bouts of resistance, were reduced to a reluctant labour
force. Increasing pressure on the land within the colony meant that by
1812 only 18 per cent of whites owned land, while virtually all had in
the 1770s (Giliomee, 1989a). As Khoikhoi were deprived of their
remaining land, their ability to decline to work for whites disappeared.
They were kept as servants on white farms by a variety of tactics on
the part of the farmer. These included the withholding of wages,
impounding of the servant's livestock and detention of the family of
an employee.

The new British administrators, in spite of some sympathy for the
Khoikhoi needed the consent of the frontier farmers to secure order
and the labour of the Khoikhoi to secure meat supplies for the growing
Cape settlements. The outcome of their intervention was therefore to
bolster the labour-securing practices of white farmers. Indenture for
Bastaard children of servants until the age of twenty-five was introduced and, as we have seen, at the end of the eighteenth century a
pass was required for Khoikhoi and slaves to move between farms and
to towns in the colony.

An ideological construct – white space – had been created in
southern Africa by dint of conquest. There were still more black people
than white living in this space, but most blacks had to obtain permission, in the form of a pass from a white employer or owner, to

move within it. The white presence was now territorially anchored: even while its landscape remained largely alien to European eyes, there was now a discrete portion of southern Africa within which whites considered themselves possessors rather than visitors. Concomitantly, and within this space, by the early nineteenth century, race had become a more concrete determinant of status and class. Khoisan and Bastaards – the original territorial possessors and their offspring – were now merging into an undifferentiated servile class only slightly above the level of the slaves themselves.

Afrikaner identity

It has been argued that the material relations which were formed within white space in the early period of colonization were portentous. There is also an assertion that Afrikaner nationalism, which would later combine with a concern over the preservation of established material relations to bring about the apartheid system, had its origins in the period between white movement inland and the early nineteenth century (Sparks, 1990; De Villiers, 1988). The seeds of an exclusivist Afrikaner identity are said to have been sown among the Dutch-speaking trekboers and farmers of the early colony; conflict with the British nurtured its growth.

The bonding elements which have been identified in the generation of a collective Afrikaans identity on the frontier include the Calvinist religion and the nagmaal, a kind of festival associated with it (see below); the need for collective defence against a visibly different, and much more numerous black group made hostile by white conquest and competition for land and cattle; and common antipathy to the attempts of first the VOC, and then the British, to extend control (but not protection) over the independent-minded trekboers. To this list De Villiers (1988) adds the common belief that retreat into the interior was a way to solve the problems of poverty and harassment by the British law (a belief apparently manifested in the Great Trek of the 1830s).

Yet it is not necessarily the case that a prototype *Afrikaner* identity was formed in response to these forces in these early years. The factors listed above helped to forge a bond among settlers of the frontier, but their independence was often a stronger force than their collective spirit. The rise of a collective sense of ethnic Afrikaans solidarity, and particularly nationalism, must be placed later in South Africa's history. The identity which emerged at this time was that of settlers in a relatively hostile colonial environment, not that of a nation in the making.

The rate at which farms were taken up in the interior was not related to market fluctuations, which leads one to conclude that it was primarily the desire to be the master of one's own land that motivated whites to settle there (Guelke, 1989). Once there, many had little contact with Cape Town. Trips to the town were occasioned by specific needs – for ammunition, tobacco, coffee, tea, sugar, baptism, or to sell a surplus. From the Zuurveld along the eastern frontier, a return trip would take about three months (Guelke, 1989). The low density of settlement in the first half of the eighteenth century and the remoteness of the frontier necessitated an independence of spirit and an ability to be a 'jack of all trades' rather than a sense of communal solidarity.

However, isolation and independence were not unalloyed. The nagmaals tempered the trekboer's exclusion from wider society. These were intermittent gatherings of the settlers of the frontier regions for the purposes of Calvinist religious renewal and reassertion, the marketing of home-produced goods and the enjoyment of social intercourse. Calvinism itself was an important bonding factor, but as Du Toit (1983) points out, it did not serve an Afrikaner sense of being *the* chosen people, but a more diffuse conception of being chosen in contrast to the heathens of the region. It did not therefore necessarily encourage an exclusivist Afrikaner identity as distinct from the later British presence. While religion was an obvious component of white identity on the frontier, it could not be said to have welded together a *nation* in the sense that Turner's American nation was supposedly forged on the equivalent US frontier.

The absence of VOC authority, emanating from Cape Town, in the more remote districts is also said to have served the waxing sense of Afrikaner frontier identity, since the settlers substituted for central authority by running their own form of government involving paid officials (landdrosts) and part-time burgher administrators (heemraden). The VOC presence *was* weak on the frontier, and it was indeed resented. The Company, on the one hand, tried to monopolize, or at least supervise, trading relations with the Khoikhoi, like it did in the west, but on the other hand, was not able to offer the acceptable aspect of authority on the frontier – protection from indigenous enemies. The Company was not only perceived as a wholly negative influence by many, but was also incapable of punishing insubordination in the remote districts when challenged. And challenged it was in 1795 when the eastern settlers rose up in a rebellion which was finally to be put down only by the new British administrators.

The independence of spirit and rebelliousness of the frontier is often held as an example of new traits developing among its settlers

(Sparks, 1990; De Villiers, 1988). These traits may have represented the emergence of a different identity from that of the more stable west, but it was not yet an ethnically defined and exclusivist Afrikaner identity. This was not shaped by white settler antagonism to blacks or burgher antagonism to the VOC in this period, but by resistance to British interference in a late nineteenth-century context (see Chapter 2). In the late eighteenth and early nineteenth centuries, there certainly was a clear distinction between Dutch-speaking settlers and their new British administrators. Settlers were perceived by British officials as sharing some of the attributes of Africans. In Barrow's account, 'Euroafricans as well as Africans must be codified specifically in relation to British aspirations; prior Dutch claims and 150 years of Dutch colonialism must be discredited' (Pratt, 1992: 61). Thus, Dutch-speakers were disparaged for a lack of the spirit of improvement. The same tendency is seen in contemporaneous British accounts of Dutch colonies in the Caribbean and Spanish America, upon each of which Britain had similar colonial designs. But these perceptions were not, until later in the nineteenth century, and in a very different imperialist context, enough to stoke widespread ethnic antagonism in the Cape.

The administrative actions of the British which had the most far-reaching effects on settlers penetrated in two main directions – the protection of Khoisan 'rights' and the attack on slavery. The centre-piece legislation regarding the Khoisan was Ordinance 50 of 1828. This abolished passes for the Khoisan, stated their right not to be forced into service and to own land, and made parental consent a condition of child apprenticeship. Contracts were required for work of over a month, and were not to extend beyond a year (Elphick and Malherbe, 1989). Slavery was undermined first in 1808, when further trade in slaves was halted, and finally abolished in 1834.

These moves on the part of British administrators have been credited largely to liberals in Britain in the case of slavery, and in the case of the Khoisan, to missionary influence within the colony (Elphick and Malherbe, 1989), although there is also a materialist argument that Ordinance 50 represented an early attempt to establish free-market labour relations (Newton-King, 1980). But the impact of the legislation was never as dramatic as its instigators would have liked. Elphick and Malherbe point out that it did not alter the essential nature of the Cape economy – 'namely its reliance on cheap, immobile labour' (1989: 52). In spite of Ordinance 50, the *de facto* position of Khoikhoi servants remained essentially unchanged. In fact slaves were often treated better than contracted Khoikhoi since they represented an asset of their owner (Stockenstrom, cited in Elphick and Giliomee, 1989b: 452).

The lack of *de facto* change can be put down to official unwillingness to stir up the wrath of the white settlers of the colony. This was the element of the Cape's population in whose interests the government was most concerned to act. Whites were the wealth-makers, and the guarantors of political stability and minimal costs for the officials at the Cape. As Crais (1992: 95) puts it:

> What became increasingly clear to both the British colonial elite and a rising number of bureaucrats was that economic growth in the colony would ultimately rest not on free labour, but on its opposite. Counter to their most cherished ideals, economic growth and human progress depended on subjection and the violence which accompanied the denial of freedom.

The British administrators therefore trusted markets and missionary intervention, rather than their own direct intervention, to improve the position of the Khoisan in line with liberal thinking. Indeed, when further legislation entered the field from the official camp it was to be emphatically on the side of white employers.

Even the abolition of slavery in the colony cannot be said to have dramatically changed its social characteristics. Following emancipation, slaves were bound to the same master for four years to make the transition easier for their owners. After this interval, many had no option within the prevailing social structures but to continue working full-time or on a casual basis for their accustomed 'employer', although, around Uitenhage and Albany, most became waged townsmen (Crais, 1992), contributing to early urban growth in the frontier district. Well after the formal abolition of slavery, within the colony, illicit slave-trading continued, and on its frontiers, even some slave-raiding took place (with some Xhosa participating by selling captives).

Despite the practical ineffectiveness of the British moves against white despotism, they generated disgust and apprehension on the part of some white settlers. After all, unquestioned, and often violent, domination of black labour had, by the early nineteenth century, become a cornerstone of white settler identity along the frontier (Crais, 1992). It was clear that the general trend of British policy was more favourable to the black inhabitants of the colony than that to which settlers were accustomed. Specific incidents, out of which much was later made, such as Slagtersnek, where British officialdom intervened forcefully against settlers for their maltreatment of a servant (see Chapter 2), were a manifestation of the trend. That the trend was resented by many is clear. That it became a focal point in the early nineteenth century for the emergence of Afrikaner identity in opposition to British official interference is far less clear. Indeed, for most of the late eighteenth and early nineteenth centuries, the new

British administrators of the colony co-operated with Dutch-speaking local officials in their organization of warfare against Xhosa. It was later Dutch-speakers who would use the events of the period to create a sense of Afrikaner nationalism, not those who lived at the time (Thompson, 1985).

Conclusion

This chapter has been an attempt to trace back the origin of South Africa's racial order and to address the question of an early emergence of Afrikaans ethnic awareness. With regard to the former issue, if one can question the extent to which later social structures emanated from eighteenth-century ones, one cannot doubt that in the eighteenth century a social order based to a great extent on pigmentation was created. In examining the mode by which this racial order originated, Elphick and Giliomee (1989b) place emphasis on the official intervention of the VOC. A racial order, they argue, was created rather than emerged. The legal structures of the VOC, imposed in the first years of settlement, provided the skeleton of the society that was to grow in the Cape. It was this basic form that was to be adapted over the following two centuries of geographical expansion and economic development. The legal status groups of the early Cape – freeburghers and Company servants, Khoisan, slaves and, later, free blacks – were the precursors of the racial categories which characterized subsequent South African society.

Such an argument may not, however, be sufficient in explaining the origins of South Africa's racial order. It emphasizes administrative structures and an official moulding of the social perceptions of the population. But the members of this population brought with them, and generated further, ideas wherein could lie the origin of a racial structuring of society.

We have seen how Europeans constructed Africa and Africans in their own conceptual schema as in many ways the inverse of what could be expected of European civilization. African landscapes, and indeed peoples themselves, lacking their own intrinsic purpose in the world, could be put to more productive, European, use. But this use was not simply material. Colonization, as Fanon (1963) showed, also has a profound psychological dimension. Cohen (1980: 33), following Foucault, puts it thus:

Africans served Europeans as a convenient mirror, or as a screen onto which they projected their own fears about themselves and their world. The encounter with Africa in the seventeenth century occurred in an era that emphasized [particularly for Dutch colonists, however lax they were] order, self-discipline, self-abnegation, sexual restraint and Christianity. These were difficult ideals. The Europeans' failure to realize these lofty goals, or even their temptations to deny them, created serious inner tensions to which the contact with Africa gave an emotional release.

Europeans 'were constrained by law and convention to act in a certain manner, but their fantasies tempted them to doubt their civilized humanity and revealed instead their own animality' (Cohen, 1980: 33–4). A process of projection then, could mean that 'the African [instead, was] depicted as animalistic, sexually lustful, lazy and religiously unregenerate' (Cohen, 1980: 33–4). Africans therefore became what Europeans were not, or at least what they covertly wished to be, but overtly wished to avoid becoming.

Once established on African soil and embroiled in the power relations of colonization, further attributes of the African other became solid in settlers' general perceptions. Since Africans refused to acknowledge dispossession and the conversion of land to private European uses, their appropriation of what Europeans now considered their own made them inclined to 'thieving', while their unwillingness to work for their colonizers consolidated notions of their inherent laziness.

If such psychological and cultural forces were at work, they certainly blended well with material desires. The process of conceptually extracting the indigenous Khoisan 'out of economy, culture and history too' (Pratt, 1992: 53), to reconstruct them as a vital, projected other, as an antithesis of conscious European values, allowed colonial appropriation to be underwritten and the Khoisan to be legitimately reduced to servility and labour.

The actions of the VOC then, could be seen as not so much initiating, but guarding and bolstering burghers' own preconceptions, not only of what *should* be, but of what *was* a natural social order. The view of society entailed in VOC legislation already saturated the white society that the VOC administered. 'The pattern of racial relationships established in the eighteenth-century Cape must be seen in the light of the formation of the Cape colonist as a whole, the form of his inheritance from Europe and the exigencies of the situation he had to face' (Legassick, 1980: 68). During the VOC period, 'power radiated from the body of the white master [himself]. This was power as property, as objectified in the discourse of patriarchy ... slaves and peons became the mere extensions of the colonial sovereign' (Crais, 1992: 87).

European social values brought ashore at the Cape were, however, modified by its VOC-ruled, slave-owning society. Here, settlers readily adopted racial attitudes which favoured them by slotting them into a social hierarchy according to their skin colour and European background. Once established, such a hierarchy would be defended against, on the one hand, the physical threat of those defined primarily by their race, and, on the other, the cultural threat of a loss of European identity in Africa. The consolidation of white racism on South African soil stemmed initially from fear – the isolated colonizer's fear of the other, of the colonized, dispossessed and enslaved, and also, perhaps, the fear of what lay within the colonizer's own psyche.

Racial attitudes on the frontier derived initially from those in the western Cape and, despite a period of relative social fluidity, became more extreme with increasing competition between Xhosa and settler societies for land and grazing. Along the frontier, after a brief spell of Dutch-speaking hegemony on the Cape side, 'two societies with radically different ways of perceiving the world around them' were brought together. 'The British came from a capitalist and industrializing society centred on the individual and an economic system oriented around the production of commodities for exchange. In Xhosa society, in contrast, the overwhelming majority of goods remained within the community and circulated according to principles of reciprocity and redistribution.' The result of the two societies' interaction was 'the construction of "working misunderstandings" which often collapsed into violent [culturally *and racially* defined] conflict' (Crais, 1992: 100).

As Xhosa, too, began to be dispossessed by whites, missionaries and some administrators, with varying motives, developed the aim of 'civilizing' them and incorporating them in white society. As far as some officials, such as the Governor D'Urban, were concerned, to make the Xhosa other more like themselves, domination must precede assimilation. But, despite some vocal objections, the dominant settler conception held that they were to be kept outside of white social structures, and even outside of white space, unless they were servicing whites' labour needs (see Lester, forthcoming).

Prior to white settlement on the frontier, different Bantu-speaking polities had dispossessed each other (as well as Khoisan) of land; but certain shared cultural assumptions, including that of communal land tenure, the importance of reciprocity and exchange between patron and client, and the lack of an obvious physical difference between dispossessed and dispossessor had facilitated a high degree of subsequent assimilation. The colonial interaction between white settler and Xhosa was of an entirely different nature. Apart from the simple desire for land, powerful conceptual constructions associated with physical and cultural difference, notably over 'ideas about land tenure, labour, marriage and the causes of disease' (Wilson, 1982a: 268), plus the salient fact that Xhosa numbers were not only much greater than

white, but growing much more quickly, made the assimilation of colonizer and colonized unacceptable to the vast majority of whites.

The shifting frontier zone did not, as in the 'frontier thesis', represent the seedbed of racism in South Africa, since racial conceptions
associated with European cultural traits, slavery and the VOC order
were already established in the southwestern Cape. Nevertheless, despite
much interaction for the material gain of both white and black along
the frontier, the region did see the consolidation of racially defined
identity, largely because it was coincident with cultural identity. Although there was increasing class differentiation within the white
population, and indigenous societies were never as egalitarian as is often
believed, race assumed and retained paramountcy in defining social
relations across the whole of the colony in the early colonial period.

Within the white population of the colony, by the early nineteenth
century, discrepancies in outlook were emerging between British administrators and the slave-owning settlers – differentiated by their
language, religion, subsistence mode of production and sense of relative
independence from authority – but they were not yet being expressed
as significant ethnic cleavages. Despite legislation which was relatively
liberal, the British administrators generally upheld fairly fixed racial
relations, favourable to the settlers, based on a controlled labouring
function for blacks in white space.

While they are significant, the importance of early colonial racial
conceptions and material structures for South Africa's later development must not be overemphasized. 'There was nothing in Cape society
to suggest a race consciousness stronger than in many, perhaps most
colonial societies of the day, nor anything that particularly prefigured
the later elaboration of apartheid' (Freund, 1989: 334). While, elsewhere, similar systems were subsequently diluted by succeeding
economic and social developments, in South Africa the system was
modernized, and white space maintained, as far as possible. The racial
order was significantly changed as a result of South Africa's interaction
with a world economy, its witnessing of an intra-white struggle and,
most importantly, the incorporation of a numerically superior black
population in rapidly developing industrial and urban structures from
the nineteenth century. The gap between early colonial social and
spatial structures and those of late twentieth-century apartheid – a
more deliberate ideological imposition – is even greater. While the
pre-industrial period as a whole laid the foundations for later systems
of segregation and apartheid then, it did not dictate their form.

2

Colonial
Expansion, Industrialization
and Afrikanerdom

This chapter is divided into three sections, each dealing with one of the most fundamental transformations of the nineteenth century. Section one examines the processes and more conscious decisions by which not only African, but also white polities to the east and north of the Cape Colony were deprived of political independence, and often, ownership and control over land. Section two describes the evolution of systems for the control of African labourers in white space during South Africa's first industrial revolution. Section three accounts for the emergence of Afrikaner nationalism in the late nineteenth century.

1 Colonial expansion

Introduction

The land, both as symbol and as reality, has had resonant implications in the history of South African society. Possession of land was, since 1652, a theme of contention between racially and ethnically defined participants, and remains so today. Whites sought not only to deprive blacks of their possession of land, but also to transform fundamentally the nature of land ownership itself. While Africans had practised a form of unequal communal tenure (see Wilson, 1982b) associated with landscapes of dispersed, self-sufficient homesteads (kraals), over much of the region whites substituted a landscape of individually owned, enclosed farmsteads and trading communities. But this was no smooth transition: the landscape was fiercely contested.

The nineteenth century brought to fulfilment the white appropriation of African soil and the minerals beneath it. By the end of the century there was no enforceable African claim to most of South Africa. The magnitude of the transformation was hidden from the view of most whites. J.M. Coetzee (1988) has shown how two strands of white literature emerged, reflecting this fact. The 'pastoral novel', exemplified by the writing of Van den Heever, is permeated with the assertion of white ownership of the land by right of occupation. Boer and soil are bound together and the Boer *is* South Africa – 'the land lives in the culture of the farmer people through the plough'. The 'empty landscape' novel, exemplified in the work of Olive Schreiner, portrays a South African landscape that is silent and forbidding. There is no recognition of a black occupation, indeed blacks are silent through most of white writing. This silence is imposed over the presence of the dispossessed. It reflects, according to Roy Campbell, the 'curbed ferocity of beaten tribes' (quoted in Coetzee, 1988: 10). Yet the menacing and brooding presence of Africans lies just outside the thin boundaries of white society, and it is a recurrent image in white South African thought; available to be manipulated for political purposes.

Gunner (1988) provides an account of the black literary response to dispossession. Sol Plaatje, writing in *Mhudi* at the end of the era of black dispossession, used the past as a source of inspiration and strength, harking back to a time before the frontier gave way to white advance, when Boers respected and feared their African neighbours. An indication of the nature of the intervening transformation, and of its impact on Africans, is present in the writings of R.R.R. Dhlomo and Benedict Wallet Vilikazi. In these, the ability to adapt to the industrial present is demonstrated by the experience of migrant mineworkers. Vilikazi also 'wrestled with the question of how to reinterpret the Zulu past and how to write in a society where his own people were becoming increasingly dispossessed and displaced' (Gunner, 1988: 223). One response was to eulogize the paramounts who had presided over a powerful and independent Zululand, or resisted white incursion: Shaka, Dingaan, Mpande, Cetshwayo and Dinizulu. Many educated blacks hankered for a mythologized past in which possession of the land by black communities provided a power and a tranquillity no longer to be found, especially in the industrializing cities.

While the literature of the late nineteenth century can tell us something about how attitudes across the most significant racial divide were shaped by African dispossession, it does not tell us how that dispossession came about. In order to comprehend the magnitude of the transformation which took place in the ownership of the land, and the use that was made of it in southern Africa during the nineteenth century, it is useful to simplify what was a complex series of interactions between different polities into two broad stages. The first stage was mainly to do with competition over grazing land: on the one hand, between settlers along the eastern frontier and the Xhosa and,

on the other, between Dutch-speaking trekkers, establishing republics
to the north of the colony, and surrounding African polities. During
this stage, which lasted from the late eighteenth to the mid-nineteenth
century, the loss of African independence often occurred through
indirect, as well as direct means, the role of labour flows, missionaries
and trade being particularly important. In the second stage, beginning
in the 1860s, mineral discoveries were seen by the British colonial
administrators as necessitating a new geographical and economic order
in the region. Those African, and even independent white polities,
which had until now retained their autonomy, had it removed in the
late nineteenth century, generally by overwhelming British military
force.

Colonial penetration in the 'first stage'

A seemingly tangled web of co-operation and conflict between white
and black, Boer and British, and between African chiefdoms grouped
under paramounts, characterizes the early nineteenth century. But
certain events stand out as microcosms of the broader interactions
occurring, and they have a clear spatial dimension. There is an obvious
distinction between the colonially 'settled' western Cape, where
Khoisan dispossession had already occurred, and the turbulent frontiers
to the north and east, where whites were encountering much more
formidable Bantu-speaking polities.

In the east, the zone where disputes over land and cattle were
initially felt most acutely was the Zuurveld – in summer, an area of
rich and nutritious grasses, which turned sour in the winter. Here,
after a series of inconclusive skirmishes interspersed with periods of
trade and barter with white settlers, the Rarabe Xhosa chiefdoms under
Ndlambe were finally cleared across the Great Fish River by a more
aggressive British administration in 1812 (Fig. 1, p. 18; and Mclennan,
1986). There was to be a total of nine wars between the colony and
various groupings of Xhosa chiefdoms, caused largely by the vagaries
and inconsistencies of British colonial policy and periods of increased
competition for grazing land brought on by drought (see Mostert,
1992 for a compelling general narrative, and Lester – forthcoming –
for an analysis of official strategies on the frontier), but being the first
all-out assault on Xhosa territory and sustenance, this action was the
path-breaking one.

The British authorities tried to consolidate their influence over
rebellious frontier settlers and Xhosa in 1820 by importing some 5,000
civilians from Britain and placing them as settled farmers along the
disputed tract between colony and Xhosa. The settlers were the first

significant British civilian presence on the eastern frontier. They provided a backdrop for further British colonial intervention against the
Xhosa in the area. Few of them stayed on their isolated allotments
long. Most drifted to the nascent towns of Albany District, as the
Zuurveld was now known, and found their new livelihood in transport
riding, trading, craft or hunting. By May 1823 only 438 of the original
1,004 male grantees remained on their rural sites, the infertility of the
soils and the unaccustomed hazards of frontier life, including Xhosa
raids and three successive seasons of the crop disease rust, drought
and flood, having driven the rest away. Where they failed in the bush
though, they generally prospered in the towns, turning tiny colonial
'dorps' like Graaff-Reinet into entrepôts of new trade (Peires, 1989a).

While the British settlers were acting as 'apostles of free enterprise
and free trade' (Peires, 1989a: 472) within the extremity of the colony,
rumours were filtering down from the northeast, carried by traders,
trekboers, missionaries and hunters, of great upheavals among the
Bantu-speaking peoples with whom white settlers had not yet made
contact. It seems likely that a combination of ecological crisis, brought
on by the structure of pastoralist agriculture, population growth and
drought, and competition over a trading monopoly with the Portuguese
at Delagoa Bay precipitated a change in the structure of the north-
eastern polities around the turn of the nineteenth century (Guy, 1980;
Hedges, 1978; Wright and Hamilton, 1989). Certainly the chiefdoms
of the Ndwandwe under Zwide in what became northern Zululand,
and the Mthethwa under Dingiswayo along the east coast underwent a
militarization of the amabutho (originally groups of men, organized
by age to hunt elephants), a centralization of state power over
neighbouring clans and a period of intensified conflict, known as the
mfecane, which resulted in the regional hegemony of the Zulu, under
Shaka. Militaristic consolidation of clans into more centralized structures led to a diaspora of peoples from an epicentre in Natal. For
instance, an intrusion of Matiwane into the Cape Colony was met
with repulsive force in the belief that these refugees were themselves
the imagined 'rampaging' Zulu. Debate over the causes of the upheavals, however, remains intense, with Julian Cobbing preferring to
blame European-inspired slave-raiding from Delagoa Bay and the
frontiers of the Cape Colony rather than the internal activities of
African polities themselves (Cobbing, 1988), but his innovative interpretation has not been universally accepted.

The lack of recorded evidence of these developments beyond the
limit of direct European involvement means that no interpretation will
be definitive. At the time, a hazy awareness of significant upheaval and
of the rise of powerful groupings in a not too distant hinterland

permeated the frontier zone and presented yet another insecurity for the British settlers there.

Boers in their thousands had already, singly and in groups, escaped the confines of the colony to inhabit 'Transorangia' to the north, alongside the Griqua, Khoisan remnants and groups of Tswana. But the decision of some 15,000 to embark upon their own enterprise of state construction away from British territory added a new and profound dimension to the course of social formation from 1836. The collection of parties moving out of the colony extended the sphere of white influence to the north and hastened the pace of conflict with, and dispossession of, Bantu groups. After the Great Trek, the geographical spread of white settlers achieved the envelopment of the two largest black polities – the Zulu and the Xhosa – thus paving the way for their eventual conquest.

The decisive collapse of the western Xhosa's means of independence came in the 1850s. The loss of pastures, the destabilizing conflict with the colony, the psychological impact of a steady undermining of Xhosa culture, and the toll of cattle lungsickness resulted in the invocation of a form of spiritual assistance – that of their ancestors. The context of the 1850s was a particularly propitious one for the prophecies of a young girl, Nonqawuse, and her guardian, Mhlakaza, to become widely accepted (Peires, 1989b). She foretold that sacrifices of cattle (many already seemingly forfeit to lungsickness) would bring forth hordes of ancestor warriors who would banish the whites and restore plenitude to the land. Such prophecies were not unprecedented in Xhosa society, and they subsequently occurred in other parts of the world where indigenous societies were under threat (see Wilson, 1982a). The circumspection of many Xhosa was treated as treachery by a growing force of believers as cattle slaughtering gained momentum. Various chiefs sent emissaries during 1856 and 1857 to Nonqawuse at the Gxarha River mouth to ascertain a date for the resurrection, but a sequence of such dates passed and finally the participating Xhosa realized their predicament: thousands starved, their basis of subsistence was destroyed and their only option was dependence on the colony where eager employers were waiting for their labour. Despite nearly a century of resistance, the Rarabe Xhosa was the first Bantu-speaking polity to be dispossessed. The Gcaleka Xhosa to the east retained possession of their land and control over their labour until later in the nineteenth century.

Further north, in the wake of the mfecane, the trekkers, who had eventually established two new Boer republics – the Transvaal (later, South African Republic) and the Orange Free State – initially became involved in a complex series of alliances and conflicts with nearby, centralized African groupings. Most immediately, the Transvaal settlers were in dispute over land with the Ndebele (an offshoot from the Zulu kingdom), whom they subsequently drove out of the region entirely. In the 1840s, Orange Free State burghers both purchased land from the Griqua and fought the Basotho, under Moshoeshoe's leadership, for possession of grazing land between the Caledon and Orange Rivers (Worden, 1994). Neither of the republics, however, was strong enough to enforce its will over the stronger, post-mfecane, centralized polities of the region, such as the Pedi in the north and the Basotho bordering the Orange Free State (see Marks and Atmore, 1980a; Davenport, 1991). Their conquest would not occur until later British intervention.

Certain agencies were responsible for preparing the ground for African political subjugation, both to the east of the Cape Colony's frontier and around the trekker republics, in this early period. Labour contracts, for instance, between white farmers and individual Xhosa, made it increasingly difficult for the Xhosa chiefs to maintain the cohesiveness of the group (although in polities further from the colony's frontier, greater chiefly control was established over migrant workers' movements – see Beinart, 1982; Delius, 1983). Missionaries from the white colonies mostly viewed conversion and the adoption of Western parameters of civilization as proceeding concurrently (William Shaw, cited in Peires, 1989a: 487), and even the influential pro-Xhosa missionary, John Philip, recognized that he was extending British influence and the Empire. In an innovative account, Comaroff and Comaroff (1991) have shown how Tswana cultural practices and sources of authority were subtly modified to reflect an awareness of the colonial power manifested by missionaries, well before colonial conquest itself. Traders were also influential in eroding the underpinnings of precolonial African societies before their final subjection, by allowing individuals within African polities to by-pass traditional chiefly control over trade, and amass wealth on their own behalf (see Colenbrander (1979) and Kennedy (1981) for the role of trade in the Zulu kingdom).

Individual African responses to contact with white society in this early period depended to a great extent upon the structure of their rural communities (Beinart, 1982), and the nature of their pre-colonial political functioning. A comparison between Mpondo (Beinart, 1982) and Mfengu (Bundy, 1972) is illustrative. The Mfengu had already had their chiefdoms destroyed during the mfecane before they met white colonists. As refugees from Natal they were accepted by the Xhosa, but as inferiors in the hierarchy of distribution. Having no independent political structures and little independent means of subsistence, the Mfengu were especially receptive to colonial culture, particularly conversion to Christianity (see Cobbing (1988) for a radical reinterpretation of Mfengu origins as captured Xhosa). Many became allies of the colony in subsequent wars against the Xhosa. By comparison, although Mpondo adaptation occurred in the second phase of colonial penetration, when industrialization of the interior was well under way, chiefly power was not only intact, but able to dictate the terms on which Mpondo would migrate to the colony. Chiefly direction of the processes of incorporation even extended to the collection of wages by the chief on behalf of workers from his area.

For Zulu-speakers in Natal, too, even though they were under tenuous colonial rule, there was still a relatively high degree of autonomy until the later nineteenth century. Atkins (1993) traces the attempts of refugees returning from places of shelter from the mfecane or escaping the marriage restrictions of the Zulu king to the north, to reconstitute their accustomed lifestyles in the region. From their position of numerical strength and their ability to attain access to land, many of them were able to resist incorporation in the colonial economy as wage labourers, or, when they did participate, to do so to some extent on their own terms. It was this ability which lay behind the constant refrain of 'the Kaffirs are lazy', coming in the second half of the nineteenth century from the colonial settlers of the region.

Colonial conquest in the 'second stage'

'As late as the 1870s the subcontinent was divided into a large number of polities, chiefdoms, colonies and settlements of widely differing size, power and racial composition, without political unity or cohesion' (Worden, 1994: 5), but by the end of the nineteenth century, the lands of what had once been the independent African polities had generally been reduced by a combination of war and peaceful, but insidious, processes to areas reserved on European terms for continued African occupation. During the intervening period, not only the Sotho, Tswana, Griqua, Gcaleka Xhosa, Zulu and Pedi, but also the white settler republics of the Transvaal and the Orange Free State, had been subjected to a form of British imperial control.

The explanation for this expansion of imperial intervention, with its commitment of vast British resources, lies in mineral discoveries; first of diamonds in Griqualand West in 1868, and then, in the 1880s, of gold in the Transvaal. By raising the prospect of a self-sustaining, and even organically expanding economy within a united southern African whole – in other words a confederation – the discoveries made the independent Boer and African polities of the interior seem much more significant thorns in the side of the British colonial administration than they had previously appeared.

The aim of a confederation of white-ruled polities in the region was not a new one; initially, it had been motivated in London by a desire to reduce imperial commitment and involvement in colonial vicissitudes by granting fairly cohesive self-government to the region, including the Boer republics. After the 1870s though, diamond mining shed a new light on the British administrative aim. A political confederation of colonies and republics would be a significant step towards the goal of smooth economic functioning, particularly by allowing for the administrative integration of the diamond mines and their labour source areas, and the reduction of the harassment that the labour received as it traversed the Boer republics towards the mines.

Basutoland was taken under British authority in 1868, after Moshoeshoe, concerned at the increasing white interest in the region, had seen the writing on the wall, and requested British imperial protection. Griqualand West was annexed in 1871 and a rebellion there put down in 1878. Carnarvon's annexation of the bankrupt Transvaal (weakened by war with the Pedi) in 1877 and Bartle Frere's appointment as the prospective first Commissioner of a federated South Africa, were further milestones in the infusion of the idea of confederation into policy. A dispute within the Xhosa polities gave a pretext to wage a savage war on the remaining independent Gcaleka Xhosa in 1877–78, but the first major setback came in 1879 when a British column, moving to eradicate the independent Zululand's impediment to the scheme, was defeated at Isandhlwana. The eventual submission of the Zulu though, still did not leave the path to confederation clear.

In the northern Transvaal, the Pedi, who had successfully fought off Boer attempts at control, were defeated by British soldiers with Swazi help, shortly after the Zulu war, and during the first British occupation of the Transvaal. However, despite the profusion of blood spilt and the enormous sums of money spent, confederation was still not achieved. In 1881, Transvaalers rebelled and defeated British regiments at the Battle of Majuba. With the prospect of a costly war to regain control of the Boer republic, confederation was abandoned.

Abandoned, that is, until the gold discoveries of the 1880s made it seem possible once more to outweigh the costs of conquest with the economic dividends of a united colony. Southern Bechuanaland had been annexed in 1884 to secure sources of timber, grain and labour supply to the Kimberley diamond mines, but Southern Tswana resistance was only finally crushed after the gold mines had provided further reason for confederation, and following the Langeberg 'revolt', in 1897.

The Cape Colony, having enjoyed responsible government since 1872, was opposed to this second, gold-led drive for confederation, seeing in it a threat to its own economic status. But the greatest obstacles to the new push for confederation remained the Boer republics. Their leaders were rather less concerned with economic rationality for the region and rather more preoccupied with maintaining their independence from British influence. The mines also brought mixed economic blessings for the republics, along with their political uncertainties. In the 1880s, farming had still been the dominant sector in the republics and, despite regulations restricting African labour mobility and farmers' own initiative in securing 'apprentice' labour, acute labour shortages set in once the mines were functioning. By the end of the century only prosperous farmers were able to attract sufficient labour.

The republics' attempts to contain industrialization and to control the flow of entrepreneurs and labourers entering the diamond and gold fields, constituted a serious obstacle to British plans for confederation, and provided the backdrop to the 1899–1902 Anglo-Boer War (see section three, pp. 67–9 of this chapter). Once this last and most bloody, intra-white colonial war was over, the nature of the British colonial role in the region had shifted anyway, making confederation a redundant concept (see Chapter 3).

While the confederation policy was still being pursued, African polities, once conquered or absorbed within colonial structures, responded in different ways to the opportunities that presented themselves. During the second half of the nineteenth century, an independent black commercial peasantry emerged. Bundy has done most to draw attention to the struggle of this peasantry to compete in an emerging market economy for agricultural produce. Mfengu in the Herschel district of Ciskei, for example, 'made considerable adaptations, departing from the traditional agricultural economy and emerging as small-scale commercial farmers' (Bundy, 1980: 209). Marks and Atmore (1980b) note that many African polities had already had experience of producing an agricultural surplus during and after the mfecane; not for sale, but to provide tribute to a neighbouring and more powerful group. In the 1860s the emergence of commercial participation in agriculture in Herschel was indicated by the presence of new ploughs and wagons and the increasing diversity and quantity of crops produced. The boom stage came with the expansion of the diamond town of Kimberley in the late 1860s and 1870s, when Western houses, furniture, clothes and artifacts were adopted, some going so far as to employ servants.

Increasing prosperity for some, however, coexisted with greater desperation for those squeezed out by the growing concentration of landholding. From 1883 the number of passes issued to wage-seekers leaving the reserve significantly increased. What had been the fate for some soon became the fate of many, despite an ephemeral economic upswing for the region following the Witwatersrand gold discoveries and the miners' demand for riders, grain, oxen and wool. From 1895 to 1899, drought, locust and rinderpest conspired with the colonial authority's poll tax and fluctuating market prices to inflate the numbers of destitute and increase the rate of emigration. The social stratification evident in the 1880s had become pronounced by 1900. White farmers, facing similar ecological and market forces, could rely on government assistance, but not the African peasant producer, neither in Herschel nor elsewhere. By 1920, Bundy writes, the reserve was easily distinguished from surrounding white areas by its evident poverty with, according to Gaoler, a large percentage of its population on 'the very lowest level of bare subsistence' (quoted Bundy, 1980: 219).

In the early twentieth century, a new, political phase of resistance began with the founding in 1912 of the forerunner of the ANC (African National Congress), the SANNC (South African Native National Congress). It was the creation of the solidly middle-class Africans, John Dube, Pixley Seme and Sol Plaatje. These were representatives of a relatively new phenomenon – a cohesive section of African society which had used a European-style education and a willingness to adopt white cultural mores, not only to improve its own social and material position, but also eventually to speak out on behalf of Africans with more difficult access to white opinion. Lodge argues that its mobilization in 1912 was a response to the closing off of opportunities for the social advancement of Africans following the Union of the two colonies and two ex-republics to form South Africa in 1910 (Lodge, 1983). The Cape's assimilationist constitution had held out the potential for the advancement of educated Africans not only to social grace, but also to political power. It came as a bitter pill when the Act of Union not only failed to extend the Cape constitution to the other provinces, but removed the potential for black Members of Parliament at the Cape and substituted white representatives.

In its early stages the SANNC acted primarily in the interests of its middle-class founders rather than Africans as a whole. An early complaint about segregated waiting rooms on the railways was lodged on the grounds that its members would have to share benches with uncouth rural Africans (Lodge, 1983). The organization operated to defend class privilege for a new social group, as much as to fight denial of the wider racial group. Yet its very presence denoted that, by the early twentieth century, the core of Africans who had already accepted the fact of white conquest, and even a mission education from whites, were already looking for a political solution to their problems of social and economic mobility. The political approach would gradually diffuse from this core group, through 'tribal' representations, to a much broader cross-section of African society.

2 Industrialization

The infusion of capital

African dispossession by no means proceeded entirely with the growth of industry in mind. It followed from the settlers' desire for land and security well before minerals were discovered inland. But the seal was set on African dispossession by the enhanced economic and consequent political power that industrial growth would proffer to its white masters. For millions of Africans the industrial system dictated the terms of incorporation into the world created by whites in South Africa.

In the first half of the nineteenth century the growth of an export industry, centred in the Cape, was achieved with viticulture, wool, mohair, and ostrich feathers from the more arid regions, but it was the mines of the interior which generated the wealth to transform South Africa from an essentially peripheral position within the world economy to that of a 'sub-core'. The mines did not just allow South Africa's economic integration with the world economy; they also brought about an internal economic integration. As Browett (1976) points out, the gold wealth was not all returned to overseas investors; much of it was put to use in the development of new South African industries and the infrastructure necessary for further industrialization.

Despite initial Boer reluctance, by the early 1890s, Johannesburg had already become the largest city in Africa south of Cairo, and the region's industrial and financial core. Browett's (1976) survey of the economic geography of South Africa at certain intervals since 1870 (see Fig. 2) is useful in providing the outline story behind South Africa's present spatial economic relations, although its terminology and simplicity are somewhat outdated. In 1870, the only major regional 'core' in South Africa was Cape Town, with Durban representing a minor regional core. Surrounding the two towns were belts with the highest white population densities and commercial farming. Lying beyond these areas were zones of medium population density, the inhabitants of which participated in commercial livestock farming, and which contained fairly well developed urban structures for the period. Two 'resource frontiers' were just emerging in the 1870s, with diamonds attracting settlement at Kimberley, and copper in Namaqualand.

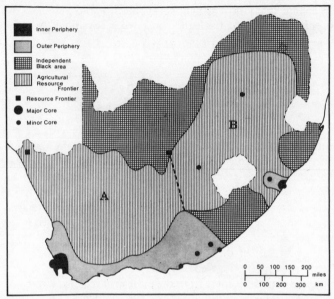

2.1 Development Regions, 1870: the pre-industrial period

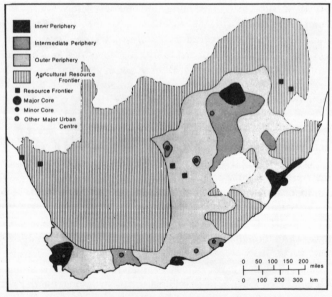

2.2 Development Regions, 1911: the transitional period

Figure 2 J.G. Browett, 1976, 'The Application of a Spatial Model to
South Africa's Development Regions'

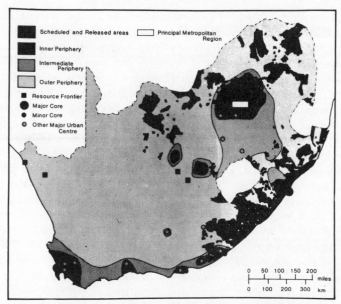

2.3 Development Regions, 1936: the industrial period, 1911–36

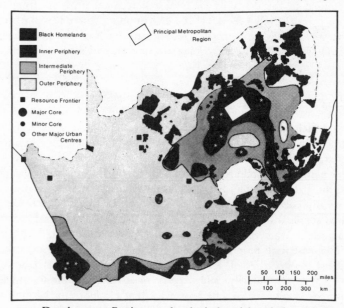

2.4 Development Regions, 1960: the industrial period, 1936–60

(reproduced from *South African Geographical Journal*, 58, 2, pp. 118–29)

Browett's next description is of the idealized South Africa of 1911, where the impact of the diamond and gold mines over the preceding forty-one years had had dramatic effects. A result of the spatial concentration of newly-discovered resources had been increasing differentiation in the geographical distribution of economic assets. South Africa's space had also become better integrated through the stimulation of regional specialization, in response to growing market opportunities. Both trends were the outcome of an infusion of capital, catalysed by the mineral discoveries. The appearance of the new mineral-based cores had provided first an incentive for British imperial control and conquest, and, later, magnets for black population shifts, and had brought into being a pattern of migrant labour that has formed a key characteristic of South Africa's human geography. By 1911 there were three major cores, Johannesburg being the largest. Below these Browett envisaged six minor cores lying outside mainstream economic growth, but still experiencing expansion. There was intensive economic activity using railway networks around each of the major cores and around Port Elizabeth, and it was these areas which had the highest employment densities and the most extensive urban structures. Regions lying beyond these immediate hinterlands responded to the demands for local and regional products from the minor cores (Bundy's Herschel is a case in point, where it was African rather than white farmers who responded). Each of the major cores in 1911 was more cohesively joined to its own periphery by the flows of black migrant workers moving to and from it, than it was to the other cores.

In the late nineteenth and early twentieth centuries, dramatic changes were occurring in the physical and social landscape of the areas which were evolving into 'cores'. An informal type of urban segregation was emerging within the white population (for example, the large gardens and elaborate design of the residences in Parktown overlooking Johannesburg contrasted sharply with the small plots and gridiron pattern of the dwellings in Vrededorp, physically and metaphorically beneath it – Van Onselen, 1982). But the consequences of spatial segregation by race were far more dramatic, being ordered and structured, rather than passively opposed, by government.

The essential premise behind the treatment of black workers resident in the cities of Kimberley and Johannesburg was that they were there temporarily, and largely to extract the finite mineral resources (Smit, 1979). The possibility that blacks could become acculturated participants in a racially shared urban environment was inconceivable to most whites. The 'fact' that Africans in the cities were to be only temporarily resident was seen as necessitating officially-ordered migrancy and urban influx control, and these in turn helped forge racial segregation in the cities.

Lemon (1982) has described South Africa's migrant labour system as a means of reconciling the social separation of races with the economic interdependence of a modern, expanding economy. He states that South Africa is unique in having imposed an institutionalized and legally entrenched migrant labour system on racial lines. But the policies of the government were not internally derived and then simply externally imposed. To a large extent they reflected and reinforced cultural and social practice on the part of white settlers, and, partially, of Africans themselves. Lemon points out that, from the 1850s, Africans in the Cape had been forced by white settlers, backed by the administration, to choose between assigned locations and service on colonial farms. Denied the previous strategy of farming on white-owned land, and facing the demands of taxation, increasing numbers of Africans came to work for white farmers.

Migrancy to the white farm was further encouraged when railway branch lines were built to areas of white farming so as to avoid black peasant producing regions like Fingoland (Bundy, 1972), thus denying Africans equal access to markets, and stimulating their resort to employment. But even while African polities like the Pedi, Tswana and the Mpondo remained independent, their paramounts had sent workers into the British colonies and Boer republics. Controlled migrant labour flows were a valuable way for African polities to secure not only consumer goods, but also firearms to resist further colonial incursion. Labour flows to the sources of white employment were expanded dramatically when the destination shifted to the mines. After 1870, first the Kimberley diamond fields and then the Witwatersrand gold mines brought forth streams of potential workers. By 1899 nearly 100,000 Africans were on the gold mines alone, many from farther afield than the four states of the region themselves (Lemon, 1982).

Kimberley's significance extends beyond the centripetal force it exerted on African workers. The closed worker compounds which were built there to prevent smuggling of diamonds and establish control over the African workforce, set the mould for other mining, and then manufacturing concerns. The first step on the road to racial discrimination in the new, industrialized South Africa was a revolt by white prospectors and merchants in 1875, to protest at undercutting by Africans.

After 1876, larger mining companies (which, as costs rose with the depth of excavation, were becoming increasingly centralized) introduced registration passes and fixed contract terms for workers, but the 1841 Master and Servants Laws were invoked to restrict the practice to black miners, who could now be arrested if found in the area without the proper pass. Developed by white prospectors, the pass system was further institutionalized by the Cape administration when the area came under its jurisdiction. Organized mining capital very much had the ear of this administration, particularly when Cecil Rhodes (who, with the De Beers Company, had established a virtual monopoly over diamond mining) became Prime Minister.

Strip searches of workers for hidden diamonds began from the 1880s, but further strike action by white miners, ironically with initial black support (Wilson and Ramphele, 1989), led to the further restriction of this practice to Africans. Closed compounds for African workers followed, not just to prevent smuggling, but to enable direct supervision and control of the companies' workers and to allow wage savings, justified by the bulk provision of food and accommodation (Turrell, 1984). It was the political power of the centralized mining houses that made such controls over the workforce in the Cape possible, and it was the racial status differences established in the pre-industrial period that enabled only white workers to combine successfully in resistance to the worst of them (Turrell, 1987).

In the Transvaal, the overall cost structure of the gold mines was critical for the development of further aspects of discrimination in the mining workforce – lower wages for Africans and job reservation. If owners could cut their overheads, then the less lucrative seams could be mined profitably. It would have to be the unenfranchised and 'uncivilized' African worker who bore the brunt of the attempt. In 1887 the Chamber of Mines was formed on the Rand to encourage uniform policy and practice of labour recruitment across the colonies and republics. Its first attempt to impose a standard African wage disintegrated under the force of competition for labour in a period when it was still relatively scarce. But subsequent government controls over recruiting enabled employers uniformly to cut African wages by 20 per cent in 1896 and a further 30 per cent in 1897 (Davenport, 1991). The white Transvaal Miners' Association was formed after a 1902 strike to resist further cost-cutting piece-work rates, which were now to be applied to whites as well.

After the Anglo-Boer War wages were again cut due to the fall in production and the need to exploit lower-grade ores. In combination with the growth of job opportunities on the railways, the wage cuts contributed to another shortage of mineworkers. The Chamber's temporary response was the introduction of Chinese workers, whose presence was resisted by white miners who were afraid that oriental labour would eventually take their own jobs. The first job reservation system was applied against these Chinese workers, but it was subsequently extended, under white labour pressure, to cover Africans. By 1907, African labour had met the shortfall and the machinery for its recruitment was functioning again, but the difference in conditions of work for white and black had firmly taken root.

Urban structures

Agricultural towns were already racially segregated to some degree in terms of area of residence and type of accommodation, but Kimberley's pattern of white workers in boarding houses and homes of the town proper, and blacks in segregated compounds 'was an unfortunate precedent for South Africa's first industrial town to set' (Worden, 1994: 39). Where Africans did settle according to unauthorized initiative – in backyards or vacant lots rather than in controlled locations, like established servants, or in compounds – vociferous demands from white townspeople for official urban segregation ensued. Rapid black urbanization was perceived as a threat to the established order of town life for South Africa's white population. The increase in the urban African population represented, for many, the demise of 'white civilization', ever held to be in tenuous occupation in an African environment. Out of the fear of this threatening black 'other' on their streets (and in their businesses) developed a defensive conceptualization of Africans as truly 'belonging' only in the countryside. It was

> expressed in written documents, and its sheer frequency [suggested] the depth and power of the needs it [served]. In general, it [went] something like this: the noble savage, whatever the difficulties attending the conditions of his existence, is none the less noble. Uproot him, transplant him to an urban situation in which he becomes a wage-labourer, and his moral collapse is swift, inevitable and complete. ... Thus the black migrant worker is judged a moral disaster in terms of the value system that made him a migrant worker in the first place. (Wade, 1993: 7)

The fear of urban racial integration in South Africa is set in comparative colonial context by Christopher (1983) who argues that the precedent for the segregated South African township can be seen in the fortified towns at Flint, Conway and Caernarvon, built by Edward I in thirteenth-century Wales. The basic premise is that English colonists, in an effort to maintain the dominant political and economic position of the English townsman, always resisted integration with the different cultural groups found in their colonies. Generally, the fear of the colonized is at the heart of the colonial settler psychology. Equality between the colonizer and colonized, in any respect, would serve to bring the spectre of a violent overthrow of the colonial yoke and its representatives closer. Physical, and particularly cultural, disparities between colonizers and colonized, and a superiority in the numbers of the colonized, contribute to the ruling group's disquiet over urban assimilation (for a deeper and far more influential analysis of colonial and anti-colonial psychology, see Fanon, 1963).

However, there was significant variation in the level of urban segregation in South Africa's early cities, even between cities in the British colonies of Natal and the Cape (Christopher, 1990). Prior to the Union, each of the four administrations in South Africa pursued separate policies of urban planning. While the Cape's pre-industrial towns were less rigidly segregated than others, the 'natural' segregation of wealth and class tended to assume a racial composition anyway. Many ex-slaves were clustered on mission stations, while, from 1847, the eastern districts of the colony had municipally managed locations and part of the Coloured population outside the white towns. In Cape Town the expanding migrant labour system was responsible for the appearance of compounds separated from the white residential areas, Kimberley being invoked as a model for African migrant control. From 1901 to 1904, an outbreak of bubonic plague in parts of the country brought about what has been labelled the 'sanitation syndrome', in which fears for the health of the (white) population informed official attempts at urban segregation. In response, separate location construction took place in Cape Town, while in Port Elizabeth Africans were shunted from their homes to the township of New Brighton. By the early twentieth century the Cape had joined the rest of South Africa in implementing pass laws and influx-control regulations and it was engaging in the resettlement of illegal black squatters.

Under the rather more severe Natal administration, Africans were discouraged from town locations early on and directed into barracks, under a system known as 'togt'. From 1873, to stay in town, Africans seeking day labour in Durban and Pietermaritzburg would have to register and wear a badge. The scheme was soon extended to cover all Africans present in the town, and was accompanied by an attempt to provide barrack locations for single male workers to live in while they were there. Marks and Atmore (1980b) explain the system as an attempt at security on the part of an early colonial presence which was weak compared to the strength of African polities in the region. Subsequently, revenues from a municipal beerhall monopoly were used to construct segregated African townships for the city.

Barracks were the only early accommodation for indentured Indians brought to Natal from the 1860s to work on the sugar plantations – a form of employment rejected by the nearby Zulu (see Richardson, 1986). By the late nineteenth century, the impulse for segregation here was primarily directed against the Indian population, growing as traders established themselves alongside indentured labourers. In response to Indian trading competition, the local state pursued 'residential segregation, political exclusion and commercial suppression' (Swanson, 1983; for a more general appreciation of the Indian presence in South Africa, see Swan, 1987; Richardson, 1986; Brain, 1989 and 1994).

Blacks were housed in the towns of the Boer republics by their employers or in locations built near, but outside, the town. There was some differentiation between the republics, the Transvaal being less efficient in its racial ordering of urban space (and also having Indian residents, who were banned from the Orange Free State). In Johannesburg, the 'sanitary syndrome' led to old African slums being razed in the early twentieth century, and their inhabitants removed to the location of Klipspruit. However, a high proportion of Africans remained living neither in compounds nor in formal townships, but in freehold or leasehold accommodation in Sophiatown, Martindale, Newclare or Alexandra. These were rather anomalous townships: due to the specific circumstances of their historical development, blacks within them could own the plots on which they lived (see Lodge, 1983: 156).

No general model of South African city development, let alone colonial city development, can accommodate the specific influences which contributed to the moulding of each city's form in the late nineteenth and early twentieth centuries; rather, like a palimpsest, the influences were layered one upon another over time, and while some of those influences may have been more universal, others were local and contingent. Nevertheless, in each of the territories of South Africa, the first industrial revolution, brought about initially by mineral extraction, had set in train fundamental social changes. While white townspeople were forced to readjust to a far larger, non-servant African presence, no longer silent and externalized, no longer physically as well as conceptually 'other', but economically vital and on their doorstep, their politicians groped for a policy to order urban space and provide the social controls necessary to reassure them.

Segregationism

Industrialization brought about a contradiction central to South Africa's subsequent social, economic and political development – that between large-scale African labour requirements, inclining social structures towards racial integration, and ideologies and administrative systems of spatial separation. The African labour presence in the cities could only remain temporary and separate if there were enforceable regulations overseeing arrivals to the urban areas, and territories set aside outside the cities where Africans could reside when not employed in them. The Cape Prime Minister, W.P. Schreiner, summarized the official attitude towards African workers: 'let them do their work, receive their wages, and at the end of their term of service, let them go back to the place whence they came – to the native territories, where they should really make their home' (quoted in Swanson, 1977: 399). The diffusion of this view – segregationism – helped put an end to a competing vision of racial relations – that of assimilation.

George Grey, the governor of the Cape Colony from 1854 to 1861, had pursued a policy of partial racial integration on white terms, to make the Xhosa 'a part of ourselves, with a common faith, common interests, useful servants, consumers of our goods, contributors to our revenue' (quoted in Davenport, 1991: 221). The material basis of such 'liberal' thinking is set out by Trapido (1980), but many 'philanthropists' adopted the same assimilationist ideas more out of a concern to benefit Africans, by introducing them to the implicit and unquestioned advantages of European civilization. Their premise was a humanitarian view of a universal human nature. But that nature was defined firmly along European lines. In other words, Africans, to become civilized, must submit to European precepts of civilized behaviour. In this sense, humanitarianism preceded the final domination and conquest of the Xhosa, just as late eighteenth-century European naturalization of the Khoisan and their landscape had prefigured their own dispossession (see Chapter 1).

Under Grey, the Cape, with a new non-racial constitution based on a property franchise qualification, witnessed the development of mixed-race schools and hospitals, in which whites and Africans were treated identically, and Grey himself even paid for forty sons of Xhosa chiefs to be educated in a mission school of the colony (Wilson, 1982a). Meanwhile, a debate on the merits of assimilation was taking place within Xhosa society, between, on the one hand, Christian converts and those who had attended colonial mission schools and, on the other hand, 'reds' – those who continued Xhosa traditions such as smearing oneself with red clay (Wilson, 1982a).

Within the colonies, while assimilation could guarantee the required African labour supplies, the threat of an integrated urban African workforce, particularly in Natal with its numerically overwhelming African population, was influential even before the advent of rapid urbanization. In 1852 a commission was set up in Natal to investigate the colony's 'Native Policy'. The commission revealed a strong segregationist discourse among white respondents. However, spatial segregation for peace and security was to be tempered by the colony's labour requirements (Thompson, 1985).

Shepstone's Natal 'Native Policy' is most often cited as the original in large-scale, formal, spatial segregation. From 1845 into the 1850s, the reservation of areas for African occupation was systematically pursued in the colony. The reserves were ruled by appointees subject to Shepstone himself, under what was described as 'traditional law'. Despite a British government grant, ostensibly for their development, Shepstone, in an attempt to ensure the colony's labour supplies, allowed the reserves to stagnate. The reserves came to embody stores of relatively cheap labour reproduction. Yet Shepstone himself was not an early segregationist ideologue. He was a pragmatist, an administrator whose brief and desire was to ensure that the most efficient systems of administration were implemented in the interests of the white colonial settlers and the British government. He, unlike later South African administrators, was not attempting to implement a pre-formulated ideological programme.

The Cape Colony's Glen Grey Act of 1894 represented a more systematic attempt to implement a coherent 'Native Policy' in one area. It is often interpreted as being assimilationist in nature (Davenport, 1991; Graaff, 1990), since it gave African producers in the Transkei (later Ciskei too) small plots of land, and by alienating the land from the remainder of the local African population, encouraged migration to supply the colony's labour needs. But Rich (1981) has argued that it had an important influence as a precedent for later, segregationist, rather than assimilationist, notions of reserve administration. For the first time under the Act, areas with separate administrations were deliberately set aside for African occupation; areas which would nevertheless remain functionally linked, through labour supplies, with 'white space'. The architect of the Act, Cecil Rhodes, saw Africans as children just emerging from barbarism. For him, it was futile to imagine that these vessels would yet contain the standards of western civilization (Parry, 1983). Turning segregated plots of eight acres (little enough to bar qualification for the Cape franchise by dint of property) over to Xhosa, and leaving the Kholwa (Christian convert Africans) out of the scheme's provisions, effectively signalled the replacement of official attempts to amalgamate black and white societies. Instead, attempts to enforce their separation ensued.

Segregation then, already established in Natal, became accepted in the Cape by the end of the nineteenth century, as a device to ensure that African social advancement in an industrializing economy should not undermine white supremacy. It was a means of both regulating unskilled labour and entrenching white political control, and it was legitimated by the racial 'science' of the era – a form of Social Darwinism (see Dubow, 1995 for a comprehensive account). The strand of thought which had Africans as an inferior branch of an evolutionary chain prevailed in nearly all publications in the first decades of the twentieth century, even in a history written in 1920 by Silas Molema, an African himself (Thompson, 1985: 95). The prominent late nineteenth-century white historian, Theal, thought that the intelligence of individual Africans depended on the amount of white blood their ancestors had acquired in North Africa before the Bantu migration to the south. With such immutable differences between the races 'proven' by the contemporary practice of anthropology, assimilation was bound to fail, since Africans were incapable of absorbing the European traits of civilization. In accordance with the pursuit of its alternative – segregation – the Cape franchise qualification was raised under Sprigg in 1887 and under Rhodes in 1892, excluding thousands of African voters. Journalistic resistance by educated Africans like Jabavu (in themselves an anomaly for the 'scientific' theory) proved ineffective, and by 1910 the Cape had liquor laws preventing sale to Africans, segregated residential locations and compulsorily segregated education.

The rejection of the prospect of equality between races was, for most whites, an implicit assumption, and it was maintained in church and state through the ensuing industrial era (Giliomee and Schlemmer, 1989). For Smuts, writing in the 1930s, the 'Native Question' was 'a matter decided for me in far-off days by my temperament and outlook', which were those of a white South African brought up in the late nineteenth century, and which 'cannot be affected by what passes or happens today, but of course I see the rocks ahead quite clearly' (cited in Ingham, 1988: 189).

It was Milner's post-Boer War Native Affairs Commission (responsible for the production of the Lagden Report), established to design a pattern for the reconstruction of the region, which encouraged the universality of segregation and portrayed it as a more coherent ideological programme. According to Giliomee and Schlemmer (1989), it laid the foundations for the system of segregation adopted deep into the twentieth century.

Ashforth, who has paid particular attention to the assumptions implied by the report's language, argues that it was part of a 'search for a formula, expressible in terms acceptable to "civilized" opinion in the mother country and the colonies of South Africa, by which labour for capitalist enterprise could be secured' (1990: 27). The reservation of land for 'Natives', it was implied in the report, required a reciprocal gesture on their part: the offering of their labour, for the mines in particular (Ashforth, 1990). The commission's proposals included the construction of locations for Africans near their centres of work in the white areas, with passes to control the influx of workers to these locations and a one-year limit on their residence there. When not employed in the white towns, Africans would reside in their own reserves, where they would be free to practise agriculture.

By 1910 and the union of South Africa, 'segregation' had already entered the language of official discourse to describe such a system, and it was being promoted, though with different emphases of rationalization, by British administrators, capitalists and Afrikaner political leaders alike. In 1913 a piece of legislation was enacted which helped to reify the conception of the Native Affairs Commission in a united South Africa. The philosophy behind the 1913 Land Act derived from the inevitable outcome of colonial dispossession. By the 1870s there was already a shortage of farming land for both whites and Africans. Squatting, sharecropping and labour tenancy were commonplace, but in the 1880s and 1890s, a new class of white entrepreneur began, for the first time, to exclude both white and black smallholders from the market. Smallholders were transformed into squatters – a wholly different legal phenomenon. Given the orthodoxy of racial attitudes, both white officials and white society in general favoured action to ensure that, if there had to be squatters, white squatters should be favoured over black. Thus, African land occupation across the country was limited to designated reserves comprising 7 per cent of South Africa's land area. Parcels of land already owned by Africans outside these reserves became known as 'Black Spots', and their inhabitants lost all security of tenure even though many remained for some time. The misery of those forced to leave is graphically portrayed in Sol Plaatje's *Native Life in South Africa* (1915). The reserves, to which they were forced to move, would provide the basis for large-scale African segregation through the twentieth century.

3 Afrikanerdom: the formation of an ethnic identity

The late nineteenth century, then, saw increasing tension, primarily between white and African, but also between white and Indian. However, it is a great (and often repeated) error to assume any kind of intraracial group solidarity as a backdrop to the history of inter-racial group conflict in South Africa. Urbanized Africans were still attached closely to their fractious traditional polities (see Beinart (1988) for the extent to which this was still true in the mid-twentieth century, and Horowitz (1991) for a contemporary analysis). Indian solidarity was impeded by differences of caste, status, region of origin and of treatment by other racial groups. As the nineteenth century drew to an end, white fractiousness, too, was developing into a vital and politically portentous phenomenon, through the emergence of a strong Afrikaner identity.

Twentieth-century nationalist movements invariably shared (and share) certain core characteristics which facilitated the mobilization of a large mass in the cause articulated by an intellectual leadership group. These characteristics were: an implicit externally derived, but internally manifested, threat to the culture, especially religion and/or language of a body of people; a constructed, but widely perceived history, the interpretation of which rests on the shared experience of 'the group' as opposed to alien 'others'; a threat to the economic fortune of most members of this historically defined group; and the creation of a set of symbols by which the group is demarcated and exhorted to act (see Hobsbawm, 1990; Maré, 1992; Greenfeld, 1992; and Smith, 1991).

All of these features played a part in the development of an Afrikaner nationalist ideology in the twentieth century. All were emerging in the decades at the end of the nineteenth century, but many of the symbols which defined the group's historical experiences were drawn from the early nineteenth century. Characteristics of late nineteenth-century Afrikaners were subjected to a conceptual time leap, and used to describe people of the early nineteenth century who were, in fact, very different. Not all commentators on South Africa have yet realized the falsity of this conceptual atemporality. De Villiers says of the early nineteenth-century British repossession of the Cape,

> in Afrikaner terms the Enemy had arrived; the Afrikaners were about to enter their Eeu Van Onreg, their Century of Wrong, which would open and close with war and defeat but which would serve to consolidate the tribe and form the volkseie, the fierce group cohesiveness, that drives them to this day. (De Villiers, 1988: 73)

But the *Eeu Van Onreg* was the publication of a twentieth-century Afrikaner intellectual attempting to mobilize an Afrikaner constituency, not a phenomenon that was consciously experienced and identified by the Dutch-speaking population of most of the period in question.

Throughout the nineteenth century, members of the Dutch-speaking population resented, and sometimes resisted, British interference in the ordering of their lives, but in the early decades of the century there was no cohesive 'Afrikaner tribe', as such, to mobilize against the British. The *Eeu Van Onreg* was part of a much later attempt to create such a group. It is the characteristics of this attempt which are of most importance in the story of Afrikaner nationalism.

The reconstructed nationalist past

The traditional narrative of the emergence of an Afrikaner ethnic awareness represents an acceptance of a history created in the late nineteenth and early twentieth centuries. It has the actions of the British, intent on political and economic modernization, turning the nineteenth-century Cape into a laboratory in which the 'distillation of Afrikanerness' (Sparks, 1990) occurred. The distillation is held to have proceeded from incidents of British repression of the Boers, notably, Slagtersnek, when Afrikaner rebels were hanged, at the second attempt after ropes broke, in 1815, and the later Anglo-Boer War. With nascent group identity repressed and language and culture threatened by Milner after the war, plus the growing 'poor white' problem, the necessary result is held to have been a widespread nationalism held latent until 1924 and 1948, when it achieved political expression.

This outline of the common approach is a crude one, but the emergence of a sense of affinity, of a shared identity or an 'imagined community' (see Anderson, 1991), is much more subtle than a catalogue of historical events, no matter how exhaustive, can indicate. As with frontier ideology, Afrikaner nationalist ideology is a complex and non-unitary phenomenon, with material as well as ideational dimensions. A proper account of it must therefore be a spatially and temporally differentiated one.

The early nineteenth-century British administrators, settlers and missionaries did indeed introduce more forcefully a set of ideas in contradistinction to those held by most Dutch-speaking frontiersmen, but in a less heavy-handed and far more contradictory way than orthodox accounts allow. The Enlightenment movement in Europe had set in train a set of social philosophies which influenced the early nineteenth-century British administrators who arrived to take up residence in the Cape (see Mostert, 1992; Crais, 1992). Philosophies of liberalism, utilitarianism and humanitarianism were introduced by those with political influence to a closing frontier environment. Humanitarianism lay behind intervention by the colonial authorities in Khoisan labour–master relations. Nevertheless, there is a distinction to be drawn between the ideological leanings of the new political elite and the change which they effected. Despite the new labour regulations, John Montagu, the Colonial Secretary at the Cape from 1843 to 1852, felt compelled to say that colour 'still forms a bar to social intercourse and intimate relations far more formidable than any rising either from diversity of origin, language or religion' (cited in Elphick and Giliomee, 1989b: 558).

Although the British assumption of political power over the Cape did not bring about great material improvement for most of the colony's black inhabitants, it did set up a contrast between white governors and white governed more apparent than when the VOC or the Batavian Republic were the administrators. The difference in language alone was enough to ensure this, since there was no significant English-speaking presence among the governed prior to 1820. The English literature of the period indicates that a slighting perception of the Dutch-speaking population was held by many English-speakers in the colony. Around the turn of the nineteenth century the Afrikaner came increasingly to join the Hottentot in being portrayed as idle and degenerate in popular writing, as the dominant discourse of the Cape became a British one. Boers were commonly characterized as lazy and malicious, their life of inactivity achieved at the expense of their slaves (Coetzee, 1988).

However, the forging of a greater distinction between colonial rulers and colonists did not automatically lead to conflict and the sharpening of an identity of opposition. Rather, co-operation between authority and settler was the norm in the early nineteenth century, with incidents of outright opposition on the part of the latter the exception. When the contested Zuurveld was systematically cleared of Xhosa in 1812, it was Boer commandoes under British command who were the most effective participants. There was conflict between Boers and representatives of British authority in the early nineteenth century, but it was exaggerated in scope and significance by a late nineteenth-century generation of Afrikaners embroiled in a deeper conflict of interest with the British authorities of their own time.

The incident at Slagtersnek became central to this late nineteenth-century construction of an Afrikaner history. The Afrikaner political establishment came to hold a mythology constructed on two key foundations: the historical suffering of the volk under the British yoke, and the persistent threat to the volk posed by the numerically superior black population. Both were sustained by the interpretation of Slagtersnek that was adopted in the late nineteenth century (Thompson, 1985). On the one hand, the incident was held to be a manifestation of ethnic conflict between British rulers and a nascent Afrikaner volk. (In fact, the administrators on the scene of the rebel hangings, and most closely involved, were themselves Dutch-speakers.) On the other hand, the episode resulted from the challenge posed to Afrikaners' status relative to blacks, because the hanged men had rebelled over laws limiting their behaviour towards their Khoisan servants.

Before the 1870s Slagtersnek was not treated in histories as a prominent event in the forming of South African society. During that decade though, the phrase wrongly attributed to relatives of the hanged men, 'we can never forget Slagtersnek', was repeated frequently enough for one to believe that it was indeed a formative event. In the 1870s Slagtersnek was being reinterpreted in the light of a contemporary form of British imperialism much more thrusting than that which existed at the time of the incident itself. The British policy of confederation was threatening the independent Boer republics. To the Boers who had struggled to build these republics, the rebels of 1815 became heroes of an earlier struggle against British domination much like their own, and therefore, symbols of a historical continuity of resistance by the mythical volk of which they were a part. No matter that the lifestyles of the Slagtersnek rebels, the Bezuidenhouts and their allies, hardly corresponded with the 1870s ethnic leadership's ideals of religious observance and racial purity, nor that most Boers at the time of the rebellion wanted nothing to do with it; the myth would provide historical legitimacy for the present struggle. Even though the incident of Slagtersnek itself was a relatively insignificant interruption to 'normal' frontier life, the interpretation of it subsequently adopted, proved, in the late nineteenth century, a powerful mobilizing factor for Afrikaners.

While the volk's early struggle with the British was a largely constructed history, there was a real historical experience, shared by many Boers through the nineteenth century, which helped provide support for a nationalistic tendency. By the second half of the century, the continuance of the Boer custom of divided inheritance, which had initially fuelled the push of white settlement eastward, became impossible for many families; fragmentation had already reduced inheritances to uneconomic sizes. A class of poor and landless Dutch-speakers began to emerge, and to provide support for the nationalism that would give it dignity, and perhaps protection from competition in the labour markets of the expanding cities.

An earlier Boer response to landlessness was the trek to the north, beyond the confines of the colony. In the interpretation of the past which helped foster a sense of Afrikaner national identity in the late nineteenth century, the Great Trek was seen as even more important than Slagtersnek. This interpretation had the Trek as an expression of the volk's urgent desire to be rid of the yoke of British interference, and to manifest their ethnic solidarity in the form of a new and pure Afrikaner state. In fact, while the British did institute changes on the frontier which were highly significant in the decision of some 15,000 Boers to emigrate, their impact was not directly to hammer a new nation into shape.

The British desire to establish the 'solid prosperity of a thriving and industrious population' (quoted in Peires, 1989a: 498) on the frontier was translated into a uniform and effective land tax, the abolition of monopolies and a revamped Land Board to give title and collect payment. There was to be a thoroughgoing shake-up of the relatively anarchic VOC frontier political economy. The appointment of resident

magistrates and Civil Commissioners to replace landdrosts and heemraden represented a decisive shift of power in favour of the British and
at the expense of Boers in the country districts. Anxiety about further
changes was a major impulse for many who decided to leave the colony.
A frontier farmer of the 1830s expresses the sentiment:

> now we have a civil commissioner to receive our money for government
> and for land surveys, a magistrate to punish us, a Clerk of the Peace to
> prosecute us and get us in the Trok [gaol], but no Heemrad to tell us
> whether things are right or wrong. ... The Englishman is very learned.
> ... They and the Hottentots will squeeze us all out by degrees. (Quoted
> in Peires, 1989a: 498)

The aim of the 1830s emigration was to 'generally reconstitute the
way of life of which the revolution in government had stripped [the
migrants]' (Peires, 1989a: 499). New implementation of rent collection,
including arrears, the threat to established methods of dealing with
black labour, and the legal intervention of the British, seemingly biased
towards those who were not white, were already establishing dissatisfaction among burghers by the 1830s. The revelation that compensation
for the loss of slaves after abolition (worth four-fifths of their value)
could only be collected in London, added insult to injury. As an early
promise of laws to channel mfecane refugees into 'useful labour'
receded, and abolition approached, preparations to leave the colony
were made. They were hastened by the advent of the sixth frontier
war with the Xhosa.

In the interpretation of the late nineteenth-century Afrikaner
nationalists, in their decision to leave the British colony, the trekkers
were upholding the volk's staunch racial integrity and antipathy to
racial intercourse. In fact, Tregardt, one of the Trek's leaders, had
lived in Xhosa territory under Hintsa before leaving the frontier, and
many Boers expressed their disgust at the British murder of the
paramount chief. The old prospect of an alliance with Xhosa arms in
a fight against the British was revived at times by the generation of
Boers which supplied the Trek. Legassick (1980) argues that most of
the Boers of the period were prepared to concede equality to the
independent African nations, while defending the exploitation of their
own black labourers. Equality, though, may be too strong a word. The
respect Boers had for African polities was based more on the force that
they could muster than on an ideological recognition of equal worth.
Nevertheless 'there can be no doubt that the emigration was a response
to specific policies of the colonial government rather than an Afrikaner
nationalist reaction to British rule or a response to the breakdown of
black–white relations on the frontier' (Peires, 1989a: 499).

The late nineteenth-century reality

Despite the mythology of a later generation of Afrikaners, nationalism was not a prominent feature of the consciousness of Boers in the early nineteenth century. Adam and Moodley (1986) state that the first real ethnic political mobilization of Afrikaners in fact occurred at the Cape in 1872. During this year 'responsible government' was granted by the British government to the Cape Colony, with a franchise qualification set, after intense debate (primarily over the extent of African participation it would allow), low enough for even the poorer sections of the white population to vote.

Since 1820 the incoming British settlers had largely stayed clear of agriculture, leaving Afrikaners predominant in the agricultural sector. With the Cape now setting its own economic policy, these farmers mobilized to safeguard their material interests. Their virtual mono-ethnicity gave their political mobilization an obvious ethnic dimension. They mustered around the pursuit of low taxes, agricultural credit, secure and cheap labour supplies and further state support for the sector. In the late nineteenth century though, the conception of ethnic struggle within the Cape extended beyond the farming sector and into the financial realm. Butler (1987) and Giliomee (1989a) have traced an intensifying conflict between British-based and local Afrikaner banks, fought over the custom of the predominantly Afrikaans farmer. The fact that smaller banks with a more local and Afrikaans identity, in spite of receiving greater sympathy, were losing out at the end of the nineteenth century to the better terms offered by the bigger 'foreign' banks, fed into the growing sense of Afrikaner ethnic defensiveness. By the turn of this century, then, materialistic concerns were intricately and inextricably interwoven with ethnic identity for a core group of Afrikaners in the colony.

But the political mobilization of Afrikaners was not restricted to the Cape in the late nineteenth century. Davenport (1991) has charted the creation of a politically expressed ethnic identity in the South African Republic (SAR) and Orange Free State. Here, Afrikaners had constructed independent states following their emigration from the Cape Colony. The leaders of the republics had found it difficult to inculcate a national pride during the years in which they were left alone by the British, but when confrontation with the British administration of the Cape Colony developed, a catalyst for ethnic mobilization was provided from without.

Britain had already annexed the trekkers' republic of Natal in 1843. In 1852, realizing that economic dependence on the Cape Colony and Natal would continue, it had recognized the independence of the SAR and in 1854, that of the remaining trekker republic, the Orange Free State. But the new phase of imperial expansion in response to mineral discoveries was about to begin. In the year that Britain annexed Basutoland – 1868 – a play about Slagtersnek was first performed in Cape Town, and a Bloemfontein journalist advised his readers to 'Think of Slagtersnek' (Thompson, 1985: 126).

The 1815 incident was cemented in the infant mythology in 1877 with the British annexation of the SAR and the Revd S.J. Du Toit's publication of *Die Geskiedenis van ons Land in die Taal van ons Volk* (*The History of Our Land in the Language of Our People*) (1877, Cape Town). Du Toit was a key participant in the formation of Afrikaner national identity in the late nineteenth century. He was based in Paarl, the town which became the hub of Cape nationalism, and edited its nationalist paper, *The Patriot*. In his influential book, six pages were devoted to the 'Uprising of Bezuidenhout', with the rebels portrayed as heroes resisting British tyranny. The Great Trek was interpreted as a direct consequence of the precedent of resistance they established.

By the end of the nineteenth century, the interpretation of Du Toit had found apostles among authors who were sympathetic to the republics striving to resist expansionist British imperialism. Sympathizers were galvanized particularly by the success of the Transvaal in shaking off the British yoke in the first Anglo-Boer War of 1881, when the Boers inflicted a major defeat on British line regiments at Majuba. The two major thrusts of twentieth-century Afrikaner nationalism – anti-British and anti-black – had crystallized by the 1890s, in opposition to the British 'unnatural and stupid policy of equalising born masters and born servants' (Thompson, 1985: 130).

The ideological momentum developed in the late nineteenth century soon generated political organization. The first branches of the Afrikaner Bond were formed in the Cape in 1880, with a Kuyperian theology as defence against 'liquor, lucre and redcoats' (Davenport, 1991: 93). Du Toit played a major role in the organization of the Bond. Initially, the organization was not approved of by the republic's leaders, but branches were subsequently set up in the Transvaal and the Orange Free State. Du Toit was eventually displaced as the leading light of the organization by Jan Hofmeyr, after the latter had gained control of the Transvaal branches.

The mixed reception of the Bond by Afrikaners reveals their divided political outlook in the period. Although a certain momentum had been given to the adoption of political ethnicity, the structuring of political views according to ethnicity was by no means universal by the beginning of the second, and major, Anglo-Boer War. When gold was first discovered in the Transvaal, many Cape Afrikaners, including

Bond members, feared the potential for economic competition from the SAR and placed their allegiance with the British colony rather than with the Afrikaner republic. In 1889, when the potential for Cape farmers and speculators to profit in central Africa was realized, Hofmeyr even pledged Bond support for Cecil Rhodes in his scheme to extend British influence northwards. Thus Rhodes, the arch British imperialist, became involved in a parliamentary alliance with the Afrikaner Bond in the Cape Parliament.

The Rhodes–Bond political alliance was maintained in the Cape, in economic opposition to the Boer republics, until the 1895 Jameson Raid. The raid was a bungled attempt by Rhodes to stir a rebellion of uitlanders ('outsiders' – mostly English-speaking prospectors and traders) in the SAR. The rebellion would be ignited by an incursion of armed men, led by Jameson, and it was hoped that the Boer republic would collapse. In fact, the conspirators were rounded up and the raid led to an irreversible split between Rhodes and the Bond in the Cape. Cape politics now reflected the wider division in the region between ethnically defined political competitors. The split between Rhodes' Progressive Party and the Afrikaner Bond presaged the violent conflict between the British and the Afrikaners in the subsequent Anglo-Boer War.

By the 1890s the Republic's export value exceeded the Cape Colony's, meaning that 'imperial paramountcy would soon become a meaningless phrase' (Davenport, 1991: 187) if the South African Republic remained independent. The inevitable Anglo-Boer War of 1899 to 1902 was fought, then, 'to determine which white authority held real power in South Africa' (Davenport, 1991: 198). If British control could be established over the gold mines, the labour supplies and infrastructure necessary for their efficient exploitation would no longer be impeded by the independent Boer polities. Added to this, British financiers, particularly nervous after the recent collapse of the Baring Brothers financiers, could rely on the gold deposits as the biggest single source of the standard on which money was based – on the eve of the war gold supplies at the Bank of England were falling again (Worden, 1994: 26).

When Milner was appointed as governor at the Cape, the drive towards war began in earnest. For Milner, as with other British Cape officials, war with the SAR would not be purely an economic matter. The republic's government was perceived as 'not one "friendly" to, and prepared to collaborate with, British imperial interests. Control over the polity of the Transvaal as much as over the economy of the mining industry, was crucial' (Smith, 1990, quoted in Worden, 1994: 26).

The ensuing war, pre-emptively initiated by President Kruger of the SAR, 'entrenched a bitterness between Boer and British which was to endure throughout the twentieth century' (Worden, 1994: 28). British scorched-earth tactics, in a systematic attempt to end prolonged guerrilla resistance, resulted in the deliberate destruction of over 30,000 farms. In British 'concentration camps', set up to deny succour to Boers continuing the fight, over 26,000 Boer women and children died (Spies, 1986: 214) through disease and neglect. By creating thousands of martyrs for the cause of the volk, and uniting the ethnically homogenous republics against a powerful enemy, the war was a major stimulus to further Afrikaner nationalist mobilization, across what was to become the whole of South Africa, the Cape included.

The settlement of the war also contributed to Afrikaner ethnic formation. Milner's avowed aim of Anglicizing South Africa after the war led to a policy of outlawing Dutch instruction in government schools and promoting everywhere the use of English. During the attempts by Afrikaans political leaders to vitalize Afrikaner ethnicity in the 1880s and 1890s, many Dutch-speakers had placed their identity largely within class, religious or territorial boundaries, rather than ethnic ones, as the Rhodes–Bond alliance demonstrates. But the war and this policy of deliberate repression of 'Afrikaner-ness' helped generate a focus on precisely that ethnicity as the prime marker of identity.

Yet, the emergence of a political constituency willing to back a nationalist political programme within the Afrikaans population also had a great deal to do with economic conditions which were developing both prior to and after the war. What ultimately galvanized a general, politically expressed Afrikaner nationalism was the disproportionate impact of economic distress on a broad section of the Afrikaans population. With an economic battle to be fought, and the participants clearly defined by their culture and ethnicity, ethnically based political mobilization was inevitable. The growing shortage of land had been creating a squatter (bywoner) class around the old eastern frontier through the second half of the century. With the industrialization of the Rand, commercial farmers across the country began to utilize fully the land they owned so as to supply the expanding urban markets. Landless Afrikaners found their rural options narrowed as landowners began to evict unprofitable tenants, and the volk's drift to the cities began, as individual families felt the broad shifting structures of economic development impinging upon their lives. For those who retained ownership of the land, increasing profits were available, with government aid in credit, research and training for farmers, plus the expansion of road and rail networks around the turn of the century.

Prior to the Anglo-Boer War, the presence of dispossessed Afrikaners in the cities, and their obvious impoverishment compared to the traditionally urbanized English-speaking population, had already helped to stimulate an urban Afrikaner political and cultural awakening (Giliomee and Schlemmer, 1989). The movement received extra boosts with the agrarian rinderpest crisis of 1890, which ejected more poor white smallholders from the land, and the attack on Afrikaner life, property and culture during and after the war.

In the rural regions, which provided the sources of the migrants, there was particular resentment at the fact that black tenants and sharecroppers were becoming wealthier than many of the Afrikaners being forced out. One white landowner was nearly beaten up when he remarked that he could get more out of one of the African families on his farm than he could out of seven bywoner families (Keegan, 1986). Anti-British and anti-black feeling defined a sense of independent identity, this time in the cities. For poor Afrikaners, urbanization brought both an obvious material disparity with urban English-speakers, and an erosion of material superiority over Africans. The material concerns of the migrants dovetailed perfectly with the ideological fervour of ethnic 'revival' promoted by leaders like Du Toit. As urban slums containing a mixture of poor whites and blacks sprang up, first in the eastern Cape, then throughout South Africa, the challenge to an established racial order was concentrated on a large section of the Afrikaner population.

Political ethnic mobilization represented a way of pulling Afrikaners out of their new, urban predicament. As the material gap narrowed between urban Afrikaners and Africans, a wider group came to adopt an ideology and a theology which stressed the innate differences between the races. Even if material security could not be assured, at least psychological dignity could be. The Afrikaner nationalist emphasis on Calvinism stems from the late nineteenth century. Afrikaner historians of the period tried to give expression to the implicit differences that they felt existed between their 'volk' and blacks by stressing religion's role in the formation of an Afrikaner people. In 1882 and 1898 respectively, F. Lion Cachet and J.F. Van Oordt traced the Calvinism of the volk back through a continuum of opposition to both secular British and heathen black (cited Thompson, 1985: 85–6).

With a reinterpreted past, a recent experience of ethnic suffering at the hands of the British, an ethnic intelligentsia leading a nationalist revival, and a new material predicament, Afrikaners really were beginning to feel a sense of innate difference, and to forge a separate political identity, by the turn of the twentieth century. This nationalist identity was to reach its apotheosis in the formation of the apartheid system after 1948.

Of great importance too (although it has been relatively neglected), was the development of a separate Coloured political body through the same period in which Afrikaans identity was solidifying. Prior to the 1890s, many Coloureds (descendants of Khoisan, slaves and various mixed-race unions) in the Cape, and particularly in Cape Town, felt that the distinctions between them and whites were lessening. The Cape franchise gave them the same political rights, and some had achieved a degree of success in business. But with the late nineteenth-century raising of the franchise qualification – primarily in order to exclude Africans – and with increasing competition in the growing urban arena for work and custom from rural migrants, sections of the Coloured population felt themselves being squeezed from above and below. On the one hand, local authorities were becoming increasingly concerned to protect poor whites from Coloured competition and, on the other, urbanizing Africans were proving an additional threat to established Coloured economic status. For Coloureds, 'there was simply too much to lose through identification with Africans' (Goldin, 1989: 248). Intensifying Coloured identity, then, was both a reaction against greater white discrimination and 'a rear guard action' to preserve what distinction there had been between Coloured and African. Both were resorted to in an attempt to restore the possibility of Coloured–white integration.

Given that this inclusivity was its goal, late nineteenth- and early twentieth-century Coloured mobilization was not nationalist in the sense that white Afrikaner mobilization was: Coloureds generally sought to be a part of another established identity – white, as opposed to black – rather than to construct a distinct sense of Coloured being. However, one of the consequences of the 'elaboration of segregation' (Dubow, 1987) (discussed in Chapter 3), was the increasing remoteness of this particular ideal.

Conclusion

By the beginning of the nineteenth century, the Cape Khoikhoi, despite the granting of *de jure* equality with whites, represented a distinct *class* as well as a racial grouping. Following their dispossession,

> the 'coloured' survived because they possessed only their labour power. Cape liberalism gave them equality before the law, access to the courts, protection against lawlessness, a free labour market, and in all other respects permitted a high degree of discrimination. They were emancipated from slavery, but not from poverty, ignorance and disease. As the legal gap narrowed, the social gap between them and the colonists widened. (Simons and Simons, 1969: 29)

The nineteenth century brought crucial transformation to all of South Africa's social groups, as agents largely from Britain extended the economic and social patterns of capitalism to incorporate them and their territories. The industrial systems forged under white administrations set the conditions on which both Africans and Afrikaners would be brought into 'modernity', just as the farming systems of the Boers had forced the Khoikhoi into a particular social niche within white space in the eighteenth century. Africans in the nineteenth century, like the Khoisan before them, found their labouring function entrenched not only in social relations, but also, through the regulation of migrancy, in spatial relations, by law, both in the colonies and the republics. An uprooted African peasantry was made available for work in white space through cultural and military conquest, annexation, taxation and, finally, market competition. Despite a mid-century assimilationist discourse, racial discrimination became an inherent and largely unquestioned principle of government in both republics and colonies, even if it was theoretically disallowed by legislation in the latter.

But the systems which characterize South Africa's human geography as a whole – migrant labour, influx control and spatial segregation – were not uniformly imposed on South African society. They evolved incoherently through the century from a configuration of regionally and locally specific processes. There was no centralized, overarching attempt to order South Africa's spatial flux – its urban growth, its labour flows and the distribution of its races – until the twentieth century. This was not just a consequence of South Africa's division into four separate states for much of the nineteenth century; it was also the result of poorly connected elites, each striving to manage threatening change within their own localities. South Africa in the early twentieth century represented a summation of varied local efforts to fix a racial order into dynamic social, economic and spatial relations. Each of these local agents was, directly or indirectly, under the influence of the British Empire, with its own inconsistent Colonial Office policy.

While the localities of the nineteenth century were not well physically connected for most of the period, they were articulated by a fairly universal hegemonic group ideology. It owed its origins to white distinctiveness and conceptions of the African 'other' at the early Cape, but it had developed and been entrenched by the experiences of warfare, industrialization and urban growth. The novels of J.M. Coetzee, André Brink and Christopher Hope all impressionistically convey a white incapacity to 'become African'. The Boers early on adopted an African mode of production and an affinity with the African landscape and soil, but their consciousness was derived from Europe, as was their cultural expression of it. The black African presence was still 'silent' in most white minds, despite the massive transformation and integration of social and material life, at the end of the nineteenth century. Even the physical presence of Africans in their cities was made more remote, externalized by segregationism in urban planning.

The ideological legacies of the eighteenth century – the assumption of exclusive white access to power, land and wealth, and the expectation of service from cheap black labourers – were made tangible in white space through industrialization and urbanization in the nineteenth century. With the option of armed resistance gone by the end of the century (though there was a last Zulu revolt, largely over taxes, in 1906; see Marks, 1970), and economic competition on equal terms disallowed, most blacks either tried to maintain a subsistence in the reserves, worked for white farmers on the platteland (white-owned rural farmland) or worked, with varying degrees of compliance, in the white towns. Afrikaners, meanwhile, had responded to the uneven material and ideological consequences of the closing of the frontier, and the penetration of British capitalism and imperialism, with the development of an ethnic particularism. A nationalist tradition was invented and became established in the late nineteenth century. The impression that the 1950s generation of Afrikaner political leaders made on South African society and space could never have been so deep without a profound sense of national identity and destiny, inherited from the late nineteenth century, and extending beyond mere racial consciousness.

3

The Germination of
a System

Introduction

The seeds of the twentieth-century system of white domination and
segregation had been planted in the nineteenth century by African
dispossession and early industrialization. The structures by which that
system would be administered germinated with Milner's post-Anglo-
Boer War reconstruction, and took firm root across the nation during
the period from South Africa's formation as a nation state in 1910 to
the Second World War. The bulk of this chapter is split into two main
sections to address the most salient characteristics of this period. In
the first, the ideology of segregationism and the legal and spatial
structures which resulted from it are traced through the first half of
the twentieth century. The second section interprets the increasing
political success of Afrikaner nationalism. This movement reached its
apotheosis in 1948, with the election of a regime determined, with the
policy of apartheid, to shore up white supremacy and uplift the volk
through the second half of the century.

But before the elaboration of a segregationist system can be properly
explained, it is useful to introduce, in the next few pages, the institutional and class struggles that South Africa experienced from 1910
to 1948. These struggles provided both the context, and an important
impulse, for legislation firmly entrenching an edifice of segregation.

Class and institutional struggles,
1910–48

The British Empire, the South African state, English and local capital,
and black and white labour were the main structures and agencies
whose interaction shaped mid twentieth-century South African society.
Through their dynamic relationships they provided the context for the
political and economic struggles which prefigured apartheid. Immedi-

ately following union, the South African state was led by two Boer generals, Botha and Smuts. Their government deliberately acted as the vanguard of a sentiment of reconciliation between British and Boer. The debates within white politics for the next decade and a half were to centre around this government's compromising and conciliatory stance towards South Africa's English-speakers and the British Empire.

An alliance between wealthier Afrikaner farmers, mostly in the Cape and the Transvaal, and English mineowners formed the backbone of the governing South African Party (SAP). While the party ran the country, the Chamber of Mines, through its command of finance and economic organization, effectively ran the economy (Terreblanche and Nattrass, 1990). The obvious challenge to inter-ethnic harmony came from nationalistic Afrikaners led by J.B.M. Hertzog. Their main grievance was the leverage exerted over South Africa's political economy by English-speakers within the country, and the British government without. The anti-alliance group remained within the Cabinet until 1912, when it broke away under Hertzog and, in 1914, formed the Nationalist Party (NP).

In 1914–15, nationalist Afrikaners led a rebellion against the government when it decided to enter the First World War as an ally of Britain, and to invade German Southwest Africa on Britain's behalf. Throughout the twentieth century, the Afrikaner nationalist tradition would continue to be represented both by formal political and parliamentary organizations – the descendants of Hertzog's party – and by extra-parliamentary, and often violently inclined, more extreme groups (see second section of this chapter, pp. 93–105).

While the state, representing an alliance of ethnic elites, was ideologically and politically challenged by Afrikaner nationalists between 1910 and 1924, a more tangible challenge came from increasingly well-organized workers in the economic sphere. In 1918–19, Afrikaans, English and African workers struck in response to a decline in living standards. The result was limited gains for the white workers and the repression of their black counterparts. Racial differentiation within the workforce was consolidated with the Industrial Conciliation Act of 1924 which restricted the advantages of new collective bargaining structures to unionized whites and Coloureds, to the exclusion of Africans.

The divergence between white and African worker experience was not solely due to legal discrimination. In the early twentieth century, Africans had little experience of industrial organization, while whites were more able to draw on European traditions of workerism. The difference was reflected in the formation by whites, in 1921, of the Communist Party (CP) of South Africa, founded in the belief that 'capitalism and white domination ... rested on the four pillars of racialism, nationalism, jingoism and reformism' (Simons and Simons, 1969: 270), and that workers' collective action could undermine these pillars.

White workers, as the CP hoped, did come together against capitalists spectacularly in 1922, but they were in violent opposition to their African counterparts. In November 1921 the Chamber had responded to a falling gold price and rising costs by announcing its intention to eliminate the colour bar in semi-skilled work, thus facilitating the employment of cheaper black labour in jobs previously reserved for whites. The announcement raised the possibility of some 2,000 white jobs being retrenched. White miners came out on strike in January 1922 and organized themselves into unofficial commandos along the Rand. Even CP members, in their encouragement of the strike, adopted a racist stance. Their specious argument ran as follows: support for the miners in their attempt to protect the colour bar was justified, since the strike, by opposing the employment of blacks at lower rates, could be seen as a necessary step to raise levels of pay for all workers. Hence the paradoxical slogan sported on workers' placards: 'Workers of the World Unite and Fight for a White South Africa'.

The state's economic dependence on the mines ensured that it would have to back the mineowners' drive for continued capital accumulation (Ingham, 1988). Smuts authorized police action against the union commandos, which resulted in three deaths at Boksburg. The union proclaimed a general strike, and Smuts announced martial law. Several days of bitter fighting ensued which, combined with the heavy handling of previous strikes in 1913 and 1914, the wartime rebellion and the shootings of Africans at Port Elizabeth and Queenstown in 1920 and 1921, gave an impression of the government's hands being stained with blood, and of Smuts himself as an autocratic ruler (Davenport, 1991).

The NP and the Labour Party (LP) had shared sympathy for the strikers in the early stages of their struggle. The brutality of the ensuing conflict helped mobilize a union of anti-capitalist and Afrikaner nationalist sentiment which swept an NP–LP alliance to a victory over the SAP in the 1924 election. Terreblanche and Nattrass (1990) describe this result as the first serious challenge to colonial capitalism in South Africa. 'The [white] artisan had won the struggle for recognition within the white power structure. New industrial laws, the "civilized labour policy" and the LP's presence in the coalition government marked his absorption in the ruling elite' (Simons and Simons, 1969: 327).

The new state stood firmly for white labour and small Afrikaner farmers. However, the political position of unskilled white workers (predominantly Afrikaners) was still in doubt. The allegiance of this class was the prize fought over by the left-wing trade unions and the Afrikaner nationalists.

In an attempt at greater autonomy, the new government encouraged import substitution with a Board of Trade, and in 1928 a nationalized Iron and Steel Corporation (ISCOR) was established. The trauma of modernization and urbanization for the white poor, 80 per cent of whom were Afrikaners, was moderated by a welfare state. Small Afrikaans farmers had not only the assurance of cheap black labour supplies through the denial of black trade-union membership and the 1925 Wage Act; they were also cushioned by state financial support. Poor urban Afrikaners were eligible for state-protected employment on the railways or in government (the beginnings of a highly significant trait). With incorporation in the state sector and the help of the post-depression boom, the 'poor white problem' had been as good as eliminated by 1939. Furthermore, the radicalizing potential of the CP and the white trade-union movement had been effectively neutralized by the government's action in taking white labour under its wing (Davenport, 1991).

The tension between the alliance of class forces represented by the 1924–33 state on the one hand, and mining capital on the other, has been seen by some writers as part of a wider conflict between foreign and domestic capital (Legassick and Hemson, 1976; Bozzoli, 1978; Rogerson, 1982; and O'Meara, 1983). Domestic agricultural and industrial classes had a powerful ally in the state, with its capacity for economic intervention. The NP's hold on government allowed it to divert English capital's surplus into investment within South Africa (Nattrass, 1981, cited in Lemon, 1987), notably for the government's main economic constituencies – agriculture and domestic industry (see also Davies et al., 1976).

Unfortunately for the Pact government, a close understanding with domestic capital and a fervent desire for economic self-sufficiency and detachment from imperial influence were not enough to ride out the economic depression which struck the world economy in the early 1930s. Although South Africa was relatively insulated from monetary collapse by its gold reserves, it could not help being articulated with the world economy, and the depression had significant domestic political repercussions.

In the early 1930s the international demand for South Africa's exports began to fall as consumption overseas plummeted. The government, however, refused to devalue like other affected countries, not only on the grounds that it was demonstrating its cherished independence from external influence, but also because devaluation would raise the price of imports. Speculation that South Africa would nevertheless devalue led to a drain of local currency as money was invested on the London Stock Exchange. (After devaluation this could then be converted back at a profit.) The speculative drain itself eventually contributed to the decision finally to abandon the gold standard and devalue in December 1932.

In 1933, with Hertzog fearing a loss of the next election, an approach was made to Smuts for a coalition of the NP and the SAP on certain terms, including South Africa's autonomy, the retention of the national flag, equal English–Afrikaans language rights, the safeguarding of white farmers and workers and the maintenance of 'white civilization and political separation' (Davenport, 1991: 276) in 'Native Policy'. Such terms for coalition were acceptable to many in the NP (especially in the two northern provinces), but to others, particularly in D.F. Malan's Cape section of the party, coalition on any terms with the party of English capital and imperialist collaboration was a betrayal. Ultimately though, not just coalition but fusion was to occur between Hertzog's NP and Smuts's SAP, creating the United Party (UP), while Malan was to lead most of the Cape caucus of the old NP, plus northern sympathizers, into the Gesuiwerde, or 'purified' NP (from here on, simply NP).

The fusion government bore the brunt of social tensions arising out of the most rapid secondary industrialization and urbanization South Africa had yet seen and, with Smuts in government once again, the English establishment was readmitted to political power. The Cabinet considered a programme of more liberal policy options towards urban blacks, which for many Afrikaners represented a threat to the established order.

During the war, with white workers lost to the army, the job colour bar was openly flouted, with the tacit approval of the English liberal element in government. A first, tentative step towards permanently filling skilled posts with blacks was the Native Education Finance Act 1945, which freed black education from its reliance on finance raised solely from black taxes. The reforms which were envisaged beyond this, especially those suggested by the UP's Fagan Commission, set up to investigate the changes required of 'Native policy', went a long way towards losing the UP the 1948 election. Government officials were contemplating, by the end of the war, the stabilization of complete African families in the cities, village-building for the landless in the reserves and the issuing of passes which would be voluntarily applied for, and linked to, secure employment (Davenport, 1991). In private, some Cabinet ministers may even have considered ending the traditional migrant labour pattern altogether, reversing the established principle of temporary urban African residence (Wolpe, 1988).

Such thinking was induced by a dawning recognition of the need of the expanding manufacturing sector for a stable African workforce and a more wealthy domestic market for its goods (dependent on a better-paid black population). It was further stimulated by the 1946 strike of 70,000 African mineworkers, in response to rising expectations, the cutting of rations and an attack on their union. The strike, like that of 1922, was crushed by the state, but the African workers of 1946, unlike their white predecessors, were not subsequently to gain access to government.

It was urban employers who required a stable urban African workforce, but it was the UP government which would shoulder the responsibility of supplying it and face the threat of a loss of white electoral support. The NP's Sauer Report – rival to the UP's Fagan Report – represented an early 'spelling out of the gospel of apartheid' and 'seemed to offer more security on more familiar lines' (Davenport, 1991: 312–13). While improving the conditions of African workers may have furthered the interests of manufacturing capital, mining capital, white labour and white farmers were generally protective of their dominance over black labour. Such was the prelude to the assumption of power in 1948 of Malan's NP, and its alternative programme of apartheid.

1 Ideology, segregation and the urban arena, 1910–48

By the beginning of this century, the Cape assimilationist discourse of the mid-nineteenth century had been effectively replaced throughout South Africa by a Darwinian scientific racism. Scientific racism held that 'the relative position of "pure races" along the evolutionary scale was "immutable"' (Dubow, 1987: 82), with the qualification that white civilization could potentially 'regress', notably through 'miscegenation'. In the 1920s, though, on the Witwatersrand, a new 'breed' of liberal anthropologist began to identify the differences between African and European as cultural, rather than as objective degrees of civilization. Bantu Studies – the anthropological project that was to occupy many university departments through the first half of the twentieth century – had begun. Liberals like Alfred Hoernle and Edgar Brookes found, in the rather ambiguous phenomenon of 'culture', a quality which would always progress, eliminating the fear of a regression of civilization. For liberals, the concept of culture represented a compromise wherein blacks were held to be at present inferior, as acknowledged by general white opinion, but with the capacity for advancing, in the context of an urbanized, industrial society, to a state in which they would meet the white population's cultural standards. Most liberals agreed on the essential distinction between adaptable cultural, and immutable racial differences. However, because of the cultural gulf which separated whites from Africans in South Africa at the time, many liberals argued, along with white society in general, that the policy of segregation should be continued, at least for the foreseeable future. In the 1920s 'segregation appeared to be beyond the realm of political dispute' (Dubow, 1987: 9).

From the late nineteenth century to the 1920s, segregationist Acts had seldom been interpreted as 'integral elements of a united ideological package' (Dubow, 1989: 39), although English-speaking liberals had fostered the idea of spatial segregation as a protective shield against further black dispossession. But by the 1930s, it was becoming increasingly clear that segregation was being implemented, under Afrikaner nationalist patronage, to counter English liberal hegemony and to ensure continued white dominance over blacks in the cities.

In the atmosphere of threatening African worker mobilization, particularly under the Industrial and Commercial Workers Union (ICU), the concept of a cultural gulf between the races could be invoked to stem the threat of radicalization by promoting a return to traditional African 'tribalism' in the reserves. The segregationism of the 1920s and 1930s was an attempt to 'bolster a more conservative system as a means of social control' (Worden, 1994: 77) against an alarming alternative focus – militant African workerist resistance. Heaton Nicholls, MP for Zululand, expressed the fear behind the 1920s segregationist drive succinctly: 'if we do not get back to communalism we will most certainly arrive very soon at communism' (cited in Dubow, 1989: 71).

Liberals in the 1930s and 1940s, then, had to re-evaluate. The liberal principle of 'protective' segregation for Africans had been used instead to uphold white political and economic dominance against the threat of African proletarianization. It was also ensuring the impoverishment of the reserves. The liberal historian, W.M. Macmillan, was highly critical of the early twentieth-century form of urban segregation, arguing that it was founded on an insufficient rural base. Reserves such as the formerly successful Herschel in the eastern Cape were being noticeably eroded as their occupants' numbers swelled (Macmillan, 1931). Such criticisms provoked the government response of 'developmentalism' – the aim of improving the reserves with agricultural demonstrators, soil conservation and instruction. But the level of financial commitment ensured that, for most rural Africans, the material impact of the policy was insignificant.

Out of the abuse of traditional liberal ideology grew a new oppositional or counter-hegemonic ideology (or rather, an old one resurrected). Assimilationism assumed greater legitimacy among liberals as the 1930s, and particularly the 1940s, progressed. If Africans were only to be subjected to white privilege and power under segregated institutions, their best hope for advancement lay with greater integration into white social and political structures. The basis for the new liberal critique of segregationist trusteeship was well expressed by Patrick Duncan at the beginning of the 1930s:

> The people of South Africa – the European people – will not give up the idea that the country is theirs, the only home they have for themselves and their children. They do not consider that they are here as invaders with no title as against the natives but that of conquest. ... But of course, it is not really a question in the end of title, legal or moral. In the end it is a question of survival in numbers and on that ground our prospects here do not look very bright. But the point here which makes our position different from most is that we are here as a minority having built up the country out of barbarism and established the conditions under which the other race could flourish in peace, and we claim the right to rule not as trustees but as a dominant and civilized race ruling their own country and with it the subject race which partly for comfort and partly for the embarrassment of the rulers will persist in inhabiting it. ... That works alright so long as the under race is content with its primitive state and does not feel the stirrings of national and political feelings. When they do – as they are beginning to do here now – the trouble begins and grows apace. What the end will be, whether we will slowly evolve into a Jamaica or be the ancestors of a new brown race no one can tell. But it certainly seems unlikely that the white man will be able permanently to maintain the outlook to which he clings now. (Quoted in Ingham, 1988: 173)

The fundamental problem liberals encountered in their move towards assimilationism was its unacceptability to the body of white opinion. Political and social assimilation could not proceed in a spatially segregated landscape, and as long as the town was seen as a 'European area in which there is no place for the redundant native' (Davenport, 1971, quoted in Christopher, 1983: 146), the segregated landscape would remain. Over and over again, liberals in parliament, and as Native Representatives, tried to explain how hunger and poverty in the segregated reserves and the industrialization of white areas were fostering the influx of Africans so resented in the cities (Lewsen, 1987: 103–4). Some argued for a settled urban black population, independent commercial black farmers, and the abolition of the migrant labour system and influx-control regulations. But, by and large, their protestations fell on deaf ears, both in parliament and in the wider society. Inter-war liberals in Craddock, for example, felt embattled and defensive, 'unable to transform a body of ideas into practice because they could not appeal to the perceived interests of a sufficient number of the enfranchised' (Butler, 1987: 97).

However, liberals were not a group completely extraneous to wider white society. Usually, publicly or privately, they shared the fear of 'miscegenation', and 'friendly personal relations across the colour line were rare, though meetings were fostered by official occasions and letters were exchanged' (Lewsen, 1987: 104). (The misunderstandings accompanying such cross-racial correspondence in the subsequent apartheid era are well represented in the epistolary *Not Either an Experimental Doll*, ed. Shula Marks, 1987, The Women's Press, London.) Nevertheless, parliamentary liberals were instrumental in effecting minor adaptations of segregationist structures, for example, in persuading Smuts to extend legal recognition to African trade unions during the war.

The liberal desire for African tutelage and progression within a more integrated urban environment represented one extreme of white ideological influence on urban policy. At the other extreme lay the well-established principle of Stallardism. This was a philosophy of urban African administration developed in the late nineteenth century, but enunciated more coherently in the early 1920s by the Stallard Commission. The Commission had recommended that only the temporary sojourn of economically useful Africans be permitted in the cities, and that they be efficiently despatched to the reserves once their term of work had expired. In the 1940s, Smuts's government found itself tugged part way towards the liberal extreme by manufacturing interests' desire for stable, skilled and semi-skilled African labour, and towards the Stallardist extreme by mining capital's continuing need for cheap, unskilled migrant workers (Maylam, 1990).

The continuing impact on public opinion of the 'sanitation syndrome' was a decisive factor in favour of maintaining Stallardist segregation. In the first half of the century unhealthy living and working conditions, long hours of work and inadequate nutrition, all conspired to make a large proportion of both the black and white urban population susceptible to infectious and nutritional disease. But, in whites' minds, disease became particularly associated with the proliferating black presence in the cities, and 'the imagery of infection and epidemic disease provided a compelling rationale for major forms of social control and, in particular, the segregation of African locations' (Marks and Anderson, 1988: 176).

But the general white belief in segregation stemmed from a blend of material interests and more opaque cultural assumptions. Historians vary in the emphases they place on the two influences, and before considering the practical implementation of segregationist policy prior to 1948, it is worthwhile to consider interpretations of its ideological substructure in more detail.

Sparks (1990) argues that segregationist assumptions derived from the transplantation of a European culture to unfamiliar African territory, and that culture's inability to adapt to, and absorb, exotic African cultural forms. Thus segregationism represented an attempt to keep Africa and Africans, constructed as a malignant 'other', at bay, to preserve what was innate to European identity in a very different environment. In a study of the segregation within Port Elizabeth, Robinson, 1996, places the emphasis on the central and local states' own, more specific, programmes in extending and maintaining power through the division of urban space. On the other hand, Marxian historians stress the functionality of segregation, and its compatibility with white material accumulation (Wolpe, 1972). It can be argued that segregationist ideology developed as a justification for the material privilege of a group defined by race, and, some would argue, class (Marks and Trapido, 1987b).

J.M. Coetzee's overview of *White Writing* (1988) finds that early twentieth-century South African literature echoes the historical problem of 'Europe in Africa'. Africa lacks a depth of meaning to the European eye (Butler, cited in Coetzee, 1988). In Europe, the long historical association between landscape, language and culture allowed the 'historical resonances' of the past to be carried continuously through, giving succeeding generations a secure foundation for their sense of identity. The African landscape, though, lacked this association, having no historical meaning yet conferred upon it (the Africans' own association remaining inaccessible, and therefore silent, in European representation). Coetzee argues that literature carried 'the burden of finding a home in Africa for a consciousness formed in and by a language whose history lies in another continent' (Coetzee, 1988: 173). Extending a literary critique to the political sphere, that consciousness transplanted meant that whites strived to realize a European lifestyle on the African continent. Such a project could be effected only through the segregation of Africans, so that white society could maintain its cultural form unchallenged.

Counter to the abstractedly cultural premises of such an interpretation, runs the firm materialistic interpretation of Marks and Trapido (1987b). For them, segregation emerged to 'solve the problems of industrialization'. It was a finely balanced system which supplied the material requirements of an industrializing capitalist society, using an accessible, cheap, black proletariat. For the cities, it ensured large numbers of unskilled workers from the reserves. These workers were complemented by a core of skilled, stabilized and 'incorporated' urban, white workers. The costs of the unskilled African labour were kept low by the independent reserve base which would ensure its reproduction. The costs of social control would also be minimized under segregationist structures, through the administrative incorporation of chiefs (see Marks (1986) for considerable elaboration). The system gave white farmers control over African tenants and labourers in white rural areas, and protected white urban workers from cheaper African competition through urban influx-control regulations. The segregationist premise was, then, a natural one for most white classes to adopt, since it was in their own material interests.

Segregationism allowed material functionality by supplying the cities with their labour needs, but it also facilitated white political and cultural security, preventing a threatening, large-scale African proletarianization by containing the spatial base of this labour in the reserves (Dubow, 1989). The practical application of the principle and the spatial forms resulting from it, provided the structures which the apartheid ideologues would seek to consolidate.

The implementation of segregation

Before 1948 there was much greater differentiation in the application of spatial segregation than after. Nevertheless, from the 1920s, the general direction was towards increasing centralization of control over spatial form and the standardization of segregationist policy. Maylam (1990) argues that the 1923 Natives (Urban Areas) Act (see below) in particular, paved the way for apartheid planning. However, prior to this, the Housing Act 1920 gave assistance to municipalities for building housing estates, but only racially homogenous ones. The Act was an early, formal incursion into the already informally and partially segregated housing market. Before 1923, the 1913 Land Act already provided a legal basis for universal and systematic segregation in the rural areas (although there was no legislation to remove blacks from land owned prior to the Act until 1939).

The 1923 Natives (Urban Areas) Act itself supplemented the rural legislation by decreeing that urban African 'locations' should be separated from their white towns. The 1923 Act was passed by the Smuts government, under the influence of the Stallard Commission. Under the Act, the African locations would be funded through a separate Native Revenue Account. Thus Africans could be excluded from white-funded urban amenities for which they had not contributed taxes. Johannesburg and Kimberley were the first cities to respond to the new legislation by proclaiming segregated areas. Cape Town followed in 1926 and Durban in the early 1930s, although, by 1937, only eleven towns systematically implemented influx controls to the segregated locations. While the machinery to do so was there, it was not used with 'optimal efficiency' (Maylam, 1990) until after 1948.

Hertzog's NP–LP government was to follow up the 1923 legislation with more systematic rural segregationist measures. The 1927 Native Administration Act finally committed all of South Africa to a twentieth-century form of Natal's old system of rural segregation, decisively denying the Cape assimilationist tradition. The Governor General was now the supreme chief over all Africans. The government had the power, *inter alia*, to appoint chiefs, define boundaries and alter the composition of 'tribes'. Chiefs and headmen became government agents, paid according to the taxes they collected.

The imposition of authoritarian rule over the reserves was, however, characterized by a degree of flexibility on the local scale. Chiefs who proved not to be easily coerced into the role prescribed for them under the Act were treated largely according to local initiative. The strategy of paramounts such as Solomon in Zululand and Marelane in Pondo-land was to try to win formal recognition as representatives of their peoples from the white authorities. In particular, they shared a concern that chiefly control over natural resources, concessions, traders and tariffs be continued under the new system (Beinart, 1982). Their methods coincided at some points – for instance, the organization of spectacular, traditional royal hunts which were an expression of the chiefly status being ignored by the authorities. By and large, their claims were dismissed, but this did not preclude local flexibility in the granting of some concessions. For example, in a number of cases, the chief was allowed to continue to collect death duties from his subjects.

In order to maintain the return of migrants to the reserves and to restrict the urban black population, influx controls for women were made available to municipalities in 1930, although they were difficult to implement since passes for women were not yet necessary. 'Urban stability' was further enhanced in that year by the passage of the Riotous Assemblies Act, a 'security backstop' (Davenport, 1991) for the body of segregationist legislation. In 1934 a powerful tool was made available to enforce segregation in the poor, racially mixed, inner-city areas, particularly of Johannesburg, with the Slums Act (Parnell, 1988, cited in Christopher, 1990).

One of Hertzog's conditions of fusion had been more complete political segregation. This was achieved in 1936, after a legislative struggle, with the Representation of Natives Act. This legislation finally removed African voters from the Cape electoral role, and placed them on a separate role to elect three white representatives to the

House of Assembly. Four senators were to represent Africans nation-wide. The Act represented the end of the Cape assimilationist tradition in practice. As partial compensation for the loss of the common vote, the land area of the African reserves was to be extended from 7 per cent to 13 per cent of South Africa's total area under the 1936 Native Trust and Land Act.

Smuts's 1923 structure for urban segregation was consolidated with the 1937 Native Laws Amendment Act, which implemented, at the local authority's discretion, influx control to the 'locations' outside white towns. An African migrant staying in the location was permitted fourteen days to find work (reduced to three days in 1945). If the municipal returns showed a surplus of local labour, individual Africans could be 'rusticated' (Lemon, 1991b), that is, sent back to the reserves. At the same time, controls over women's entry to the urban areas were reinforced. By the time Hertzog left the government in 1939, a legal system holding back African advancement in the political, economic and spatial spheres had been designed and was being implemented with varying degrees of effectiveness across the country.

Following Hertzog's departure from the government on the outbreak of war, Smuts's post-1940 segregation measures were largely directed against Indians in Natal. Their ability to trade and occupy land on equal terms with whites was successively diminished by the Trading and Occupation of Land Act 1943 and the Asiatic Land Tenure Act 1946. But Smuts was to implement one more major piece of urban African segregationist legislation before leaving office. The 1945 Natives (Urban Areas) Consolidation Act created the Section 10 legal category of urban African – that is, those who may claim permanent urban residence by virtue of their having resided in the urban area continuously since birth or lawfully for the last fifteen years, or by having worked there for the same employer for ten years. The clause was only available where requested by the local authority.

While the discretionary nature of most of this urban segregation legislation permitted much local variation until the 1950s, one feature was growing universally apparent in, or rather outside, South Africa's cities in the 1940s. This was the sprawling squatter settlement. The proliferation of shacks was particularly noticeable during the war, when resources were diverted away from formal house construction in the locations. Post-war industrial expansion generated further migration from the impoverished reserves, but little urban housing was con-structed even after the war due to municipal reluctance to finance building through rate rises. There was also lingering uncertainty over the permanency of large-scale urban African residence, since the ex-tended life of the gold fields was still in doubt (Lemon, 1991b).

The cities around which squatter settlements grew differed widely in their application of the segregationist doctrine. Apartheid's standardizing impact in the 1950s cannot really be appreciated unless one has a knowledge of how varied the spatial dispensation for Africans, Coloureds and Indians was before 1950. In 1936, one-third of Cape Town's population lived in racially mixed residential areas. African passes to enter the city were introduced in 1909, but, once there, they could buy or rent anywhere until 1913. From 1919 they required exemption to live outside the location. The first buffer zones between African locations and white residential areas were introduced in the planning of Langa location. Between 1933 and 1948, African employment in the Western Cape increased by 534 per cent (Olivier, 1953, cited in Cook, 1991). Eighty per cent of the Africans who had been attracted to the city lived in informal shacks along the railway line after Ndabeni location had been cleared for redevelopment in 1935. The African Nyanga township was planned beyond the built-up area, to tidy the spatial pattern, in 1946, but the city's plans for segregation of its 'Coloured' community were deferred following vociferous protests from the Malay Coloured population (Cook, 1991).

In East London, Africans had been restricted to three locations prior to 1923, and within them, they were mostly accommodated in owner-built shacks on council rented land. By 1948 these locations had the highest rate of tuberculosis in South Africa, provoking opposition to local segregation by African trade unions and in the press. Commissions reported on the problem in 1937 and in 1949, and they were followed by the building of Mdantsane township where the bulk of the town's African employees now live (formerly within the 'independent' Ciskei homeland's boundary). In the pre-apartheid period, local fears were directed more against the Indian population. The *Daily Dispatch* of 16 August 1928 expressed fears of the town developing like Durban, a 'town in the python coils of an Asiatic menace' (quoted in Fox et al., 1991). Coloured segregation was encouraged, but not enforced, by the construction of the exclusively Coloured township of Parkside (Fox et al., 1991).

Durban's segregation policy, as we have seen in Chapter 2, was unusually systematic in that separate provision was in place for each race's finance and administration. Most municipalities relied on a series of *ad hoc* measures rather than coherent, segregated planning bodies when implementing spatial segregation. In Durban the Native Beer Act of 1908 had given the municipality a monopoly over the brewing and sale of traditional African beer. The revenue from the scheme was directed into African housing, thus 'satisfying a capitalist precept that the user must pay' (Davies, 1991: 76). A Native Administration

Department was established in 1910 to regulate African influx to the municipality. Durban's administrative and housing scheme came to be known as the 'Durban system' and was used by the 1923 Act as the model for a national structure. Yet Durban, like every other major city, had a housing shortage, the inevitable accompaniment of which was the informal construction of shacks on the periphery of the controlled urban area (Davies, 1991).

The degree of consideration behind urban planning for blacks is demonstrated nicely by Pietermaritzburg. Here, before 1923, there were only council barracks and peripheral slums for blacks. The response to the 1923 Act was the construction of Sobantu location, the 'sanitary syndrome' dictating its placement well outside the pretty colonial town and adjacent to the refuse dump. The municipal sewerage works was a later addition to the township neighbourhood (Wills, 1991).

Despite the variation in urban segregation prior to 1948, from informal and incomplete separation in Cape Town to Durban's tightly controlled system, all of South Africa's cities and towns displayed some form of spatial exclusion along the lines of race, inherited from the late nineteenth-century colonial era and elaborated to cope with an increasing rate of urbanization. As segregationist legislation from the central government accumulated from 1920 to 1948, local authorities' discretion in urban policy was incrementally undermined. First came the Minister of Native Affairs' capacity to compel any local authority to implement any section of the 1923 Act, then the Housing Amendment Act 1944, which set up a National Housing and Planning Commission with powers to intervene in local housing policy (Lemon, 1991b). The trend of centralizing control over urban space was under way, then, even before the accession to central government of Malan's NP.

Encroaching centralization was protested by some white local authorities, but it was actively resisted by members of the black population it sought to control. Formal, organized black resistance was encouraged by the subtle modifications in consciousness and culture wrought by urbanization, the compounds and the factories in the first part of the twentieth century.

African cultural change and political responses

Migrancy served as a means of channelling new, urban behaviour patterns back to the reserves – patterns which challenged traditional African structures even more than nineteenth-century missionary activity had. But migrancy was not simply imposed upon Africans by employers and the state; it was a strategy well suited to Africans with a viable reserve base, and one with a long tradition (see, for instance,

Delius, 1983 and Beinart, 1982). A temporary sojourn working for white employers in the city or on the land enabled the retention of contact with the independent home base and often simultaneously encouraged greater co-operation with other migrants at work (Beinart, 1987). Beinart argues that traditional ethnic consciousness among migrants in some ways facilitated the gradual development of a new class consciousness in the African workforce of the 1920s and 1930s. Traditional and 'progressive' identities coexisted, with the established ethnic bond between migrants bolstering a new sense of class affinity. Ethnically 'particularist associations at work made self-protection and organization possible, rather than constraining them' (Beinart, 1987: 289). While the bulk of the less educated migrants tended to join such ethnically homogenous groups in the cities, some joined student associations with wider African nationalist affiliations. However, the feeling of class identity that developed out of ethnic consciousness did not displace ethnic awareness. Ethnic identity remains a strong motivating factor behind some of the violence in African townships today.

The urban gang was a tangible expression of African ethnic association in the cities of the 1920s and 1930s (see Van Onselen, 1982). Newspapers on the Rand and in Durban expressed concern over the proliferation of knifings in fights between ethnic gangs. Councillors also rued the 'immoral practices' of homosexuality, sometimes associated with gang coercion, in the migrant-worker compounds (Beinart, 1987). With the circularity of migrant flows, urban traits were soon transferred to the reserves. In a rural Pondoland setting, beer-drinking groups of young men borrowed a hierarchical form of organization from the urban gangs. Such groups combined with migrant worker gangs to present a continuing threat to both the white rural administration and the chiefs (Beinart, 1982: 159–60). Another cultural influence contributed to the atmosphere of crumbling stability in rural areas as the reserves opened wider to mission education and tuition in the early part of the twentieth century.

In the cities themselves, however, African cultural adaptation extended well beyond gang mobilization. In the 1930s and 1940s, the township environments of the Rand and Pretoria, characterized by poverty, overcrowding, illegal drinking dens called shebeens and pass raids, produced 'a distinctive popular culture known as "marabi"' (Worden, 1994: 62). The blending of traditional, missionary, ragtime and jazz traits produced a new, peculiarly urban form of African music (Coplan, 1985, cited in Worden, 1994: 62). But beyond music, marabi was a 'distinctive way of life, impenetrable to outsiders, which helped to deal with poverty and the "lack of visible means of subsistence"' (Worden, 1994: 62–3, quoting Koch, 1983). Parallels to marabi developed in other South African urban environments: for instance, the development of popular music, carnival and self-help organizations in Cape Town's District Six (Worden, 1994).

Adjustments in African culture and consciousness soon fed into the forms of organized resistance to white administration adopted by Africans. In rural areas, the encroachment on chiefly authority embodied in the 1927 Native Administration Act was resisted in novel ways. For example, in Pondoland, an attempt was made to reject the chief imposed by the authorities in court because he was the inheritor of a tradition represented by the nineteenth-century chief Sigcau, who had aided white labour recruiters in Pondoland, and thus 'sold' the country for his own benefit (Beinart, 1982). Rural resistance, however, was to reach its peak when the succeeding apartheid government sought to consolidate its rule in the reserves with far less flexibility.

In the inter-war period, most organized resistance came from more radical, urbanized blacks, who led the ANC intermittently from the 1920s, with many also, or exclusively, supporting the powerful urban and rural socialist movement, the Industrial and Commercial Workers Union (ICU). The ICU taught the ANC a lesson in radicalization over the period. If the ANC was to represent the expanding African industrial working classes, it would have to distance itself from the 'courtly and often pompous discourse of African politicians' (Lodge, 1983: 6) who currently led the movement. The founding of the CP in 1921 infused a further radicalizing influence, enhanced after the CP abandoned the racism of the white labour movement following the 1922 strike, and committed itself to black mobilization.

Garveyism was another radical movement in the black politics of the period, but it was distinct from the 'left-wing' tendency. While Dube, of the ANC leadership, reflected the American ex-slave, Booker T. Washington's accommodationist line towards whites, many young blacks, experiencing the appalling conditions attendant upon rapid urbanization, followed the contrary American line of Marcus Garvey, stressing black pride and perceiving black Americans as redeemers (Marks and Trapido, 1987b). In one rural millenarian movement, reminiscent of the Great Xhosa cattle-killing, black American aircraft pilots would intervene to protect oppressed black South Africans (Marks and Atmore, 1980b). Even the socialist ICU blended elements of Garveyism into its doctrines. The Garveyist movement was strongest in the Western Cape. Here, Xhosa, with their Africanist traditions, and black Americans in the docks combined to diffuse the ideas. Marks and Trapido (1987b) highlight the contrast between the thrusting radicalism of this region's black population and the conservatism of the 'organic intellectuals' of Natal, where Zulu ethnicity and the maintenance of the

Zulu monarchy's legitimacy were the most cherished ideals of African political mobilization. Resistance to the state was largely precluded by them, and their pursuit as goals was gladly assisted by the state in its support for the Zulu Society. The political quiescence of Natal in the 1930s and 1940s provided the prelude to the violent manifestation of Zulu ethnic chauvinism in Durban in 1949, discussed below.

Meanwhile, the conjunction of socialism and Africanism in the ANC rank and file was radicalizing the movement, a tendency manifested in the election of Josiah Gumede as president. The new blend of political ideology was encapsulated in one motion passed on Gumede's accession – 'the right of self-determination through the complete overthrow of capitalism and imperialist domination ... the principle of Africa for the Africans' (quoted in Lodge, 1983: 8). Some members of the ANC and South African Communist Party (SACP) came to share an understanding that South Africa contained a colonial situation for which two stages of liberation were necessary – a nationalist democratic revolution in co-operation with reformist African petty bourgeois organizations, followed by a socialist revolution (Lodge, 1983). This premise continued to be held by the SACP throughout its resistance to apartheid, but it was less well diffused through the ANC, which retained a core conservative membership. Gumede was replaced as leader by Pixley Seme in 1930, and 'with his ascendancy the ANC shifted several degrees rightwards into almost total moribundancy' (Lodge, 1983: 9). At the same time, the SACP was moving on to a confrontationist course with the government, a course which was to destroy its organizational structures in South Africa.

Although the ANC reached the nadir of its influence in the 1930s, by wooing traditional chiefs and businessmen, 'identifying them with the general good' (Lodge, 1983: 10–11), another turning point was reached in the 1940s as African political organization adjusted to the massive wartime expansion of the African working class, mainly in Johannesburg. In the wartime decade, many more blacks than ever before came to pursue their well-being in an urban and industrial context within 'white space'. From 1936 to 1946, the urban African population grew by 57.2 per cent, from 1,141,612 to 1,794, 212, overtaking the white urban population by about 75,000 (Posel, 1991: 24). The urbanization of Africans and their incorporation as a large industrial workforce in themselves presented challenges to white urban political and economic hegemony. A sense of threshold, of the 1940s being a critical and portentous time, is apparent in contemporary reports (Walker, 1948; Blackwell and May, 1947; Norton, 1948; and Robeson, 1946).

Despite Smuts's tentative reformism, urban Africans felt compelled to make their own attempts to resist the further encroachment of poverty. In Alexandra, in protest at fare rises, bus boycotts took place in 1940 and 1945, and from 1944 to 1947 a Johannesburg squatter movement culminated in the incorporation of Orlando into older housing estates to form the largest African township of Soweto (Southwest Townships). Workerist action was added to the 'repertoire' (Clingman, 1991) of resistance, with the increasing importance of African labour during the war and falling wages contributing to a series of relatively successful strikes on the Witwatersrand in 1942 and 1943. Once the war was won, however, the African mineworkers' union was destroyed in the crushing of the 1946 strike, and the Council for Non-European Trade Unions, which had been formed during the war, was severely weakened.

The ANC could not help but incorporate some of this flourishing radicalism. The Africanist element of it was manifested in 1944 with the founding of the ANC Youth League (ANCYL). The ANCYL soon developed influence over the leadership of the organization as a whole, infusing it with the spirit of Africanism. Its leader, Anton Lembede, saw, in the urbanization of the African populace, a source of mass support which, so far, the Congress leadership had shamefully neglected (Lodge, 1983). However, the Africanists were wary of that other radicalizing influence, communism. They saw in it an updated form of white paternalism and felt their own oppression to be clearly based on race rather than class.

Radicalization of black political organizations was also encouraged indirectly by the state's own actions in the 1940s. ANC members were pushed into more radical stances by brutality towards the strikers in 1946, the extension of influx-control regulations to the Cape, the creation of segregated political institutions for Coloureds and Indians, and the consistent hedging of the Natives Representative Council into a pusillanimous ('toy telephone' to the government) role.

Coloured and Indian responses to segregation

While African organizations were being moulded into more militant forms in the 1940s, the political position of Coloured and Indian populations was more ambiguous. Coloured political identity and mobilization had been spurred by the post-Boer War settlement, when the Coloured franchise was confined to the Cape and withheld in the northern republics. Political protest was organized by the African Political (later People's) Organization (APO). Ethnic mobilization was aided by the fact that Coloured voters were influential in at least six Cape Town City Council seats (Marks and Trapido, 1987b). With the lingering influence of scientific racism's classifications, Coloureds were able to utilize their perceived status as a race more advanced than Africans: 'the advantages of a separate identity for "Coloureds" came to be appreciated' (Marks and Trapido, 1987b: 29). That the APO could benefit from drawing such a distinction became clear when Coloureds were exempted from carrying the passes introduced for Africans with the 1923 Act.

The Indian population was subject to much greater internal class differentiation. There was little sense of an Indian communal identity in political discourse until the state defined such a community by its discriminatory legislation. Indian South Africans in the late 1940s though, had the advantage of international leverage, the Indian government being willing to act on their behalf in a global arena – the United Nations – when legislation was enacted against Indian land occupation and trading rights. To a certain extent this compensated for a lack of the cultural ties with Afrikaners that Coloureds had (Marks and Trapido, 1987b).

After Union in 1910, a South African-born, Indian political elite had begun to mobilize against the separate registering of Indians in the province of the Transvaal. These clerks, interpreters, teachers and professionals provided the personnel for Gandhi's first 'satyragraha' campaign. Later organization, however, mostly revolved around the property rights threatened by Smuts's government, and there was little linkage with African political movements. Indeed, the 1949 Durban riots were a traumatic experience of involvement with Zulus. A minor affray between an Indian and an African set off Zulu attacks on Indians in the city, leaving 142 dead. The conflict of culture between Indian and African had been steadily exacerbated by exploitation of Zulu workers by an Indian petty bourgeoisie, and state-manipulated competition between African and Indian entrepreneurs. Continuing white invective and incitement against Indians probably gave extra impetus to the conflict (Marks and Trapido, 1987b).

From segregation to apartheid

The period from 1910 to 1948 was one in which the political and spatial groundwork for apartheid was laid, but in a varied and inconsistent manner. While centralization of control over South Africa's space was progressing through the period, it was only partially accomplished by 1948, and there was a great degree of variation in political and spatial structures on the ground. Nevertheless, the legal framework for a more rigid implementation of spatial and political division along the lines of race was in place by 1948.

Pre-apartheid state intervention had also precipitated an expansion of the repertoire of black resistance, a repertoire that would be a crucial destabilizing factor for future government spatial and political projects. By the mid-twentieth century, the context for black resistance had decisively shifted to an urban arena ostensibly in white space, and its general form had likewise altered from armed resistance to dispossession, through passive protest at ill treatment, to 'modern' industrial action, although more traditional forms would coexist with the modern, being particularly prominent in the reserves. At the individual level, evolving systems of white social control would continue to be met with black non-co-operation.

Apartheid's historical context included the spatial and political forms of segregation legislated over the previous fifty years, the attitudes behind them, and the methods of black opposition to them. It also included another strand reaching back half a century or more – that of a sense of Afrikaner identity, developing towards nationhood. The more fundamentally segregationist regime elected in 1948 was intent on a material and spiritual revival of the Afrikaner volk. Behind the success of the NP lay a far more coherent expression of Afrikaner nationalism than South Africa had yet seen.

2 Vitalizing Afrikaner nationalism, 1910–48

Introduction

During the 1930s, somewhat of an intellectual 'renaissance' (Sparks, 1990) emerged among Afrikaner nationalists. The scholastic elite of the Afrikaner community engaged itself in redefining and solidifying a nationalistic ideology which had its roots in the late nineteenth century. The late 1920s and 1930s provided an ideal context within which such ideologies could attain mass adherence, bringing a world economic crisis and particular material crisis to South Africa's poor white Afrikaners. There has been some debate over the motivation for the resurgence of nationalistic feeling in the 1930s, some writers emphasizing the ideological and cultural 'entrepreneurship' of ethnic leaders (Moodie, 1975; Welsh, 1987; and Davenport, 1991); others stress the material impetus behind ethnic political mobilization (O'Meara, 1983; Marks and Trapido, 1987b).

Nationalist ideology in the 1930s has been interpreted by Marxist scholars as a mental construct, built upon the solid material plight of Afrikaners experiencing discrimination under English-dominated capitalism. An alliance of class 'fractions' lay at the heart of Afrikaner nationalist mobilization, each fraction seeking to improve its material position through broader ethnic mobilization. However, liberal writers have placed more emphasis on the original divisions of language, history and religion between English- and Afrikaans-speakers, divisions which, in the first place, ensured that the impact of capitalism would be felt differentially. Such writers would not agree that the grounding of ideology in material conditions is direct. The success of nationalist ideologues in the 1948 election was brought about by a welter of subtle, non-material factors, interacting with material concerns. More recent work on the complex construction of political identity (see, for example, Laclau, 1994 and Gellner, 1994) enables a shift of focus: the identitative disorientation which feeds national mobilization is the phenomenon to be explained, and the contributors to that disorientation are necessarily and simultaneously of a material *and* ideological nature. But they are also of an intrinsically spatial nature. The tendency towards a growing Afrikaner nationalist sensibility was a product of an evident *spatial* disorientation, brought about by commercialization, industrialization and the concomitant drift to the cities. It is this spatial shift of urbanization which forms the context for the following account.

Material concerns

In the 1930s and 1940s, more people than ever before identified their political interests as lying with the NP. The pressing day-to-day, material concerns of these people, traced by O'Meara (1983), helped foster their allegiance. A cluster of Afrikaans-speaking classes came to realize that the programme of the nationalist movement, led by the secretive Broederbond and politically represented by Malan's NP, could alleviate the material problems each was facing. By 1948 the alliance was composed of a petty bourgeois leadership group – farmers and urbanized Afrikaner workers – but it was financed by, and achieved its material apotheosis in, Afrikaner-run commercial enterprises. Mobilization of the alliance was triggered largely by the blocked aspirations of the petty bourgeoisie in the northern provinces.

The frustration of this middle class was first manifested in the 1910s over the specific issue of language. English was the language of the workplace and of education, and it was English which opened doors to state employment. Dutch remained the language of 'hymn, sermon and bible' (Marks and Trapido, 1987b: 17). If Afrikaans-speaking journalists, writers, teachers and clerics were to advance in the professional fields using the vernacular, they would have to mobilize a new constituency to empower their language. The concentration on the importance of language, its centrality to identity, was in clear distinction to the politics of the established Afrikaans leadership, represented by Botha and Smuts.

In 1918, the Broederbond was established by aspirant professionals in the Transvaal to work for the interests of Afrikanerdom, but specifically, in its infancy, for the promotion of the vernacular. The institution took firm root in the province, backed particularly by the Transvaal's Afrikaner teachers (Moodie, 1975). The Broederbond 'provided a superb vehicle for the discussion, elaboration, adoption and eventual execution of what, after fusion, amounted to the independent programme of the Afrikaner petty bourgeoisie' (O'Meara, 1983: 64).

Central to O'Meara's materialist argument is that this class, in order to remove the obstacles to its advancement, needed to mobilize the support of two sectors of the Afrikaans constituency in particular: the farmers of the Transvaal and Orange Free State, who had displayed a willingness to support Smuts's UP after fusion, and urban Afrikaans workers, who were being enticed by the left-wing movements. The ideologues of the Bond therefore sought, through their covert influence in the inter-war period, to unite these forces into an ethnic coalition. Such an alliance would 'burst open the doors of economic advance' (O'Meara, 1983), presently barred to the Afrikaner petty bourgeoisie by the use of their mother tongue.

In the meantime, though, this class had to endeavour to 'participate in the industrial capitalist economy through the medium of its own language' (O'Meara, 1983: 66). A prerequisite was the generation of specifically Afrikaner capital. One man was particularly influential in this respect – W.A. Hofmeyr. Unlike the leaders of the Broederbond, Hofmeyr was based in the Cape. He had channelled capital derived from Cape commercial farmers into the establishment of three overtly Afrikaans companies – Nasionale Pers (press), SANTAM and SAN-LAM (insurance and credit companies).

By the 1930s, Hofmeyr and the Broederbond had some mutual goals. In order to drive the nationalist economic movement, the Bond needed capital to invest in the north, while Hofmeyr was seeking to extend his influence northwards from the Cape. A tension-wrought co-operation emerged from a meeting of these, and other like-minded Afrikaners, at the 1939 Ekonomiese Volkskongres. Here, the Broederbond's official 'front' organization, the FAK (Federasie van Afrikaner Kultuurverenigings), was active in creating a number of institutions to further the economic interests of the volk. The Federal Volksbelegging was set up to utilize Afrikaner capital to build up Afrikaner participation in industry and commerce. An Ekonomiese Instituut (EI) was to lead Afrikaans capital into the volk's own commercial companies, like Hofmeyr's SANLAM and Volkskas.

Economic advancement was necessary, but if the movement initiated by the petty bourgeoisie was to be ultimately successful in the political

arena, it would need the support of a significantly wider section of the
white electorate – particularly, as we have seen, farmers and workers.
O'Meara argues that it was the promise of economic salvation which
generated this support. In the 1930s, many Afrikaners, both on the land
and in the cities, were in need of material redemption. By 1939, the
state estimated that some 300,000 whites (mainly Afrikaners) were in
'terrible poverty' (Giliomee and Schlemmer, 1989: 31). The 1932 Car-
negie Commission found that one-third of Afrikaners were 'desperately
poor', while another third were classified as 'poor'. The bankruptcy of
small farmers in the 1920s and 1930s was given as the main explanation.
In 1939 Afrikaners constituted 41 per cent of blue-collar and other
manual workers, while only 27 per cent of white-collar workers were
Afrikaners. With the prospect of demobilization and redundancies
following the war, fears of further material decline for the 'poor whites'
of the cities arose.

Even from its formation in 1933, the new NP thought that it was
possible to capture this poor white voting constituency. The 1924 NP
government had sought to protect Afrikaners from the effects of
English capital, which, unmitigated, could have left most small white
farmers as poor urban workers. But fusion brought the old NP's
abandonment of that protection, and common cause between Hertzog
and 'Hoggenheimer', an Anglo-Jewish caricature and the Afrikaner
nationalist's despised enemy. Malan's new NP stood for the continuity
of the former protection (O'Meara, 1983).

Ethnic mobilization behind the new NP would confer new material
blessings upon the volk, and the FAK would create the structures
needed. The Reddingsdaadbond (RDB) was set up to pursue the lead
of the EI in raising Afrikaner consciousness of the volk's own financial
power and redeeming it from English economic domination. Membership of the RDB brought participation in cultural events, cheap life
insurance from SANLAM, burial schemes, loans, training and an
Afrikaans employment bureau. The RDB 'directed a clear message to
all Afrikaners – only as part of the Afrikaner volk, only in exclusively
ethnic and Christian national organizations would their economic interests be fostered' (O'Meara, 1983: 142). In effect, the RDB acted as the
link between poor white and Afrikaner capitalist institution that the
Broederbond sought, and which paved the way for the NP's 1948
success. The economic movement as a whole helped diffuse the
Afrikaans intelligentsia's nationalist ideology to the masses. The short-
term aim of the movement was to channel capital, derived from
northern and Cape farmers, into industrial and commercial enterprises
for urban Afrikaners (with dividends and interest as the reward for the
farmers) – a rural to urban redistribution of the volk's assets to
accompany that of the volk itself.

However, Afrikaner urban workers had choices as to where to place their allegiance and their trust in a brighter economic future. If the nationalist movement was to secure their support, it would have to compete with the leftist trade unions in the workplace. A nationalist assault on trade union structures (and even, in some cases, on the persons of members) took place in the 1930s. Nationalist mobilizers stressed that ethnicity was the common denominator among poor whites of the city. Ethnicity must therefore be the organizing principle behind an improvement in the workers' fortunes. The fact that, in 1939, almost 40 per cent of adult male Afrikaners were unskilled, compared to only 10 per cent of other whites, could be portrayed as deliberate ethnic discrimination by an alliance of 'foreign' (English/ Jewish) capitalists and English-speaking trade union leaders. For instance, the white mineworkers' union was, at one time, in an agreement with the owners which often ran contrary to the interests of its members (O'Meara, 1983). Signs that Afrikaner workers might be replaced by cheaper Africans were interpreted as an imperialist state attempt, aided by trade union leaders, to consign Afrikaners, *en masse*, to poor whiteism. Only unions of a nationalist nature could really further the cause of the Afrikaans worker.

The Garment Workers Union was particularly successful in diffusing Afrikaner nationalist ideals among its women members. Nationalist sentiment about women's role as the motherhood of the volk, strengthened by the development of domestic matriarchy on the farm and of martyrdom in the concentration camps during the Anglo-Boer War (Tomaselli, 1988), was blended with anti-capitalist rhetoric by the union's membership in the second half of the 1930s (Berger, 1987).

O'Meara argues that it was only when the Broederbond became involved in matters extending beyond ideology that it became successful in its political aims. By focusing on the material affairs of white workers, it was able to mobilize both their political support and their savings for the nationalist economic movement, which in turn generated further political support. Afrikaner nationalism and material accumulation thus proceeded hand in hand, the former leading the latter. But the origins of a specifically Afrikaans constituency itself lay in ethnic differentiation rather than material, or class, distinction.

Non-material concerns

Marxists have tried to de-personalize the forces which created a distinct position for Afrikaners under South African capitalism. For example, Marks and Trapido (1987) state that nationalism 'can best be understood as a response to the social dislocations and problems posed by the uneven development of capitalism in South Africa' (1987b: 10). But the factor which defines the unevenness of capitalism's impact – ethnicity – is already present. The distinction between those who, by and large, benefited from the penetration of capitalism, and those who, by and large, did not, was already established. It was a sense of ethnic identity which distinguished Afrikaners from other white South Africans, and this identity, while it may have been reinforced, was not created by impoverishment under capitalism. Behind it lay an ideational realm, a sense of being that was only partially connected to material status. Capitalism alone could not have wrought the mobilization of Afrikaans-speaking whites as Afrikaners, 'unless some line of ethnocentrism, however mild, was an intrinsic accompaniment of the process of differentiation. ... One need not regard this ethnic sentiment as 'primordial' or deny the degree of contingency in its formation to assert that ethnicity played an autonomous and growing role in Afrikaner politics in the 1930s' (Welsh, 1987: 200).

The Afrikaner's material situation, in a time of world economic crisis and in an environment of disorienting urbanization, was probably the key factor behind the eventual scale of nationalist support (see Adam and Giliomee, 1979), but the nationalist movement transcended economic concerns and was firmly planted in a worldview determined by ethnicity. Members of the Broederbond stressed the interrelationships between the political, economic, cultural and spiritual dimensions of their nationalism, and did not merely mobilize support for their economic interests. Each one of these forms of identity has its own 'situational salience', and while class was an important form, it was 'woven into a racial and ethnic fabric' (Welsh, 1987: 202). Ethnicity was a much more powerful mobilizer of political force than class alone could have been.

The ideologies of Afrikaner nationalist leaders in the 1930s were linked to those of contemporaneous German nationalists, themselves extremely successful at mobilizing within exclusive group boundaries. However, there is disagreement over the extent of German influence in the course of events in South Africa (see Bunting, 1969; Sparks, 1990; Moodie, 1975; Bloomberg, 1990). The most tangible link was that of the Afrikaner nationalist leaders who studied in Germany in the 1930s and who returned to diffuse new ideas of nationhood within South Africa. But a more subtle, literary link is identified by Coetzee (1988). German volksideologie emphasized the rootedness of the volk in its native landscape. Early twentieth-century Afrikaner poets also found evidence of a 'natural' bond between volk and land. They too, attempted to 'provide transcendental justification for ownership of the land' (Coetzee, 1988: 106).

The exclusive frame of reference of the Afrikaner nationalists reached its apotheosis in the 1930s when the rhetoric of the Afrikaner's communion with the sublime in the landscape became prominent in Afrikaans writing. This was a communion denied to other ethnic groups, less proximate to God. In the 1930s, literary expressions of Afrikaner distinctiveness also reflected the pressing material concerns of the volk. The 'Bauernroman', or 'Plaasroman' (farm novel) became popular in both Germany and South Africa as a rural way of life was increasingly threatened by urbanization and the penetration of commercial farming capital. In C.M. Van den Heever's *Groei* (1933), tilling the soil is represented as a 'quasi-religious act in a Lebensraum free from capitalistic relations, subject only to natural laws' (Coetzee, 1988: 76). In such novels, the tangible expression of this capitalistic threat was often the Jewish or English professional, a character who would enter the narrative as a revolutionizer of tradition, looking to buy a viable farming operation and drive the Afrikaner from his land through competition, breaking the bond of 'Blut and Boden'. 'The *Plaasroman* grows out of the Afrikaner's anxiety that he will lose his economic independence and cultural identity if he leaves the land' for the city (Coetzee, 1988: 135).

Tomaselli (1988) traces a similar genre through the Afrikaans cinema. Here, the equivalent of the wistful Plaasroman is the 'Eden film', recalling the same lost innocent sense of tranquil place: 'Once upon a time, the Afrikaner was the independent master of his own pastoral destiny. He lived, as is common in myths, in amity with nature and his surroundings. These included his Coloured servants. Neither Blacks nor the English disturbed his idyll' (Grieg, 1980, quoted in Tomaselli, 1988: 139). In the film, as in the novel, the tranquillity is shattered by British dispossession, leading to 'subsequent Anglicization, [and] the migration from the farm to the town' (Tomaselli, 1988: 139).

The importance of cultural identity was stressed by the Broederbond, an organization that was not merely O'Meara's vehicle of petty bourgeois aspiration. Moodie (1975) emphasizes the Bond's republican political leanings. There was no republican dimension in the early Cape Afrikaans-language movement, but the desire for a firm political expression of cultural independence informed a strong republican sentiment in the northern Bond. The demand for an explicitly Christian national state was added to those for Afrikaans schooling, radio time and songbooks, and, by the 1930s, was attracting overt criticism from Hertzog. The new NP's call for an Afrikaner-led republic became a clamour in the 1930s, heard even above those for language rights, segregation and economic protection for poor whites (Moodie, 1975).

Beyond the economic component of Bond activity lay a spiritual dimension, difficult to account for in a purely materialist interpretation. Urbanization was resulting not only in economic and political disorientation, but also in religious laxity. In the nationalist film genre analyzed by Tomaselli (1988), the Dutch Reformed Church pastor has a consistently ambivalent role. He is caught between the old rural and the new urban environments of the volk, attempting, despite their oppositions, to be the focal point of identity for each. In reality, though, it was the Bond which was more actively setting itself the task of maintaining 'the nation's religious character as well as acting as the watchdog over all its interests' (Bloomberg, 1990: 31) and, in line with this aim, it admitted only practising Calvinists, its members having to show 'the highest degree of religious conviction' (Bloomberg, 1990: 31). In the Bond of the 1930s there was a strong current of thought that the volk was created by God as an independent entity, and that it should remain so. A republic, divorced from British imperial interest, would be an immutable political expression of both a national and a religious entity.

Even within the Bond though, there were ideological divides. Theological fissures, in particular, split the ethnic leadership group. One prominent tendency derived its ideas from the Dutch Calvinist theologian, Kuyper. Like all nationalists, those who followed Kuyper believed that the Afrikaner nation had been forged by God, out of the furnace of British imperialism and African savagery. But they saw the nation as one among many spheres, including the family and the individual, through which God fulfilled His intentions. Each of the spheres was autonomous in its relationship with God. This tendency was most coherently represented by H.G. Stoker, a leader of the Broederbond in the 1930s. Malan himself had been a dominee of the Nederduits Gereformeerde Kerk (NGK), which sought to preserve its institutional independence from the state (hence Malan's resignation from the church on entering politics), but which was broadly supportive of nationalistic politics.

During the 1930s, Kuyperian theology faced competition within the Bond from a more secular, neo-Fichtean line of thought. Academics such as P.J. Meyer, H.F. Verwoerd (later Prime Minister), G. Cronje (author of the Bond's 'Native' policy) and, most notably, N. Diederichs, returning from German universities, brought with them a preoccupation with the volk as an organic body, held together by common historic culture. Diederichs developed a social metaphysical argument that individuals and humanity only exist in, and through, the nation. Any identitative abstraction beyond the nation, such as 'universal humanity', was too vague, in an immediate sense, to have meaning (Moodie, 1975; Davenport, 1991: 288), and any identity below the level of the nation precluded efficient social interaction. Kuyperians like Stoker and L.J. du Plessis saw this as virtually deifying the nation, and restricting the power of God over it, since it was no longer held to be one of many spheres through which His will is implemented. The nation, for them, had a value in God's scheme alongside that of the individual and the family, not greater than them.

The practical implication of both tendencies, despite the differing nuances of their theological standpoints, was largely indistinguishable: the furtherance of the volk's interests. While it was the economic movement which did most to diffuse nationalist thinking to a mass base, ideological persuasion was also influential. The constant neo-Calvinist expounding of the volk's election as a chosen people allowed a flattering sense of dignity to filter down through the Afrikaans population. There was more pride to be had in ethnic identity than in an identity founded upon other parameters.

Popular political support for the NP was also generated in the purely ideological sphere, notably with the FAK-organized celebration of the Great Trek and Blood River's centenary in 1938. The immense popular enthusiasm, and even hysteria, generated by the celebratory trek of wagons, each named after one of the Trek's leaders, is well documented by Moodie (1975). Behind the enthusiasm was a new mythology, surrounding the Vow to God taken by the original trekkers, led by Sarel Cilliers, before the Battle of Blood River. In 1838 the trekkers in Natal, in the event of a God-given victory over the Zulu, had apparently pledged to celebrate on that day in the indefinite future. The Vow was, in fact, largely forgotten until the late nineteenth century, when it was revived as part of the early Afrikaner nationalist movement. The largely mythical Vow played a central role in the 1938 celebrations which, in themselves, precipitated a welling desire for Afrikaner unity in politics. 'Afrikaners had learned in their worship at the oxwagon altars how very much they had in common as Afrikaners' (Moodie, 1975: 185).

According to Tomaselli (1988: 138):

> The radio and film coverage of the symbolic re-enactment of the Great Trek ... gave a considerable boost to the recapture of the popular pastoral memory. Four broadcasts a week over four months amplified this historic moment. It united agricultural capitalists, the urban working class and the petty bourgeois by locating both English and blacks as outsiders. (See below.)

The NP's virtual monopoly on organizing the celebrations was a vital step in wresting control over the political expression of Afrikaner-ness from Hertzog and the UP (Thompson, 1985). Malan himself skilfully incorporated an appeal to urban Afrikaners in his celebratory speech, using the 'civil religion' theme (Moodie, 1975), with urbanization portrayed as a new twentieth-century trek. The battleground on which these trekkers would have to fight was not Blood River, but the labour market, supervised by foreign capitalists and manned by an insidiously increasing urban African population. Both the British and blacks, therefore, defined the parameters of 'otherness' and thus provided a necessary space for the creation of a distinct Afrikaner identity. As Norval (1994: 121) puts it:

> [T]he process of identity formation cannot be thought merely in terms of an elaboration of a set of features characteristic of a certain identity ... an enumeration of positive characteristics will not suffice in individu- ating an identity, or in delineating its essence. In order to achieve that, an additional element is needed; namely, the positing of an 'other' which is constituted as opposed to the identity in the process of construction. This positing of an other is what allows for the closure that facilitates the individuation; or in Smith's terms, the 'cerning' of a particular identity.

Thompson (1985) demonstrates how Afrikaner historical identity was shaped by the perpetual struggle against both foes – British and black – and Tomaselli notes that the celebratory trek of 1938, by splitting into two, 'one [party] proceeding to the Voortrekker Monument site in Pretoria, and the other to the site of the Battle of Blood River in Natal, represented Afrikaner triumphs over both English and blacks respectively – two kinds of outsider' (1988: 138).

The awakening ethnic identity in the inter-war years was stimulated by a sense of affinity with Afrikaner forefathers. One man, Gustav Preller, was particularly active in bringing the mythologized exploits of these historical figures to the attention of the public, contributing to what Smith (1986) calls the 'mythomoteur', or what Anthias and Yuval-Davis (1993) call the 'constitutive myth', which describes the basis for a collectivity's identity.

Preller was a nationalistic Afrikaner with supreme leverage over the media of communication. His hagiographic biography of the trekker leader, Piet Retief, ran through ten printings and sold over 25,000 by 1930. This book alone 'moulded the historical consciousness of many Afrikaners' (Thompson, 1985: 181). Preller was more than just a writer. He was a leader in the drives to formalize the Afrikaans language and to establish an Afrikaans historiography. But possibly his most crucial contribution was to popularize an influential version of Afrikaner history (Hofmeyr, 1991). He effected this visually through writing the script and determining the appearance of the 1916 film *Die Voor-*

trekkers. This was the first popular representation of the Trek and its leaders, and some 15,000 people queued each week to see it. Its contribution to the twentieth-century version of the Afrikaner tradition was enormous. It was a vital thread in what Hofmeyr describes as 'the cultural fabrication of nationalism' (1991: 62). Preller shared the implicit assumption of many nationalists: that the biographies of key historical figures amalgamated to form a biography of the nation itself. He used all media to proselytize the nationalist faith (also being the editor, in the 1930s, of the NP paper, *Ons Vaderland*), but it was especially his visual images which made the nationalist elite's conception of identity concrete in the minds of Afrikaners in general.

Nationalist disunity

Despite the coherence of its organization and the individual flair of its leaders, the tide of Afrikaner nationalism in the 1930s did not sweep away the other political identities of the volk *en masse*. By 1939, Afrikaner nationalism had taken on new force, through a combination of material inducement and ideological fervour associated with a new, urban identitative disorientation, but it could not present a cohesive and undifferentiated front to the challenges that it faced. Regional differentiation had marked the nationalist movement from its inception, but the late 1930s and 1940s brought a plethora of political offshoots and competing factions within nationalist politics.

After fusion, Malan's NP had been able to assume control of much of the old NP's organizational structure in the Cape, but it faced a UP that had successfully retained most of the old NP's support in the Transvaal and the Orange Free State. Within the NP, the provincial party units were semi-autonomous and had divided political interests. The 'various Afrikaner nationalist movements in South African history were always constituted by a differentiated and shifting ensemble of social forces – each clearly articulating widely different conceptions and expectations of the "volk" and what "its" interests were' (O'Meara, 1983: 6). The Cape's NP component tended to be more externally orientated than those of the northern provinces, with SANLAM and the relatively wealthy vine and wool exporters articulating with the world, rather than just the domestic, economy. NP structures in the Transvaal tended to be strongly protective of the poor whites of Johannesburg and of the small farming sector from which they derived. Party members in the Orange Free State were inclined towards the interests of the province's domestic cereal producers.

Although these diverse material interests were, by and large, accommodated within the NP by 1948, ideological differentiation was far more divisive for Afrikaner mobilization. The NP leadership was thrown into a dilemma by the emergence of Oswald Pirow's fascistic New Order group and the mass recruitment of the militant extra-parliamentary Ossewabrandwag (OB) (see Marx, 1994). Both organizations shared some ideological tendencies with the NP, but each was unacceptable to the body of nationalist leadership opinion. On the one hand, the NP could hope to gain support by accommodating such tendencies. On the other hand, it could interpret their existence as a challenge to the party's fundamental values, and hope to compete successfully with them for allegiance. The OB was finally dealt with when the NP invoked the aid of its enemy, the government, to repress it, while the New Order group died out with the defeat of Nazism, but the story of the NP's relations with both indicates the extent of political deviation within the body of 'the volk' (see Moodie, 1975; O'Meara, 1983; Davenport, 1991; and Marx, 1994).

By the end of the war, the NP was the unchallenged political representative of the nationalist movement. The party was astute in quieting its membership's contentious republican clamour in the run up to the 1948 election, focusing instead on the areas of clear agreement between the Dutch Reformed Church (DRC) and the Broederbond: mother-tongue education, the communist peril and checks on African social and economic advancement (Moodie, 1975).

The NP's first overtly racial policy directive arose out of concern that the gains of the Afrikaner economic movement should not evaporate through competition with Indian traders. An early NP policy pledge was to remove Indians to their 'own areas', and prevent them living or trading in white areas (O'Meara, 1983). The wider apartheid policy arose from the mutual concerns of Afrikaners, given their marginal position in an urbanizing society and economy. Apartheid was first mooted as a vague concept by Malan in 1943, to maintain white purity and to secure supplies of cheap African labour to white farmers by further controlling African migration to the cities. Even though the scheme was vague, it was clear that it would favour each of the class components that the NP was concerned to protect.

Afrikaner businessmen, who had experienced rising African wages during the war, rendering competition with English capital harder, would be able to lower their costs. The NP would also combat the 'laziness' of African workers, supposedly induced by their sense of security with Smuts's unemployment benefit. Once in power, one of the first moves of the NP was indeed to restrict the African unemployment benefit scheme. The financiers of the volk's mobilization in the Afrikaner commercial institutions like SANLAM would also be assured of state accounts after a NP victory.

Afrikaner farmers were keenly concerned with the continuity of their African labour supplies, threatened by industrial growth in the cities. The NP Member of Parliament, de Wet Nel, said in 1944, 'just take the Free State or the Transvaal. One simply cannot get a Native to work there. The farmers are at their wits' end' (quoted in O'Meara, 1983: 177). Apartheid held out the promise of more rigid influx control than Smuts was willing to implement, and thus the retention of labour in the rural areas. The NP would also recognize the farming community's financial contribution (via the commercial companies) to the volk's economic mobilization, and the marketing board would once more be used to protect farmers rather than drive food prices down as it had done during the war under Smuts.

The poor whites, who had already left the land for the cities, sought in apartheid protection from the competition of cheaper African workers, again through stricter influx-control regulation. They could also hope for a reversal of the erosion of the job colour bar, which had occurred during the war.

The 1948 election, then, saw a crucial shift in allegiance towards the NP, from the UP in the case of northern farmers and from the LP and the UP in the case of Afrikaans urban workers. O'Meara's petty bourgeoisie now found an open forum, within the state itself, for the ideology it had developed. The success of the NP in the 1948 election, though, was owed to something more than just the successful mobilization of Afrikaners, with varying interests, as an ethnic bloc. National Party propaganda, based on the 'swaart gevaar' (black peril) and 'oorstrooming' (swamping), touched on the concerns of a wider postwar white electorate, and political and economic circumstances lying beyond the influence of the nationalist leadership, such as the perceived blood on Smuts's hands, also conspired to bring about the NP's narrow electoral victory (see Davenport, 1991).

Conclusion

Conciliation between English- and Afrikaans-speakers after the Boer War was never allowed to be complete. Just as, in the first decades of the century, Botha and Smuts's co-operation with English-speakers in the SAP was resented by Hertzog, so Hertzog's own fusion with the SAP in 1933 was resented by a generation of Afrikaners who had assumed the mantle of nationalist leadership from him. The ethnic divide was reinforced during these years by an increasingly evident spatial dynamic. English-speakers were associated with capitalism, with the commercialization of farming and with their inescapable product – urbanization. Capitalization and urbanization in turn constituted the

greatest threat to the security and stability of a predominantly Afrikaner rurality.

While ethnic sentiment was being actively politicized, racial sentiment in the white population was fully entrenched by the beginning
of the century. The 1922 strike revealed that a racially exclusive sense
of identity was still far more powerful than that of class, even after
some fifty years of blacks and whites working alongside one another
(one group, of course, supervising the other) in the mines. White fears
of the changes that industrialization and urbanization might bring were
superimposed on an established racial ideology. Together, they brought
about increasing centralization of control over segregation, although
there were still anomalies in South Africa's spatial patterning in 1948.

In the 1930s and 1940s the increasing pace of industrial and urban
growth magnified political dilemmas. Smuts contemplated the reforms
which were needed to cope with the influx of African workers that was
needed, but simultaneously resented, in the cities. However, reforms
conflicted with the prevailing racial ideology, and thus contributed to
the popularity of the NP. But this popularity was enhanced by ethnic
mobilization, coming from within the nationalist economic movement,
which was itself feeding on the material conditions and the ideological
anxiety of poor Afrikaners in the cities. Urbanization, then, was the
context for the implementation of South Africa's late twentieth-century
spatial, political and social structure. It was ultimately the changes
wrought by urbanization that made Smuts's potentially reformist
government unpopular. The threat that urban African competition
brought to whites in the lowest-paid jobs helped drive that government's reactionary alternative into power.

From 1910 to 1948, the enduring legacy of late nineteenth-century
white supremacist ideology was manifested in new spatial forms, and
transplanted to new urban environments. An 'elaboration of segregationist discourse' (Dubow, 1987: 71) took place in twentieth-century
South Africa despite the increasingly assimilationist stance being
adopted by liberals and, indeed, most of the world's governments. In
1948, apartheid planners inherited an urban form that was already
substantially segregated under central directive. But centralization of
a kind had also occurred in black resistance politics. Urbanization,
again, had wrought profound changes. A new radicalism had emerged
and, co-ordinated largely by the ANC, it found its expression in new
forms of urban resistance, forms which were added to those of the
established repertoire.

4

The Formulation of
a Structure

Introduction

There is a common perception that the 1948 change of government, and the ensuing implementation of apartheid, represented a clean break with previous social trends and political outlooks. However, a number of structural continuities bridged the period. In an analysis of the nature of apartheid, the theme of continuity versus discontinuity is revealing. This theme underlies the first half of this chapter. The second half deals with the subsequent evolution of apartheid policy, and the black resistance that it provoked.

On the one hand, apartheid arose out of a continuation of social characteristics dating from well before 1948: racial ideologies, an Afrikaner nationalist sense of identity, the structuring of material relations between races, and the spatial structure of segregation. Its impact as a body of policies was slow to take effect and the NP conception of policy in the apartheid era was often *ad hoc* rather than pre-planned (see Posel, 1991). In all these senses, apartheid represented a continuation, an elaboration and an increase in fundamentalism, but, nevertheless, founded upon inherited forms. On the other hand, in so far as apartheid marked the accession to government of a 'new breed' of Afrikaner nationalist, and the generation of new ideological legitimations for its type of policy, it represented a novel development. Apartheid was also a discontinuity if the frame of reference is taken to be the preceding decade, rather than the preceding half-century, in that it reversed the tentative reforms that Smuts had begun during the war.

At the level of the individual, too, both continuities and discontinuities were evident. Whites would continue to experience social, political and spatial supremacy, but through policies which took them ever further away from international norms, particularly once the civil rights movement began to take effect in the USA, and which generated more fundamental attitudes of both support and dissent at opposite poles of the white political spectrum. Blacks were to feel, in the most concrete sense, the discontinuities of apartheid, with the extinguishing of the glimmer of material improvement sensed during the war. Africans were to be barred more securely from the cities and to have a new, limited, state-conceived political role conferred upon them. Coloureds and Indians were to experience large-scale urban segregation and removals, similar to those which Africans had already undergone. A new distance developed between culturally articulated Coloureds and Afrikaners, and Indian politicization broadened out, from the elite group which had protested Smuts's prior discrimination, to involve a wider cross-section of the Indian population.

1 The nature of apartheid

When the NP narrowly won the 1948 general election, it brought to government an ideological standpoint that was distinct from that of the preceding government. The basic racial attitudes of the two ruling groups did not diverge in kind, only in degree, but their conception of white society differed fundamentally. Analysts who have sought a material rationale for apartheid have often overlooked such discontinuities in the nature of ruling-group ideology. Wolpe's influential article of 1972 explains apartheid as a rational response to the material difficulties of accumulation that, by the mid-twentieth century, South African capital was facing. Here, apartheid is represented as an all-embracing system, implemented on behalf of capital by a compliant state. In the early twentieth century, mining, industrial and commercial capital had still benefited from viable African reserve bases. The reserves had acted to reproduce cheaply the migrant labour that capital required. But with the gradual penetration of a capitalist mode of production into the reserves themselves, increasing inequalities undermined the redistribution of resources that had sustained a partially independent (and therefore cheap) labour force in the cities. As the communal productive base of the reserves was eroded, so the permanent urban African population increased. For Wolpe, apartheid was an attempt to keep African labour costs low in the new conditions of the mid-twentieth century, when the reserves themselves could no longer bear the costs of reproduction. If capital was to continue to pay low wages to Africans without an independent reserve base, the resulting unrest in the cities would threaten the whole political structure. Thus the state involved itself in economic relations, to maintain cheap African labour through new structures of repressive legislation. 'Racial ideology in South Africa must be seen as an ideology which sustains and reproduces capitalist relations of production' (Wolpe, 1972: 454).

The new government's ideology may have been partially founded upon the preservation of advantageous material relations, or at least, their justification, but it was not confined to this. The government was motivated by a plethora of non-material aims, coexistent with those of a material nature. Even the treatment of 'the government' as a homo-geneous and coherent bloc is false, but the differentiated components of government will be discussed later. Here, the overall direction of policy outcomes will be taken as indicating 'the government's' position.

Three basic objectives are often ascribed to the newly empowered NP (Price, 1991; Giliomee and Schlemmer, 1989; Terreblanche and Nattrass, 1990). First, the party sought to maintain a segregated society 'in keeping with the precepts of the Afrikaner politico-religious doc-trine' (Price, 1991: 23), and by so doing, to preserve Afrikaner identity. Marks and Trapido declare that it was the 'petty bourgeois obsession with racial "purity" and eugenics' (1987b: 21) that lay behind the passage of the Population Registration Act, the Immorality Act and the Mixed Marriages Act, but it seems likely that the preoccupation with racial 'purity' extended well beyond just this class. Regarding the Immorality and Mixed Marriages Acts, the

> primary intention and the practical effect ... was to take away from white men the freedom to drop out of the ranks of the labouring class, take up with brown women, settle down to more or less idle, shiftless, improvident lives, and engender troops of ragged children of all hues, a process which, if allowed to accelerate, would, in the end, they foresaw, spell the demise of white civilization at the tip of Africa. (Coetzee, 1988: 35)

A second goal was the securing of white political supremacy and economic privilege from potential internal and external threats, notably those of African urbanization and social advancement. In 1930, 90,517 Africans had been employed in manufacturing; by 1955, there were 342,150. The permanent African population of the cities was now larger than the white urban population and Africans were beginning to assert a strong moral claim to political participation (and, implicitly, therefore dominance) in the new democratic conditions of the post-war world. Their steadily progressing assumption of positions of economic power posed a long-term political threat to white control over government (Giliomee and Schlemmer, 1989). White political and economic supremacy could only be obtained by halting African urbanization, extending the migrant labour system from mining to manufacturing, and deflecting urban African political claims. Those urban Africans who were seen by the NP as being already 'detribalized', were initially to be allowed to remain in the interests of the economy, but this urban labour force would have to be utilized fully before others would be allowed to join it (Posel, 1991). Subsequently, however, for Prime Minister Verwoerd, 'the survival of white civilization in South Africa' became 'of more importance ... even more important than expanded industrial development' (Rhoodie, 1969, cited in Giliomee and Schlemmer, 1989: 36).

The NP's third overriding aim was to elevate the Afrikaner community into a position of social and economic equality with, if not dominance over, the English-speaking population. A three-pronged programme would be pursued until the 1960s. New discriminatory legislation would be applied to Africans and extended to Coloureds and Indians in order to preserve the hegemony, as members of the dominant racial group, of the poorest Afrikaners. The bureaucracy and the parastatal sector would be enlarged in order to generate specifically Afrikaner employment, and welfare programmes would be instituted to redistribute wealth within the white population for the uplifting of poor (Afrikaner) members of the racial group. The success of these measures is indicated by the fact that in 1970 Afrikaner per capita income was 70 per cent of that of the English-speaking population; in 1946, it had been less than half (Terreblanche, 1989, cited in Terreblanche and Nattrass, 1990: 12).

These three considerations were undoubtedly prominent in the minds of apartheid's administrators, but they were never coherently expressed as a programme of administration in the way that is often implied. Apartheid was not the unified conceptual model it is often thought to have been. The influential nationalist editor of *Die Burger* from 1954 to 1978, Piet Cillie, described apartheid thus: 'A system? An ideology? A coherent blueprint? No, rather a pragmatic and tortuous process aimed at consolidating the leadership of a nationalist movement in order to safeguard the self-determination of the Afrikaner' (quoted in Giliomee and Schlemmer, 1989: 63). Beyond the often conflicting interpretation of policy within government circles, Posel shows 'that the powers and interests of central and local state institutions, individual African workers as well as mass organisations, individual employers as well as organised commerce and industry, must all be taken into account in explaining how Apartheid took shape' (1991: 18).

Legitimating apartheid

Even if the conception behind apartheid policies was not entirely clear, and the policies themselves were pursued in vacillatory ways, apartheid as a broad strategy could still be legitimated, for whites, through a variety of media. A further step in the 'scientific' differentiation between races was one such medium. The initiative came in the 1950s from Afrikaans university departments of anthropology. 'The departments of "Volkekunde" ... were expected to contribute to the theory and practice of apartheid. They have generally done more or less what was expected of them' (Kuper, 1988: 35). The scientific racism of the late nineteenth and early twentieth centuries was generally unacceptable by the 1950s. Blatantly racist language and argumentation was therefore largely avoided by apartheid theorists. Anthropology provided a new rationale for the emphasis on racial differentiation, or rather, resurrected an old one through the use of the ambiguous word 'culture'.

In the 1920s 'culture' had given liberals a less rigid means than Social Darwinism had allowed of explaining racial differences. But the concept was now used to maintain that these differences were immutable, ignoring the possibility, stressed by the earlier generation of liberals, of their diminution over time. W.M. Eiselen was a leader of the field. He held that blacks were not inferior to whites according to any objective standard, but that they were culturally different. Apartheid sought merely to preserve the cherished cultural identity of each group, thus preventing mutual cultural degradation. Thus 'Eiselen and his students – and their students – were in search of a fundamental alternative to race in the ideological edifice of South African "Native policy". With different emphases and in different ways they chose to identify "culture" as the alternative basis' (Kuper, 1988: 45). Such a mutually protective policy would require a separation in space based on adequate resources for each racial group. 'At its most idealistic apartheid was a projection of the aims of Afrikanerdom onto others. All must wish to survive as distinct ethnic units, with their own language, religion and traditions' (Kuper, 1988: 46).

While anthropology provided a secular, academic justification for intensified segregation, the Dutch Reformed Church (DRC) ensured that 'apartheid had many of the trappings of a moral crusade beyond the more bland social engineering designs of the previous Fabian segregationists' (Rich, 1989: 292). The Church's theology was, by and large, derived from the Kuyperian notion of separate spheres of divine intention, only boundaries were now drawn between the spheres of nationhood to coincide with those of racial group. With the evangelization of apartheid by the DRC, its broad support within the Afrikaner community was, to a large extent, assured. Its wider legitimacy was mainly to be achieved in the field of education (discussed below).

At the same time that apartheid's legitimacy was being secured for whites within South Africa, the world was moving away from the principles which had supported the colonial segregation upon which it was built. In the 1950s, a momentum of resistance was building up against racial oppression in the USA, as well as in many of Europe's colonies. Apartheid was implemented by 'a more insular governing elite that now relied far less heavily on the external Commonwealth supports, and drove segregationist ideology into an ethnocentric creed to try to fit a new world order of declining European colonial empires and resurgent African nationalism' (Rich, 1989: 292). Outside South Africa, racist suppositions were gradually – usually, almost imperceptibly – being dropped. Inside, after 1948, a modified racist mythology was cocooned, and propagated ever more fervently by politicians, radio broadcasts, teachers, textbooks, and, from the 1970s, by television (Thompson, 1985).

New policies

The first concrete changes to emerge from the handover of power in 1948 were largely brought about by the NP's concern to safeguard specifically Afrikaner interests. But these interventions were soon followed by those directed at securing the racial order as a whole. On assuming power, the NP leaders began a minor purge of the senior civil service, the army and the police. Nationalist army officers, who had resigned on the outbreak of war, were reinstated, and the use of Afrikaans was insisted upon, to the detriment of those English-speakers who were not sufficiently bilingual. English street names were changed and the military establishment at Roberts Heights near Pretoria was renamed Voortrekkerhoogte (Le May, 1971), reflecting a common tendency on the part of new regimes to stake their place (literally) in spatial nomenclature (David Smith, personal correspondence). The nationalist economic movement's goals were brought closer to fulfilment with the transfer of municipal bank accounts to Afrikaans institutions. Afrikaans financial houses also received a boost from central state contracts which helped, by 1980, to establish them on a par with English-owned interests (Marks and Trapido, 1987b: 21).

The state's preservation of the volk was not confined to the economic sphere. In 1927 sex between African and white had been banned. In 1950, the new government extended the ban to cover intercourse between a white and any 'non-white' person under the Immorality Act. Not content with this, in 1957 'intimacy' (falling short of full sexual intercourse) between members of two different racial groups was also banned.

The NP's centralization of control over South African society was the most prominent departure from the characteristics of government prior to 1948. Legislation was introduced to penetrate every area of social relations. The Immorality Act is an extreme example on a personal level, but centralization also occurred on a broad economic scale. After 1948, the government's influence over the economy increased dramatically with the development of parastatal corporations, initially constructed to aid in Afrikaner economic upliftment. By 1974, the state was responsible for 45.6 per cent of total investment in South Africa, and 29.6 per cent of industrial investment (Rogerson, 1982), largely through corporations such as ARMSCOR (arms), ISCOR (iron and steel), ESCOM (electricity), SENTRACHEM (chemicals), SASOL (oil from coal) and NATREF (oil refining). With its participation in these concerns, the state sought to occupy 'the commanding heights of the economy' (Weiss, 1975, quoted in Rogerson, 1982: 48).

A more subtle kind of centralization lay behind the government's intervention in the education system. If apartheid was to function, its ideology would have to be secured through schooling. The 1953 Bantu Education Act was the most prominent piece of legislation in this regard. This not only pegged expenditure on black education back to the level of black taxes, it also provided an apartheid epistemology. The structures of knowledge that the education system conveyed were to be tailored according to racial group. F.H. Odendaal, the administrator of the Transvaal province, told its school principals 'we must strive to win the struggle against the non-white in the classroom rather than lose it on the battlefield' (Thompson, 1985: 59–60).

Within the white education sector, Afrikaners, separated in their own schools, were given a 'Christian National Education'. Bloomberg (1990) argues that the Broederbond's innate Calvinism and sense of ethnicity was solidified into a firm Christian–Nationalist ideology in the late 1920s and early 1930s, largely in response to the growing influence of Potchefstroom University theological academics, and in opposition to the old NP's fusion with the secular and Anglican SAP. With the extension of the ideology from the Bond to Malan's newly empowered NP, its influence over Afrikaans education was ensured. The History syllabus, for instance, focused around the story of God's revelation of purpose; a God who has 'willed separate nations of people' (quoted in Thompson, 1985: 50). Afrikaner teachers, many of whom were Bond members, were organized into unilingual professional associations which were 'among the most reactionary forces in South African society' (Thompson, 1985: 51).

African education under the Bantu Education Act was more restrictive than that given to the protégés of the nationalist leaders. Prior to 1948, a large part of African education was conducted under the auspices of church and mission schools. The relative freedom of content and interpretation they allowed was construed as a challenge to the envisaged role of Africans under apartheid. The 1953 Act forced most of these schools to close and transferred the administration of state African schools from the provinces to the central Department of Native Affairs, which would in future devise syllabi and regulations. Coloured and Indian education would also be centralized in the 1960s, but the immediate threat of 'non-white' social advancement lay with the large and expanding African population.

African primary school tuition, contrary to the demands of African political leaders, was to be given in the mother tongue, rather than in English. In 1959 the Minister of Bantu Education outlined the rationale: 'The Bantu must be so educated that they do not want to become imitators, that they will want to remain essentially Bantu' (quoted in Giliomee and Schlemmer, 1989: 93). The education that was deemed suitable involved lower spending than on whites, fewer, and lower-qualified teachers and – the centrepiece grievance – a syllabus designed to complement the apartheid model of society. Of the version of History that was taught to blacks, even in the pre-apartheid period, Z.K. Matthews said,

> if it was difficult for us to accept the white man's account of his own past doings, it was utterly impossible to accept his judgements on the actions and behaviour of Africans, of our own grandfathers in our own lands. Yet we had to give back in our examination papers the answers the white man expected. (Quoted in Thompson, 1985: 66)

By the 1950s, Coloured teachers in Cape Town were dictating two sets of notes to their classes. One was headed 'For Examination Purposes Only', and the other, 'The Truth' (Thompson, 1985: 67–8). Discriminatory education was extended beyond the school sector and into Higher Education with the paradoxically named Extension of University Education Act, which provided for segregated learning in these institutions.

Through the new education system, it was hoped that the segregationist impulse would be instilled in the minds of young South Africans. To complement this conceptual differentiation, the state would legally enforce greater communal separation. But before racial discrimination could be legally entrenched, the NP had to establish a legal basis for differentiating between the races, a task which was by no means clear-cut after 300 years of racial mixing. Nevertheless, each individual would have to have a racial category assigned to him/her, so that the discriminatory laws, which applied to racial groups as a whole, could be enforced. This groundwork was laid with the 1950 Population Registration Act, described by Cohen as a means to 'systematize previously confusing and scattered legal usages and race definitions and to stop the high incidence of "passing" [usually from Coloured to white] once and for all' (1986: 21). The original criteria for classification were appearance, descent, generally accepted racial status and repute. Later, habits, education, speech, deportment and demeanour could also be taken into account. Enormous suffering was imposed (especially in the light of the Mixed Marriages and Immorality Acts), simply through a bureaucrat's decision as to which racial category an individual fitted.

Once racial categories had been more firmly engraved on the consciousness of South Africans than ever before, further legislation could be enacted to keep the categories apart. In 1953, the government responded to a court declaration that the racial reservation of government railway facilities was illegal because it did not reflect the doctrine of separate but equal which the government professed. The Reservation of Separate Amenities Act now made racially segregated facilities such as beaches, libraries, post office entrances, swimming pools, etc. legal, even if they were of an unequal standard for whites and 'non-whites'.

The NP was concerned, from its early days of power, to curtail the political rights which distinguished Coloureds from Africans. The 1956 Separate Representation of Voters Act was the culmination of a complicated series of manoeuvres to by-pass the constitutional safeguard of a Cape Coloured franchise. It brought their removal from the common voters roll and gave them as substitute four white representatives in parliament, elected on a separate roll.

The geography of apartheid

Apartheid's radical thrusts into education, personal relations and political rights was matched by its drive to remodel the South African landscape, particularly in the urban areas of white space. The Separate Amenities Act necessitated spatial segregation, but it was only really one facet of the major piece of apartheid spatial planning, the 1950 Group Areas Act. The Act demarcated the areas in which each of the races might reside in the city. For Malan it was 'the essence of the apartheid policy which is embodied in this bill' (Giliomee and Schlemmer, 1989: 87). The Durban Indian–African riots of 1949 provided an official pretext for declaring separate zones of the city for each race's occupation. For the government, the riots were evidence of the friction that is generated when different races/cultures (the terms became interchangeable) rub alongside each other in an integrated urban environment. It was inevitable that, at some places and at certain times, enough heat would be generated to start a conflagration. Peaceful race relations could therefore only occur under conditions of complete racial separation.

Practically, the planners achieved, through race zoning and the Separate Amenities Act, the prohibition of 'even the limited inter-group social contact which might naturally occur ... in churches, sports clubs and even schools' (Lemon, 1991b: 9). But in the terms of its own justification, the Group Areas Act failed dismally. Instead of reducing racial conflict, it exacerbated inter-racial urban tensions to a marked degree. Even the government's own Theron Report reached such a conclusion (Western, 1982). As Whisson puts it, 'the policy ... has been successful in creating self-sustaining barriers which make group attitudes of suspicion more likely and individual non-racist attitudes less likely' (1971, quoted in Smith, 1982b). What inter-racial gatherings occurred, despite the urban boundaries, 'have tended to be self-conscious, and it is almost impossible to be truly "colour blind" in human relationships. ... For the majority, then, race zoning has kept people from knowing or understanding one another' (Lemon, 1991b: 9). While it must be remembered that such psychological barriers between individuals of different racial groups were not new (recall, for instance, the embarrassment inter-war white liberals experienced in social meetings with Africans), apartheid's measures certainly perpetuated and probably exacerbated them. Generally, whites did not (and do not) penetrate the black areas of the cities (excepting young white males, who may have done so under the extraordinary conditions of national service). But many blacks had more of an appreciation of white lifestyles through their experience in domestic service.

The Group Areas Act's alienating impact was manifested in the subsequent design and location, according to strategic considerations, of African townships. Western (1982) notes how their open streets allowed the rapid crushing of urban resistance, while their limited access points allowed them to be easily cordoned off, to prevent the overspill of instability into white areas. A secondary effect of the Act was to distance the problems of the urban poor from white eyes, particularly high crime rates and low standards of health. Implementing the Act, as far as possible, natural barriers were used to separate racial zones. If not, industrial or commercial belts were used.

The Group Areas Act has been seen as providing a general model for the 'apartheid city', reproduced across South Africa (Fig. 3). Many of the anomalies in the generally segregated urban forms of South Africa were ironed out with its implementation. Yet, even with the unusual degree of standardization that it brought, the term 'the apartheid city' still lacks utility beyond that of descriptive simplification. While the Act 'was to be the ultimate framework of control to secure a formal city more effectively structured in the image of the social formation' (Davies, 1991: 79), the timing and the extent of its

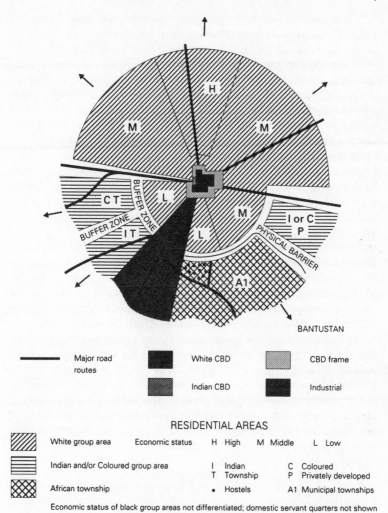

Figure 3 The apartheid city
(reproduced from A. Lemon, ed. 1991, *Homes Apart: South Africa's Segregated Cities*, Paul Chapman, London; Indiana University Press, Bloomington, Indiana and David Philip, Claremont, South Africa)

application still varied widely between municipalities. The Act only became practically applicable after it was amended in 1957. The implementation of coherent urban segregation between all races could then provide the basis for segregated education, health and social services.

Those most affected by relocation under the Act were Coloureds and Indians, Africans being already largely segregated under the 1920s urban legislation. Although many of the cleared areas, like Sophiatown in Johannesburg and District Six in Cape Town, contained slum localities, there was 'emotional plenty among the material shortage' (Hart and Pirie, 1984, quoted in Lemon, 1991: 10). Western (1981) emphasizes the bond between community and place, the two sharing a history of growth and development that was broken when people were forcibly removed from their homes. In terms of the Act's effectiveness, one example is representative. In 1951, the degree of Indian–African segregation in Durban had been 81 per cent, that of Coloured–white 84 per cent, and that of African–white 81 per cent. By the 1960s, segregation between each group, excepting black servants granted accommodation in white areas, was virtually 100 per cent (Kuper et al., 1958: 156–7; Lemon, 1987).

Municipalities varied greatly in their enthusiasm for, and degree of co-operation with, the Act. In Cape Town, where the whole of the Table Mountain area to the west of the railway line from the city to Muizenberg was zoned white, the City Council was so shocked by the potential impact on the established Coloured community, that it boycotted the public hearing of the Group Areas Committee (Western, 1981: 103–4). In the event, the 54 per cent of the city's population that was Coloured was moved to segregated areas comprising 27 per cent of the land (Fig. 4). The clearance of the racially mixed District Six, for whites-only settlement, was particularly poignant. Even if the district was crime-ridden and poor, it had been characterized by a raucous, lively, music- and dance-filled atmosphere. The bitterness of the mass removals to dusty, windswept flats outside the city and the sense of a wrenching loss of place (see Hart, 1988) still lingers. The painter Tony Grogan sums up the area's symbolism:

> It was a university of racial harmony. When authority decided to uproot and disperse this community, they switched off an oven of contentment and goodwill. Much of District Six was a slum, there was a great deal of poverty, but there was a community spirit that the most advanced urban development will never be able to buy or replace. ... District Six was one of the world's most exciting meeting grounds of people of many religions, colours and races, and its great contribution was that it proved that none of these things really mattered. (Quoted in Barrow, 1976)

After 1954, in order to deter further African urbanization in the Western Cape, and as somewhat of a gesture of reconciliation to its Coloured population, the region was declared a 'Coloured Labour Preference' zone. This meant that, if available, a Coloured applicant

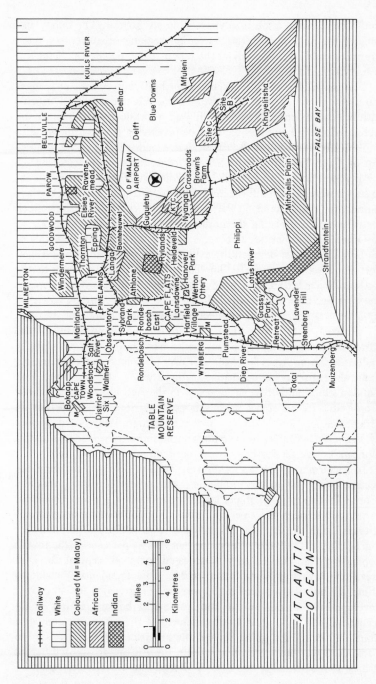

Figure 4 Cape Town's group areas (source as Figure 3)

would be awarded a job in preference to an African. The policy also entailed the removal of Africans from the region's urban centres to the Transkei and Ciskei reserves, at the rate of 9,000 people a year for five years (Cook, 1991: 30).

The range of municipal responses to the Group Areas Act is illustrated by a comparison of Cape Town's reluctance with Durban's enthusiasm. Durban City Council was a prime mover behind the tabling of the group areas legislation, perceiving it as an opportunity to diminish the threat of the city's 'Asiatic menace'. Here, the symbolism of Cape Town's District Six was reproduced in the clearance of the predominantly Indian Gray Street district. Three council representatives were sent to inform the NP's administrator, Donges, of their support for the Act and the NP expressed its gratitude to the council for its advice concerning the drafting of the bill (Maharaj, 1992).

Other local authorities across the country were ranged on a scale of support for the Act between the extremes of Durban and Cape Town. Port Elizabeth's diligence in implementing segregation prior to the Act's enforcement was commended by government ministers. Here, in 1951, 31 per cent of the population had been in the 'wrong' area. By 1960 this was down to 16.2 per cent, and by 1985, 3.8 per cent. In 1951, 1.1 per cent of the city's white population faced resettlement. Of the African population, 43.1 per cent would be removed (but not directly under the Group Areas Act); 59.5 per cent of Coloureds faced removal, as did the entire Indian population of the city (Christopher, 1991). East London's local authority was opposed to the Act, but it welcomed the promised state assistance with rehousing African slum dwellers in Mdantsane location. However, the central Group Areas Board, backed by Verwoerd, went on to overrule a local authority scheme to extend Duncan Village for further African occupation (Fox et al., 1991).

In Pietermaritzburg, application of the Act involved changing the occupants of 700 to 900 properties, and removing 9,000 to 15,000 people. Of those moved 76 per cent were Indian, 11 per cent Coloured, 12 per cent African and 1 per cent white. The council here not only co-operated with the Act, but submitted its own additional proposals for segregation to the Board. Under the Act, the 43 per cent of the town's population that was Indian was relocated to 13 per cent of the land area. The town's growing Indian middle class found itself unable to afford the housing supplied to the wealthy in segregated Indian private developments, with only the poor municipal housing estates as alternatives (Wills, 1991). A later refinement of the urban race zoning of South Africa's cities, going beyond the provisions of the 1950 Group Areas Act, was the segregation, within the African areas, of different 'tribes' (documented in the case of Bloemfontein by Krige, 1991).

The impact of the enforcement of the government's spatial ideal on the social formation was tremendous. The government's own Cillie Commission, instituted to enquire into the causes of the 1976 Soweto riots, emphasized that 'no single government measure has created greater Coloured resentment, sacrifice and sense of injustice' (cited in Western, 1981: 310). For the bulk of the Coloured population, rather than introducing a new psychological distance from Africans, to reflect the spatial distancing, the Act served to increase solidarity.

While the Act's greatest impact on Coloureds was in Cape Town, Indians were affected predominantly in Natal, and Durban in particular. Here, the Board's 1958 proposals entailed the removal of 75,000 Indians (Maharaj, 1992). A crowd of 20,000 Indians mustered to protest the measures. Even when the council balked at the financial cost of moving the established Indian population to new homes (necessary under the Act), the proposals were implemented by the Board (Maharaj, 1992). For many Indian traders, it was not just a move of home that the Act entailed. A number of traders in central locations depended on African and white custom for over 75 per cent of their turnover. To be relocated to an exclusively Indian area was often disastrous (Giliomee and Schlemmer, 1989). Even in the Transvaal, by 1966, only 7.5 per cent of Indians remained materially unaffected by the Act (Lemon, 1991b).

Although the impact of the Group Areas Act was in itself dramatic, it was to be only the beginning of the apartheid scheme for control of the city. From the 1950s, new mechanisms were added to those already in place to control African entry to, and activity in, the urban areas. The NP fulfilled its promise of tighter influx control largely through the 1952 Native Laws Amendment Act. While, in response to a 'pragmatic' line of reasoning within the party, the Act recognized the 1945 Act's Section 10 exemptions, it made a more efficient form of influx control compulsory and helped to slow down the rate of African urbanization. Other developments included the extension of passes to women, but with considerable delay caused by the scale of African protest, and the involvement of centrally controlled labour bureaux to determine who should receive passes and where they should be permitted to go. In the cities, prosecutions for being without a pass increased, and farmers received the benefits in the form of an increasing supply of convict labour. The protection of the NP's farming support base was an important motive behind these measures: 'emigration control must be established to prevent manpower leaving the platteland to become loafers in the city' (Verwoerd, cited in Lipton, 1985: 25).

African rural to urban movement was additionally controlled by the 1951 Illegal Squatting Act, aimed at the peri-urban shack dwellers who were outside the local authorities' jurisdiction for influx-control removals (Lemon, 1987). The 1952 Native Laws Amendment Act laid a basis for the distribution of Africans between towns. Movement between prescribed areas would be permitted according to labour demand.

Even where Africans were permitted in the cities, the jobs they could perform were restricted, so as to favour the poor whites, their competitors in the labour market. The job colour bar was reimposed after 1948 with more vigour. In 1959 the Minister of Labour was empowered to reserve any job in any area for particular races. Skilled work in the clothing industry was reserved in 1957, but a challenge from the courts resulted in the fixing of racial percentages instead. White job reservation was subsequently extended to ambulance driving, firefighting and traffic policing in Cape Town. Lifts were only to be operated by whites unless they were for 'non-Europeans' or goods (Davenport, 1991). The 1950s marked the 'high water mark' (Davenport, 1991) of the industrial colour bar.

While the state was engaged in limiting the quantity and the employment prospects of Africans in the cities, it was aware that many urban manufacturers required an expanding permanent labour force. During the 1950s and early 1960s, township construction for Section 10s proceeded on a considerable scale, and it was only from the 1960s that the emphasis shifted to confining African workers in the reserves by encouraging industry to move to them instead (Maylam, 1990, see below). With the rate of urbanization increasing in the early 1950s, the state sought for ways to reduce the costs of township house construction. Site and service schemes were adopted early on, as was the attempt to make employers pay directly towards the reproduction costs of their labour, with the 1952 Native Services Levy Act. Nevertheless, the bulk of maintenance costs was imposed on the Africans themselves. 'Exercise of control over urban Africans ... involved costs which the various parties wanting control were generally unwilling to bear. This was one of the major contradictions in the urban apartheid system. Moreover control not only involved large financial costs, it also generated resistance giving rise to further contradictions' (Maylam, 1990: 75). These contradictions, emerging from the inception of urban apartheid planning, were to become nearly insupportable by the late 1980s.

Even in the 1950s, the problems were bad enough. In Johannesburg, industry and commerce generally refused to subsidize employees' housing, or pay them higher wages so that they could improve it themselves. Municipal action to improve African housing was limited by the need not to tax the important mining houses too greatly. So most black urban housing in the 1950s remained neglected. The slums of Soweto were so visible, and represented such a tangible threat to the order of the city, that Ernest Oppenheimer gave a R3 million loan to the municipality for their clearance (Lea, 1982).

It was partly the presence of the slums, but also the desire for a clearly demarcated racial pattern, that led to the 1954 Natives Resettlement Act. This allowed for the removal of thousands of Africans, so far little affected by the apartheid stock of urban segregation legislation, from the homes which they rented or owned in Sophiatown and other parts of Johannesburg's Western Areas. The traumatic social disintegration caused by this action is well documented in Trevor Huddleston's *Naught for Your Comfort* (1956), London. Even legislation which was not explicitly racial in content was used for racial reallocation of urban space. Scott (1992) charts the disruption of a settled informal Indian settlement at Clairwood, south of Durban, by the implementation of 'normal' municipal industrial planning laws.

From the morass of apartheid spatial legislation, certain key principles can be discerned. There is the imposition of firmer central control over African movement to the urban areas; the attempt to extend such control, through segregation, curfews and housing provision, to the activities of Africans who have been admitted to the cities; and the requirement that African urban areas be self-financing. But even in its early stages, the developing system of urban apartheid faced certain deep-seated contradictions. Despite the government's influx-control measures, increasing numbers of Africans continued to leave the impoverished reserves and the modernizing white farms of the platteland, to establish informal dwellings or live in rented accommodation in and around the cities. The Section 10 concession, provided in response to the needs of urban employers, proved crucial in undermining entirely successful influx control. By permitting the economically 'redundant' families of workers to reside with them in the cities, it meant that, contrary to the aim of keeping the urban African presence to a necessary minimum, not all Africans in the cities were employed. Influx control was also undermined in the 1950s by the exploitation of loopholes and straightforward evasion of the law on the part of Africans (see Chapter 5) and by the fact that Africans looking for work were permitted to be in the urban areas for seventy-two hours before their expulsion. This made it impossible to monitor the illegal presence without an ubiquitous police force (Posel, 1991).

Wolpe (1988) has noted the state's actions in closing down the 'space' for the more obvious judicial challenges to state legislation. For example, the Appellate Division's declaration that the removal of Coloured voters from the common roll was unconstitutional, was finally overcome by state manoeuvrings in the mid-1950s. But the government's elaboration and intensification of discriminatory and repressive legislation helped mobilize a mass opposition far more threatening than the judiciary. The bulk of security legislation was directed at narrowing this opposition's potential for legal political action. The 1953 Public Safety Act increased penalties for protest offences, and the burden of guilt was shifted on to the accused in some political trials, with the judge's discretion limited. Ultimately, NP supremacy in parliament through the 1950s allowed the executive to override the authority of the judiciary in the matters which most concerned it (Wolpe, 1988).

In addition to restricting direct political challenges, the new security legislation had another dimension. Much of it was directed, at least partially, at controlling black urban labour. The 1950 Suppression of Communism Act has been seen in this light (Terreblanche and Nattrass, 1990). While declaring the CP illegal, the Act was used to smash the non-racial and black trade union movement. The 1953 Natives Settlement and Disputes Act banned blacks from registering with trade unions and provided emasculated works committees instead. The 1956 Riotous Assemblies Act was used not only against demonstrations, but also against strike pickets.

Despite the extensive and deeply penetrating nature of the early apartheid legislation, it did not amount to an impregnable and immutable edifice of state control. Political, economic, social and spatial planning on a grand scale was always going to be undermined by the activities of individuals collectively striving to create their own favoured conditions of living, in spite of the government's desire to the contrary. The high degree of NP influence over the structures of state – parliament, government, courts and police – facilitated impressive restructuring of South Africa's society and space in the image favoured by the party's leaders. But, as the example of influx control demonstrates, the party was never completely successful in imposing its ideal conception of order upon that society, nor upon its spatial expression. Even within the party, apartheid was not a preconceived blueprint but the outcome of competing viewpoints (see Posel, 1991). Adaptations to the apartheid structure, resulting from pragmatic struggle within and without the NP, began as soon as the NP was in power, and continued until the demise of the system.

2 The evolution of apartheid, 1948–60

Apartheid was constantly being adapted, reflecting power struggles within the ruling group, and to enable its legal provisions to cope with its changing social context and with the shifting spatial distributions of population which persisted despite the state's attempt to contain them. But a passing from one distinct phase to another has also been identified (Giliomee and Schlemmer, 1989; Sparks, 1990; Posel, 1991). The second phase was based upon a new conception of the role of the reserves, which had not featured prominently alongside the urban concerns of the 1950s planners. From the 1960s the reserves were to become the bases for 'Separate Development', as the government called it, or 'Grand' apartheid, as it has been unofficially labelled. Grand apartheid was born out of the state of flux in which administrators found themselves in the late 1950s. At this time, the inadequacies of current apartheid practice were becoming clear, but no coherent plan had yet been devised to push the apartheid concept on into the 1960s.

The first apartheid phase is characterized by Giliomee and Schlemmer (1989) as primarily an attempt to form statutory groups and implement their residential segregation. While 'advances' were made in the fields of labour and influx control and security, they were not yet part of a coherent scheme. The second phase of apartheid was introduced through the agency of Verwoerd, Prime Minister from 1958 to 1966. Verwoerd was a determined ideologue, backed by the increasingly influential Broederbond. He would help push through a more systematic policy of segregation despite the more pragmatic demands of many within the NP. The programme of the 1960s was partly prompted by black resistance, but it was facilitated by a crushing of that resistance early in the decade, an economic boom placing extensive financial resources in the government's hands (Giliomee and Schlemmer, 1989) and the more secure grip of the NP on parliamentary power (Posel, 1991).

Apartheid's second phase

The thrust of Verwoerd's innovation in policy was directed at the reserves, but his government also modified the mechanisms of urban control. First, labour repression was made more systematic. An example is the treatment of the popular SACTU (South African Congress of Trade Unions), an alliance of black unions. This was identified by the state as being related to the black Congress Opposition movement, and its leaders were banned and the organization proscribed for three months in 1961. Under the Sabotage Act, the General Secretary and eight others were forced to sever connections with the union. The government claimed that 'there are recognised federations which are representative of, and entitled to speak for, organised workers in South Africa. The so-called SACTU does not fall within this category' (quoted in Bunting, 1969: 368).

Second, steps were taken to deal with the problem of political representation for those Africans living permanently in the urban areas. All vestiges of black representation in the white political system were removed, and the forcible removal of blacks in the cities without permission was stepped up. The 'loophole' category of Section 10 was also to be narrowed in response to continuing African urbanization. African commercial concerns in the townships were limited, and redirected to the reserves, in order not to allow the trappings of permanency in African urban areas. Africans who were not required as workers were also to be removed from the white rural platteland. Here, the state and agricultural restructuring combined to break the link between Africans and the land (Marcus, 1989).

The official destinations for Africans expelled from the cities and the white farming areas were the reserves. These were now to form the centrepiece of Verwoerdian apartheid policy. They were to develop as semi-'independent' and ultimately 'independent' nations (Fig. 5). Each 'homeland', as they would be called, would be the territorial and national expression of a different African 'tribe' (excepting the case of the Xhosa, who were to have two homelands). It was this innovation which lay at the heart of the official replacement of apartheid by the policy of Separate Development.

Separate Development was by no means an easy step for many in the NP to take. Many of the Afrikaner nationalists who had helped bring the party to power in 1948 instinctively saw independent and autonomous political representation for Africans as a threat to permanent white control over South Africa's territory. Even Verwoerd told parliament that it 'is not what we wanted to see' (Posel, 1991: 231). The shift in the NP's tack, represented by the policy, was not solely due to Verwoerd's persuasiveness; it had a lot to do with South Africa's relations with the external world.

The end of the 1950s brought a changing international context for the South African government's actions. Decolonization was occurring to the north and various African peoples would soon achieve self-determination within new nation states, while racial desegregation was firmly on the political agenda in the USA. South Africa could expect increasing pressure from without its borders, to force a deracialization of existing domestic policy. It had not been long since Smuts was humiliated at the UN over racial policy. Many of the newly independent African states would be likely to follow India in using that forum to condemn South Africa. The gradual move towards apparent independence for the homelands could be presented to the outside world as a kind of internal decolonization and a recognition of autonomous African nationhood (Grundy, 1991). Within restricted NP circles, there was genuine idealism along these lines. The government-

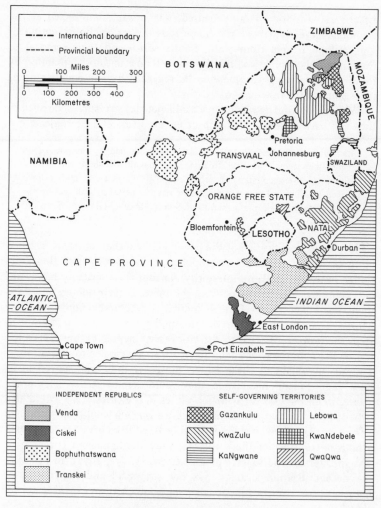

Figure 5 South Africa's 'homelands'
(reproduced from D. Smith, 1990, 3rd edn, *Apartheid in South Africa*,
Cambridge University Press, Cambridge)

appointed Tomlinson Commission of 1956, for instance, had advocated that the South African government pursue large-scale economic development of the impoverished reserves, so that they might become a viable basis for the homelands.

A 'massive programme of social engineering' (Marks and Trapido,

1987b: 22) was indeed implemented, but it was not directed at the economic development of the homelands; rather at the uprooting of four million people from white South Africa and their removal to the homelands, which would always be too poor and too dominated by the South African government to be regarded by any country, other than South Africa, as national states.

While homeland governments could not deserve such recognition, they did have a tremendous impact on the lives of their subjects.

> Sham or not, the Bantustan (homeland) policies had by the late 1970s created 'new facts'. New political institutions and the deliberate use of welfare to give reconstructed ethnic identities a material reality have created conflicting interests which now have to be taken into account in any struggle for the transformation of South Africa. (Marks and Trapido, 1987b: 22)

Ideological justification of the policy followed the 'separate but equal cultures' line of Afrikaans anthropology, shifting away from the traditional invocation of Bantu inferiority. A material rationale for homeland autonomy was also developed from the 1960s, as their political development was linked to government industrial decentralization incentives. Most analysts see the decentralization policy primarily as an attempt to stem the flow of Africans to the cities (see Chapter 5), but for Wolpe (1972) the policy was designed to create an alternative to migration as a means of obtaining cheap labour power. If industries moved to or near 'independent' homelands, they could employ Africans, at lower wages, to do the jobs set aside for whites in the cities. They could also benefit from the fact that homeland governments would not recognize African trade unions, and they would be freed from pressure to provide a housing subsidy for their workers, since the homeland government was to cater for the welfare of its citizens (Wolpe, 1972). In practice, the decentralization strategy was not successful and the degree of homeland government functionality for South African capital is debatable.

But before looking at the progress of the separate-development policy in Chapter 5, it is necessary to stress its ideological dimension – no mere expression or justification of material goals. The extent of Verwoerd's personal influence has already been mentioned. It is significant that he was Minister of Native Affairs before his accession to the Prime Ministership. His firmly rooted ideological stance was derived from his experience in that office. In his mind, the notion of preserving white society, and in particular Afrikaans identity, clearly coincided with the need to place firm limits on black social, economic, spatial and political encroachment. If black political expression must be denied within white South Africa, the shifting climate of international opinion meant that it had to be catered for in 'black South Africa', that is the homelands.

With Verwoerd's encouragement, from 1958, the Broederbond took upon itself the role of proselytizing a republic (as it had done for a period prior to 1948), within which the new vision of apartheid would hold sway. In the early 1960s the Bond had 8,000 members. By the late 1970s the figure was over 12,000 (Giliomee and Schlemmer, 1989: 94). The Bond's members, occupying virtually all of the top positions in political, civil service, church and educational structures, were in an extremely advantageous position to diffuse the new conception of separate development. All Cabinet ministers were members, as were three-quarters of the NP caucus, every principal of the Afrikaans universities and colleges, half the school principals and inspectors, and 40 per cent of Dutch Reformed Church ministers (Giliomee and Schlemmer, 1989: 95).

The state and the Broederbond's scheme of separate development was not reliant on black consultation, but blacks nevertheless proved influential in the development of the policy. The increasing scale and growing diversity of black resistance contributed vitally, in the 1950s and early 1960s, to the state's need to adjust existing apartheid structures.

Black political organization and resistance, 1948–60

The overall impact of black resistance in the 1950s was formed from the interweaving of localized and geographically differentiated strands of protest, into a fabric of broad, national-scale organization. The interaction between local and national currents of resistance is a key factor in the history of black resistance to apartheid. Black resistance has always been of most concern to the state when diverse localities were consciously articulated in their actions, and most problematic for the national resistance organizations when they were not.

The tone for black organization at the national scale was set in 1949 when the ANC conference was dominated by the movement's more radical Youth League (ANCYL). During the conference, six members of the ANCYL, including Nelson Mandela, Walter Sisulu and Oliver Tambo, were elected on to the national executive. Arrayed against the Youth League members were representatives of the more moderate 'old guard' and the communists (the Youth League had attempted to expel communists from the party in 1945 and 1947). Once in the executive, though, the prominent ANCYL representatives tended to moderate their Africanist line in the interests of compromise with other members.

The 1950s began with organization for a stayaway, directed against the Suppression of Communism Act, which, in fact, was invoked to suppress far more than just communism. The regionally fragmented response of this campaign was representative of the general geographical pattern that subsequent resistance campaigns, over the next decade, would reflect. The stayaway was particularly strong in the Eastern Cape, especially around Port Elizabeth. Natal saw relatively firm support from some quarters, but its overall response was muted by division, while the action was less successful in the Transvaal. Despite the spatial variation of this campaign, the stayaway became an important item in the 'repertoire' of resistance through the 1950s. As a tactic it was successful in highlighting the increasingly important position of Africans in the economy, and it was relatively easy to organize among the concentrated and segregated populations of the townships. Apart from the state's response, the greatest difficulty faced by the organizers of such a campaign was, and continued to be, that of mobilizing those migrant workers confined in local hostels or barracks (see Chapter 7).

During 1952, prompted by the deprivation of Coloured voting rights, the ANC leadership organized a broad Defiance Campaign. Volunteers were systematically to break the racial taboos of apartheid. As it progressed, the action's targets widened from the Separate Representation of Voters Act to encompass the pass laws, stock limitation in the reserves, the Bantu Authorities Act, the Group Areas Act and the Suppression of Communism Act. The most enthusiastic response was again from the Eastern Cape. Eventually, rioting in East London and Port Elizabeth, the government's imposition of bans on individuals, increasingly harsh prison sentences for breaking laws in protest, and the organizational confusion accompanying the spreading spatial extent of the protest, culminated in the immobilization of the campaign.

Lodge's explanation for the particularly vibrant opposition of the Eastern Cape throughout the decade centres on its industrial characteristics and the unusual form of administration it experienced (Lodge, 1983). Port Elizabeth was the fastest-growing urban centre in South Africa: Ford had established a manufacturing plant there in 1923, attracted by its port and its centrality relative to South Africa's major conurbations. The plant was soon joined by smaller, linked industries and a wider range of heavy and light manufacturing. The expanding African working population was relatively easily organized by trade unionists, being ethnically homogenous (95 per cent Xhosa) and having no internal linguistic barriers. The fact that these workers were accommodated in townships rather than in company-supervised hostels or barracks also facilitated communication and mobilization.

Port Elizabeth's local government had earned a reputation for a lax approach to influx control. Its stance was determined to a large extent by local manufacturing's need for labour supplies to maintain industrial expansion. But Africans moving to the city purely to find work were joined by those escaping the increasingly eroded reserves, and those evicted from surrounding white farms. A large squatter settlement developed which, by 1949, had the highest rate of tuberculosis in the world. By the 1950s, then, Port Elizabeth's African population was exceptional. A fairly cohesive industrial working class was found alongside the extreme poverty of peri-urban shack dwellers. This spatial 'situatedness' allowed for a particularly consistent and coherent expression of opposition to the political structures of the state, not just in the 1950s, but throughout the apartheid era.

In 1949, raised fares prompted an extensive township bus boycott, but this action was merely a prelude for the firm resistance with which the government's subsequent, more rigid, influx-control measures would be met. In Port Elizabeth particularly, 'drawing on a well-established local tradition of mass protest, the African community was able to link parochial concerns with more general political ideas: popular politics transcended the usual anxieties over subsistence which predominated in everyday life' (Lodge, 1983: 55).

During the Defiance Campaign, Natal too showed incipient tendencies towards popular mobilization. Here, however, the effectiveness of the campaign was impaired by the Zulu–Indian tension which had erupted in the 1949 Durban riots. In a later period it was to be the divide between the Zulu nationalistic Inkatha and the United Democratic Front (UDF)/ANC which would be the main obstacle to a united regional resistance (see Chapter 7).

With the unprecedented spatial extent of the Defiance Campaign, and a hingepin role in the formulation of the Freedom Charter, through the 1950s, the ANC leadership enjoyed increasing popularity. But the crushing of the Defiance Campaign had taught it a lesson: it would need a long-term programme and a means to sustain its hold over a larger and more dispersed following, if future campaigns were not to collapse in disorganization just as they achieved widespread popularity. Z.K. Matthews first proposed the drawing up of a 'Freedom Charter' of the expressed aims of the opposition movement, as a unifying and guiding force. Various oppositional bodies, including the white Congress of Democrats and the parliamentary Liberal Party, liaised, with the aim of planning local committees throughout the country, to elect representatives to a national convention. The convention, in turn, would incorporate the people of South Africa's demands into the Charter, rather in the style of the 1789 *cahiers* of France. In the event, provincial ANC branches were responsible for much of the local organization, and, at the centre, the Charter was produced by a small drafting committee, drawing on material supplied by sub-committees. (Africanists within the ANC were deeply disaffected by the influence of whites on this committee.) In 1955, the Charter was publicly presented at Kliptown, where 3,000 delegates amassed. Once the police were confident that the ANC and its allies had been given 'enough rope to hang themselves' (Lodge, 1983: 71), the meeting was broken up and 156 Congress Alliance members were arrested on charges of treason, launching the five-year 'Treason Trial'.

The tensions already implicit within the ANC became explicit in 1958, during its Transvaal Provincial Congress, when brawling broke out between Africanists and executive supporters. The Africanists had grown further distant from the executive line in the years since the Kliptown Congress. They perceived a base for their 'embittered and vengeful' mood (Lodge, 1983: 83) among the young, and especially with the migrant workers of Cape Town. For them, the ANC was too accommodating towards whites and to 'foreign' ideologies like communism. Much of their thinking derived from a realistic assessment of popular opinion: 'The masses do not hate an abstraction like "oppression" or "capitalism". ... They make these things concrete and hate the oppressor – in South Africa the white man' (*Golden City Post*, Johannesburg, 1959, cited in Lodge, 1983: 83).

Such was essentially the principle behind the Africanists' decision to break with the ANC and form the Pan-Africanist Congress (PAC). Its leader, Robert Sobukwe, believed though, that whites could be African if they altered their behaviour and thinking in line with those of Africans. The early PAC concentrated its organizational efforts in those areas where the ANC was weak – the townships around Vereneeging in the Transvaal, and the Cape Peninsula where migrant Xhosa in particular had been overlooked by the ANC. Towards the end of the 1950s, the PAC began to mobilize its first anti-pass campaign in order to wrest the initiative of resistance from the ANC.

The sum of African resistance to apartheid in the 1950s was not constituted entirely by the ANC and PAC. There was also the All-African Convention (AAC), originally founded to oppose the 1936 legislation depriving Cape Africans of the vote. Its following was largely composed of African Marxists, and its strategy was based on rural mobilization through educational and legal services, and against enforced land rehabilitation. The movement directed abuse against the

ANC for its 'collaboration' in government advisory boards, but its own influence was largely confined to Cape intellectuals.

We have seen how a regional differentiation in the extent and effectiveness of resistance to apartheid accompanied political divisions in the 1950s, and has remained characteristic. A further characteristic of subsequent black resistance also developed during this decade. This is the role of certain places as symbols of wider national opposition and as leaders by example. Soweto in 1976 and the townships of the Vaal triangle in the mid-1980s had their forerunner in Sophiatown during the 1950s. While in the former cases there was violent physical resistance against various aspects of apartheid, in Sophiatown, tangible physical resistance was weak. Yet Sophiatown was similarly significant for the wider pattern of resistance.

Sophiatown was a dynamic, vibrant, often violent, mixed-race freehold area, connected to Johannesburg. For many of the city's whites, it manifested the very threat of an ascendant and proximate urban black population that had persuaded them to vote NP. For the government, it was a standing contravention of the aims of apartheid. Not only could Africans own property in 'white space' there; racial intermixing was the most prominent characteristic of the place. It was additionally the haunt of a plethora of urban criminal gangs (see Hart and Pirie, 1984). Consequently, the government determined, during the late 1950s, to remove the African population of Sophiatown to an externalized, closely supervised, state-administered township.

The removals took place gradually and with an element of support from some sections of the settlement's population. There was no wholesale, determined resistance but there was articulate opposition nevertheless, particularly from African journalists resident in the area (see *Blame Me on History* by Bloke Modisane, 1963). The everyday non-co-operation displayed by the residents, their persistent breaking of apartheid laws in the face of repeated raids, arrests, evictions and 'rustications' (removals to the reserves) and their maintenance of a vital community spirit became known and admired by blacks (and many whites) further afield. Sophiatown's verbal and literary, if not physical, resistance, and the state's ultimate resort to coercion, informed the 'heritage of resistance', which provided the context for later struggles elsewhere.

It has been part of a more general critique of the 1950s ANC that it did not involve itself greatly in the local impact of apartheid or the localized forms of resistance, like that in Sophiatown, with which apartheid was met. Apart from its organizational structures being amateurish at this stage, Feit (1965, cited in Lodge, 1983) argues that the ANC's limitations were those of a bourgeois leadership trying to resist its own demotion to the socio-economic level which apartheid prescribed for all Africans. But apartheid itself helped to erode the distinction between an African bourgeoisie and the wider African population by lumping them together in the segregated townships of the poor and the working class: 'African townships, though socially heterodox in a number of ways, did not have the "geography of class" that was a feature of white suburbia' (Lodge, 1983: 92). While the preservation of class distinctions may have been an initial aim of some leaders in the ANC, their aims were modified by the very thing which they sought to resist – an integration with wider urban African communities. The African intellectual and bourgeois leadership was likely to retain some distinct concerns, but by immersing them in the wider problems of urban Africans as a whole, apartheid's spatial planners helped generate more universal aspirations.

Even the urban gangs, who usually preyed on their own community, were likely to pool their political interests with those of the wider community when it came to resisting apartheid. In fact, urban gangs were quite well adjusted to political protest as they had a ready-made organizational structure that could be brought into action at short notice. In Sophiatown, for instance, they helped mobilize what little physical resistance to the police there was, using their signalling system of banging on street lights to warn of an approaching police presence (Beinart, 1987; Huddleston, 1956).

At either end of the urban African social scale, then, the 1950s witnessed a convergence of political concerns. Towards the intellectual pinnacle of urban African society was the 'Drum generation' – a well-defined group of African writers and reporters who contributed to the English-language magazine, *Drum*. Together, they showed a 'social compassion and depth of anger that went well beyond their immediate class interests' (Lodge, 1983: 93). The group was distinguished by its 'raucous, zany, prolific, and frequently penetrating' style of writing (Gunner, 1988: 224). Its members included Can Themba, Casey 'Kid' Motsisi, Todd Matshikiza, Nat Nakasa, Henry Nxumalo, Ezekiel Mphahlele and Bloke Modisane (whose *Blame Me on History*, mentioned above, warranted a Penguin Modern Classics edition). 'They were urban to their fingertips. They wrote about the crowded back streets, side streets, alleys, shanties and shebeens of places like Alexandra and Sophiatown', the urban freehold areas around Johannesburg that were 'soon to crumble under the bulldozers' (Gunner, 1988: 224). African literary expression had finally followed the African geographical shift, from rural roots to the new urban arenas of white domination – a transition made with perhaps more grace than the equivalent and preceding literary displacement of the Afrikaner nationalist writers.

These African writers were not political activists, but they shared in, and represented in their writing, the vibrancy and identity of black urban culture in the 1950s (Gunner, 1988).

In the 1950s, many of the ANC's leaders had had the benefit of an elite mission education. In this respect they were most unrepresentative of the larger African community. The desire to share in the rewards that education could offer was especially strong among the poor, particularly in the Eastern Rand and the Eastern Cape. Many of the educated ANC leaders failed to perceive education as a fundamental material concern of the urban poor, alongside transport costs, food prices and housing.

Popular mobilization against the government's African education policy initially arose not so much out of the Bantu Education Act itself, as out of changes associated with it: the two-shilling monthly education levy that would be raised on urban households, the increasing pupil–teacher ratios, the falling *per capita* expenditure on pupils, the cessation of school meals and the abolition of caretakers' posts, which would involve the pupils themselves cleaning the schools. 'For an underprivileged society in which access to education provided the most common means of social mobility for one's children these were serious blows' (Lodge, 1983: 117). Once the boycott of government schools had been initiated by teachers' associations, influenced by Africanists in the Transvaal and by the AAC in the Cape, the ANC proved not to have the resources to provide an alternative education, and within the ANC there was tension over the degree of militancy that should be pursued once educational resistance had begun.

Prior to the Bantu Education Act, a tradition of student militancy had already emerged within mission schools such as Lovedale and Healdtown. Damage to school property, class boycotts and, occasionally, attacks on teachers had developed out of the issues of food and discipline in these boarding institutions. The specific problems of the 1950s were addressed through these 'older, recognised repertoires' (Hyslop, 1991: 86) of action. The Bantu Education Act precipitated the shift of these forms of resistance from mission to urban day schools, and from petty bourgeois students to an urban African, working-class youth. The Act also brought about a wider focus of anger among urban youth, from educational structures in particular to the increasingly prominent and interventionist authoritarian state in general. Yet the militants within the ANC, in endeavouring to encourage more general opposition to the state, were to find, in the 1950s and in the future, that 'men and women struggling to survive economically and to provide a better world for their children are not necessarily revolutionaries' (Lodge, 1983: 128).

The scope of resistance in the 1950s

Despite the absence of widespread revolutionary commitment, the 1950s did mark a novel phase of resistance. Lodge (1983) narrates the unprecedented level of women's mobilization both against African men's pusillanimity and directly against the influx control and land rehabilitation measures as they affected women in particular (Lodge, 1983: 139–53). Rising transport costs, crucial for Africans externalized in the townships, were protested in the bus boycotts of Evaton and Alexandra, which owed much of their success to local ANC initiative. Once again, the rift between the township community and the alienated and isolated migrant hostel dwellers manifested itself. In Evaton there was violence between supporters of the boycott and migrant Basotho vigilantes.

Resistance in the 1950s extended beyond the urban areas. This and the succeeding decade were punctuated by a series of rebellions against government attempts to restructure rural social relations. The failure of reserve agriculture, which the government intervention was designed to combat, was itself exacerbated by the government's policy of concentrating the economically 'surplus' African population in the reserves, with tighter influx control and anti-urban squatting legislation. The government's attempt to limit stock and prevent access to the land to allow its recovery could not be countenanced by those already at bare subsistence level in the reserves. The disparate rebellions of Zoutspansberg, Sekhukuniland, Witzieshoek, Marico, Natal, Tembuland and particularly the nine-month Mpondoland insurrection, taken together, resulted in hundreds of deaths but, distanced and locally inspired, they were not articulated as a general revolt. (See Lodge (1983: 269–88) for the course of the revolts in general, and Beinart (1982: 160) for the Mpondoland revolt in particular. For recent literature deepening our appreciation of rural conditions and struggles in both the nineteenth and twentieth centuries, see Beinart and Bundy (1987) and Beinart et al. (1986)).

It was not only the characteristics of subsequent resistance which were first established in the 1950s; the government's response also founded a pattern. It consistently attempted to impute blame for all 'unrest' to the ANC's incitement. The strategy was often counterproductive. Further African support was generated for the organization credited by the government with being its greatest foe and threat. In reality, however, the ANC could not, during the 1950s, marshal all the elements of resistance to different aspects of apartheid under its own direction. On the whole, it was reactive in its organization more than it was proactive.

But the importance of resistance in the 1950s lies deeper than any organizational structures. A transformation of African political consciousness lay beneath the expanding repertoire of resistance. Beinart (1987) traces, through the experiences of a Mpondo migrant 'M', the wider development of African political awareness through the mid-twentieth century. Many traditional rural ideas and values were retained by the growing urban African proletariat, but it was gradually transcending the narrow limits of ethnic identity to encompass a broader class and 'all-African', 'national' consciousness. M's political identity allowed a sympathy for both Congress's national campaigns and narrow, ethnically based strategies of rural resistance. It was through people like M that African nationalist and trade union leaders in the cities were able to 'reach the great majority of South African blacks who had not fully absorbed their generalized positions' (Beinart, 1987: 307).

Beneath even the collective level of resistance, blacks had their own individual, day-to-day forms of resistance to personal white domination and to the racism of the workplace. White stereotypes of blacks as lazy, careless and stupid workers reflect the forms of resistance adopted by people fighting an all-pervasive repression: foot-dragging, feigned ignorance, false compliance and pilfering are all everyday manifestations of non-compliance with a system of exploitation and oppression (Sparks, 1990).

Conclusion

In 1948, the government of South Africa, not for the first time, passed into the hands of an elite determined to protect and further the particular interests of a small minority of the population. Previous governments had seen the primary cleavage in South African society as being a racial one, and had endeavoured to respect and maintain that cleavage in their policy. However, the NP government, while continuing to safeguard white superiority with even more extreme measures, was additionally concerned with the maintenance of a division within white society – that between Afrikaans- and English-speakers. Its priority was the elevation of a volk threatened by modernization and urbanization, whose identity lay at the very core of its leadership's secular and spiritual worldview. Afrikaners would be protected from the economic competition of both English-speakers in the white population and blacks being incorporated in to the urban industrial economy. Paternalistic job provision and welfare distribution would ensure protection from the former, while it had long been politically legitimate to curb the activities of the latter through discriminatory legislation.

Yet the 1948 apartheid government's 'Native Policy' marked a departure from the trend which had characterized the last years of Smuts's administration. Instead of accommodating and utilizing an expanding urban African population for the sake of the economy, the outcome of compromise between competing viewpoints within the NP was an emphasis on maintaining an older pattern – the preservation of cities for their white populations, with firm control over only a strictly necessary number of black workers in the urban areas. Apartheid, then, represented both a discontinuity in the trend of government policy and a continuity in the pre-existing shape of urban society. The Group Areas Act's 'apartheid city' was built upon the segregated city of the 1920s to 1940s. Initially, each city's degree of correspondence to the 'apartheid model' was determined by the local authority's reaction to central initiative and its assessment of the potential force of black resistance (Posel, 1991), but by the 1960s, despite local variation in attitude, increasing centralization of state authority under the NP would result in a more standardized South African city form.

Attempts to develop the envisaged apartheid city were accompanied by new forms of African resistance, as the conditions of a segregated and policed city shaped more and more African lives. In particular, the residents of the townships, thoroughly urban but externalized from the cities in which they worked, mobilized around the issues of transport and education.

As the cities were being moulded to fit more closely a central design, a parallel transformation of the reserves progressed. Increasing overcrowding and land deterioration in the countryside was largely a consequence of the redistribution of the poor, the weak and the unrequired from the cities, as stricter influx control took effect. The rural decline, in turn, provoked further government intervention, which precipitated resistance of an even greater intensity and violence than in the cities.

Even though the NP government did not, as is often thought, implement a cohesively pre-planned system, the apartheid government's aggregate intention – to shape South African society and space so as to preserve an inherited, cracking mould of white superiority – involved an unprecedented degree of state intervention in black people's everyday lives. From the individual working as slowly as possible in a factory without jeopardizing his/her job and the thousands of Africans who simply would not abide by influx-control regulations, to the organization of a mass Defiance Campaign or a Ciskeian battle with police, such intervention provoked resistance. Unprecedented coercion was needed to retain economic relations based on pigmentation, and to ensure the monopoly of white political and social authority, through a modern, industrial era.

Academia searched for a way of extending the ideological justification for such a system in South Africa while it was being abandoned elsewhere. Its findings were more easily supported by the white population the more the government legislated to keep the races apart: in commuting, in swimming, in queueing, particularly in education, and even in bed. The inherent conception of a racial division of mankind, handed down to whites over three hundred years, was consolidated as they were prevented, even had they wanted to, from forming relationships and socializing with blacks, and as they were educated to respect an exclusive identity.

The legacies left by the 1950s and subsequent apartheid social engineers include more than just the obvious political problems faced by South Africans today. They also include a deliberate contribution to the lived urban and rural inadequacies of shelter, health and education for the bulk of the country's population.

5

Adaptations and Contradictions

Introduction

The turn of the 1960s brought a forceful new incentive to elaborate a firmer plan for deflecting African political claims away from the white urban areas and towards 'independent' reserve structures. The incentive came in the form of a resurgence of urban unrest, culminating in the internationally condemned Sharpeville shootings. In 1960, the relatively small township of Sharpeville, outside Vereeniging in the Transvaal, acquired international symbolism as an example of the repressive nature of apartheid. After Sharpeville, the government opted more firmly for the new interpretation of its racial policy as Separate Development and, from 1960, real steps were taken to develop separate homeland administrations. Section one of this chapter explains the context for, and the reaction to, the shootings at Sharpeville, including the nature of Separate Development and the homelands.

Yet, even the adapted spatial and political structures of apartheid rule continued to be riven by internal contradictions and fractured by the social pressures which brought South Africa into the 1970s. Section two of the chapter is devoted to introducing the evolution of these contradictions and their influence on the government's attitude towards apartheid. In turn, the impacts of continuing urbanization, of the economic constraints of apartheid, of regional (southern African) political and world economic changes, of black resistance and of socio-political changes in the Afrikaans constituency are assessed.

1 Sharpeville and Separate Development

Sharpeville

In December 1959, both the ANC and the PAC announced campaigns directed against the pass laws. The ANC's envisaged demonstrations and petitions, but seemed weak compared to the ongoing manifestation of disaffection in Cato Manor in Natal, where violent revolt was proceeding with the involvement of local ANC members (Lodge, 1983). The PAC's plan was a clearer reflection of the anger felt in many areas after a decade of NP rule. Its campaign was launched early in 1960. Volunteers without the necessary pass would offer themselves peacefully for arrest, calling for the police to act with restraint. At a variety of venues, PAC members gathered to hand themselves into custody, witnessed by supporters and demonstrators.

At Vanderbijlpark the crowds were dispersed by baton charge, and at Evaton, by low-flying jets. Aircraft failed to scatter the crowd at Sharpeville though, and the police at the local station refused to arrest the volunteers. PAC officials would not call on the crowd to disperse until the PAC leader, Robert Sobukwe, was able to address them. Police reinforcements brought the participants in the ensuing events to 200 police and about 5,000 members of the crowd. A scuffle broke out at the gate in the wire fence surrounding the police station and, as the crowd surged forward to investigate the cause, police started firing, later claiming that they were being stoned. By the time the firing stopped, sixty-nine Africans were killed and 180 wounded, most shot in the back. Only after a mass funeral of the victims did the residents of Sharpeville trickle back to work (Lodge, 1983).

Chaskalson (1991) has described the particular context of the national PAC campaign in Sharpeville. Circumstances in the township conspired to generate particularly intense disaffection with government intervention. Here there appears to be a paradox, since Sharpeville was seen as a 'model township' and had better facilities than most. The resentment stemmed from the progressive removal of residents to Sharpeville from their former 'Top Location'.

Top Location was subject to more lax administrative control than was Sharpeville. A large, informal economic sector allowed the survival of low-paid and unemployed residents in the location, but they were being squeezed out by the stricter regulation of economic activity in the newer township. Top Location's administration had also been lax in another sense: nearby Vereeniging's employers regularly overlooked a lack of workers' passes, facilitating a large population of 'illegals', who would be endorsed out of the urban area once the location was entirely cleared and removed to Sharpeville.

Even for the legal residents, relocation to Sharpeville meant a longer and more expensive bus journey to work in Vereeniging. They would also resent the more efficient policing of the township, since bans on certain political groups and on meetings of over ten people had been introduced to counter the recent urban African political organization. The very quality of Sharpeville's housing was an additional drawback, given the higher rents that had to be paid, especially with local authorities being increasingly pressurized to make their townships economically self-sufficient.

Vereeniging's industries were gradually becoming more capital intensive. For the township's youth, this meant declining opportunities. As the number of young unemployed increased, their discontent was manifested in more numerous instances of reckless resistance to authority. The same factor may also have been associated with the greater prevalence of gangs of tsotsis (young violent criminals). By the late 1950s the local authority was employing African vigilantes to expel them to Native Affairs Department labour camps. But local disorder was not caused solely by the tsotsis. The 'Russians', a migrant Basotho gang accommodated in local hostels, added their contribution. The rate of pass raids was stepped up, ostensibly to rid the community of this menace, but township residents soon found their own illegally resident relatives endorsed out of the township instead of the Russians. The disruption and menace of the raids is attested by Petrus Tom: 'People hid under beds, in toilets, inside wardrobes and in dirty washing tubs. The raids started as early as 1.00 a.m.' (cited in Chaskalson, 1991: 134).

In Sharpeville, then, it was the success of urban apartheid's implementation which generated the communal anger of the crowd surrounding the police station. The fact that similar crowds surrounded other official symbols in different parts of South Africa indicates the range and depth of official interference and disruption in Africans' lives, and the resentment generated by apartheid's attempt to level down the quality of those lives. It was a drive to collect rent arrears at the end of 1959 which provided the final spur for Sharpeville's residents to join the PAC's campaign. Elsewhere it was other local pressures that were more significant, but all were added to the already intolerable burden of apartheid's intervention.

While, due to the loss of life it endured, Sharpeville became the enduring symbol of the anti-pass campaign, the campaign mobilized far more Africans in the Cape than it did in the Transvaal. The African population of the Western Cape was subjected to particularly harsh influx control, involving the 'rustication' of Africans to the reserves in order to maintain the region for Coloured employment under the Coloured Labour Preference Policy. While the Xhosa migrant workers of Cape Town's Langa township saw opportunities in the city being closed to them by this policy, their families in the reserves were being denied land rights by the land rehabilitation policy. The settled township population was similarly suffering discrimination in favour of Coloureds, and already had a tradition of support for the Africanist ideology. The PAC campaign, then, found a large following among both migrants and township dwellers in Cape Town's environs. The campaign here also met with a violent police response, followed by riots, an extended strike supported by white liberals, a march of 30,000 on Cape Town and the cordoning off of the entire Langa township (see Lodge, 1983 for details).

On a national scale, the 1960 anti-pass campaign marked a turning point when, after ten years of apartheid's implementation, passive protest was generally transformed into more active resistance. But, despite a 90 per cent successful stayaway, organized by the ANC in the wake of the shootings, the resistance was still centred in localized islands, set in a sea of relative acquiescence.

Nevertheless, the state of turmoil into which national politics was thrown by the events of 1960 had permanent significance. Sharpeville marked a departure in the government's methods of dealing with black opposition. Prior to 1960, the courts and the law, adapted for government purposes, were used to stifle opposition. Often, nothing other than the neglect of black representations had sufficed. After 1960 though, the main opposition movements were banned and extra-legal activity commenced on a wide scale, both by black opposition movements and by the state's own security forces.

For the PAC and the ANC, banning meant exclusion from legal politics. The implications of this were clear and highly significant. If they were to continue resisting apartheid, they now had no alternative but to do so illegally. The state's use of overt violence during the 1960 campaign was also crucial for the subsequent development of resistance politics. So long as the state was willing to meet non-violent protest with brute force, and so long as white public opinion was willing to condone such a response, mere passive protest, the leaders of the ANC and PAC reasoned, would never be effective. Both movements now formed insurgent offshoots. The ANC's Umkhonto we Sizwe (MK) began a carefully controlled campaign of sabotage, avoiding, in its early stages, any bloodshed. The Poqo movement was based on the PAC's enduring, idealistic vision of inspirational attacks on whites precipitating a popular uprising. The protest politics of the 1950s, which Lodge believes was well adjusted to specific and local grievances, but had been applied ineffectually to national campaigns, was now abandoned by both organizations.

With its new strategy, however, the ANC faced enormous difficulties, not the least of which was the supervision of its own covert units, which frequently acted independently of regional and national command. When the MK leadership was captured at Rivonia, the ensuing trial resulted in the long-term imprisonment of Nelson

Mandela (already incarcerated for leaving the country without valid documents) and Walter Sisulu, among others. Seventy-two charges of minor damage, ninety-five of incendiary bombs in public buildings and seven of dynamiting installations like railway lines were levelled against the defendants. The twenty-three attacks which MK guerrillas had launched against policemen and 'collaborators', mostly in Port Elizabeth and Durban, reflected more the indiscipline of local units than the strategy of central command (Lodge, 1983). While the Rivonia capture revealed that MK was not a particularly successful guerrilla movement in its own right, the tradition of resistance that its very existence symbolized became a key factor in the ANC's revival of fortune over the next two decades.

More violent than the ANC in the 1960s were the PAC's Poqo and the white student-backed, African Resistance Movement, responsible for bombing Johannesburg's railway station concourse. Poqo was involved in a series of localized killings and skirmishes with police, resulting in 202 convictions for murder. The movement inspired particularly vehement action in Paarl, where two insurgents were killed by police, and the insurgents themselves killed a seventeen-year-old girl and a young man. Here, anger at the authorities was especially fierce, as the African men had recently been 'resettled' from informal settlements to bleak camps, and separated from the women who were 'endorsed out' of the urban area to the Transkei (Lodge, 1983).

In rural Tembuland, Poqo's actions were largely directed against Matanzima, a chief who had taken advantage of the government's patronage under the Bantu Authorities Act 1951 to establish an independent power base, and who subsequently headed the 'independent' homeland government of Transkei. In targeting Matanzima, Poqo reflected the popular opposition to his new-found status. The resistance offered by the movement, here and across South Africa, was ended with mass arrests in 1963, after effective police infiltration and intelligence.

Following the internal suppression of the two main resistance organizations, the ANC proved to be by far the better adapted to exile politics, with its necessity of mobilizing international support. The PAC was hampered by a fractious and uncompromising appearance. The ANC was thus in an advantageous position for a return, in the 1980s, to ideological and organizational influence within South Africa.

In the 1960s, black mobilization was reflected not only by the political resistance movements, but also, in an overt way, within the workforce, as trade union organization gained ground. The foundations had been laid by the Congress-linked South African Congress of Trade Unions (SACTU) in the 1950s, with its firmly expressed rejection of job reservation, exclusion of Africans from collective bargaining, racial pay differentials and restrictions on African residence and mobility – all accepted with resignation by the rival Trade Union Council of South Africa (TUCSA). By 1962, SACTU had 55,000 members, its strength rooted mainly in Durban and Natal. The specific trade-union actions of the 1960s, even after the suppression of SACTU in 1965, led to arrests, dismissals and local organizational disintegration, but, cumulatively, the strikes helped to raise the general level of African wages by the end of the decade (Lodge, 1983; Luckhardt and Wall, 1980). Lodge believes that, 'It must be admitted ... that with the adoption of a guerrilla strategy in 1961, the Congress chose to jettison a powerful weapon in the trade union organisation' (1993: 198).

The year 1960 marked the ANC's departure from previously legal activities, but it had similar significance for the security forces. A series of amendments through the 1960s and 1970s allowed the police to detain suspects for longer, and finally for indefinite, periods without trial. Behind the improvised legal edifice of repression, the use of torture, as part of the interrogation of many of these suspects, became prevalent.

The government's strategy for dealing with its black political opposition after Sharpeville had repercussions well beyond South Africa's borders. The Sharpeville shootings and the ban on domestic political opposition precipitated a growing international isolation, marked by its face-saving withdrawal from the Commonwealth and, following a referendum, its declaration as a republic in 1961. In 1963, condemnation of apartheid at the United Nations resulted in an arms embargo on South Africa. The international condemnation brought on by Sharpeville, however, also prompted a material crisis, which was of greater immediate concern to the government than ideological disapproval. After the shootings, capital, deterred by the potential for continuing instability, poured out of the country and the Rand plummeted. Sharpeville really seemed for a time to mark the crisis of an attempt to carry apartheid into the modern, interdependent world.

The economy's relative isolation prompted the government to pursue domestic development of the more capital-intensive, strategic sectors of manufacturing. Growth sectors in the 1960s and 1970s included cars and accessories, chemicals, pulp and paper, military hardware, capital goods equipment and electronic and computer manufactures (Legassick, 1974, cited in Rogerson, 1982). A second grand attempt to achieve import substitution was launched. Rogerson (1982) cites the car industry as an example. Initially, local activity was restricted to the assembly of imported components, but by differentially taxing cars with a high percentage of foreign components, the state succeeded in encouraging the local evolution of 'backward linkage manufactures' (Grundy, 1981, quoted in Rogerson, 1982: 49). As this example suggests, the initial capital flight from South Africa proved by no means disastrous for its economy. A drain of $576 million from 1959 to 1965 was converted into a $2.4 billion inflow of capital from 1965 to 1970 (Houghton, cited in Price, 1991: 24). South Africa's economic growth rates were close to those of Germany and Japan (prompting many observers to conclude that apartheid was compatible with, and even conducive to, capital growth).

The government response to progressive diplomatic exclusion and alienation was 'outward' diplomatic gestures to the rest of Africa. Jack Spence describes the years 1961 to 1974 as the 'golden years of South African diplomacy' (quoted in Grundy, 1991: 30). Confident of its control over the internal black opposition, Vorster's late 1960s government focused on ameliorating international opposition to its policies by gaining diplomatic recognition to complement its economic leverage over southern Africa. But Malawi, alone among the black-ruled African states, entered into formal diplomatic relations in 1967.

For the Western nations, the government stressed its shared commitment to the global anti-communist struggle, particularly elaborating the communist threat that black opposition to its own policies portended. Among other influences, the tactic seemed to work fairly well. From 1969 to 1986 (except during the Carter years), US policy was informed by National Security Study Memorandum 39, which recommended that friendly encouragement rather than pressure to reform should be proffered to the South African government (Grundy, 1991).

After 1960, the South African government, particularly Vorster's (1966–78), found itself channelling more of its efforts towards further limiting damage in its international relations, and to preventing another outbreak of domestic opposition. Both policy thrusts could be boosted by an elaboration of Separate Development. Grand apartheid (the package of 'independent' homelands and decentralization of industry to homeland border areas) would stem the flow of Africans joining the politicized masses in the cities, and pacify international opinion about internal black political representation.

Separate Development

Verwoerd saw homeland self-government as sufficiently 'taking into account the tendencies in the world and in Africa' (quoted in Price, 1991: 22). While outright 'independence' was not envisaged for some time, it was perceived as increasingly feasible in the light of the independence of Britain's neighbouring High Commission territories: Botswana in 1960, Lesotho in 1966 and Swaziland in 1968. The South African government appreciated that these territories, although politically independent, were still economically dependent on South Africa for the employment of their migrant workers, and without South Africa having to pay for the social costs of this labour (housing, schooling, health, etc.). This realization encouraged a more coherent plan for homeland political autonomy, leading eventually to South Africa's own conferring of 'independence' on four of the homelands. Immediately, however, steps were taken to abolish what white representation in parliament there still was for Africans, who would, in future, be represented only in their respective homelands.

In 1961, the UN General Secretary informed Verwoerd that 'independent' homelands would only be recognized if certain conditions were met. They included sufficient and coherent territory, resettlement in the homelands only on a voluntary basis, the rapid economic and industrial development of the homelands and the consistent respect of human rights (Urquhart, cited in Giliomee and Schlemmer, 1989: 101). In fact, their 'independence' remained unrecognized in virtually all but South African government circles.

The patent falsity of the 'separate but equal' rhetoric lying behind the development of homeland administrations encouraged Marxian authors to explain the homeland policy in terms of its 'functionality' to South African capital. Halbach (1988) sees the 'autonomous' homelands' significance as being progressively reduced to that of a surplus labour reservoir and dumping ground – something which had always been their implicit role. However, Lemon (1987) questions this labour pool function, arguing that a shift in labour demand, from unskilled towards skilled labour, has accompanied the evolution from competitive to monopoly capitalism. This meant that labour reproduction of the type required by the more influential employers was no longer carried out largely in the homelands, but in the urban areas (Keenan, 1984, cited in Lemon, 1987).

If not particularly functional in an economic sense, the development of 'independent' homeland structures certainly had advantages in a political sense. Overall, the policy was geared towards guaranteeing the white minority's political supremacy in the bulk of South Africa – that is, towards the preservation, in spite of economic modernization, of white space. 'Independence' enabled black citizens, who would otherwise have continued to agitate for political rights within South Africa, to be conceptually, administratively and geographically transformed into 'foreign' guest workers from neighbouring states, with no claim to political expression in white South Africa. The Bantu

Homelands Citizenship Act of 1970 ensured the legality of the transformation. With these workers now the responsibility of separate homeland governments, the South African government would no longer shoulder political responsibility for their poverty, nor for their periodic unemployment. It would also cease to be the direct provider of their welfare costs, although the economic dependence of most homeland governments on the South African government meant that it was still effectively an indirect provider.

A further, more subtle, political gain could be secured by dividing the homelands according to ethnic group – the reinforcement of latent regional identities and tribalism (Halbach, 1988) – to hinder a more unified African opposition. However, it must be remembered that the ethnic divisions, which the homeland administrations have sometimes exacerbated, have an existence independent of those structures and they do not always remain latent. 'Africans really are divided by local competitions; it is not all done by mirrors ... nationalism can result in brutal chauvinism against residents of the "wrong tribe"' (Lonsdale, 1988b). Soni (1992) believes that, in addition to further ethnically dividing resistance, the homeland structures serve spatially to divide the working class, hindering mass organization. However, while this may have been a welcome spin-off for the government, it seems un-likely to have been a key consideration in the formulation of the original policy.

In various ways, then, the development of extra political structures in the homelands was intended, or incidentally proved, to be politically functional. But the homeland governments were more than the politically expedient puppets of Pretoria. The fact that they provided an outlet for power, even if localized and constrained by Pretoria, fuelled their development and their entrenchment as independently existing entities. From the early 1970s, a prominent middle class of politicians, civil servants, teachers and businessmen began to emerge in the homelands. While having a stake in the order comparable with that of the chiefs of the Bantu Authorities Act, they showed an ability to be more critical than their predecessors (Giliomee and Schlemmer, 1989).

The development in the homelands of 'a fully differentiated state bureaucratic-military machinery, budgetary resources upwards of R1 billion to back it up and concerns and anxieties ranging from foreign affairs to winning elections' means that, in order to assess accurately the significance of Separate Development's homelands for South African political and social structures, 'a theory of the state is required' (Graaff, 1990: 61). Graaff goes on to define bantustans as states attempting to exert power over territory, a power less than that of nation states like, for example, Zimbabwe. The territory theoretically under their control may actually be more influenced by Pretoria than, for instance, Bophuthatswana's capital, Mmbatho, whose Winterveld District is economically integrated with the Pretoria–Witwatersrand– Vereeniging (PWV) region.

Pretoria's control generally tended to be tightest over homeland defence, security and mass-media policy, and loosest in the fields of education, agriculture and urban development. Despite Pretoria's influence, for the 'independent' homelands (Transkei, Ciskei, Bophuthatswana and Venda), a position 'on a tightrope between Pretoria and their voters periodically [called] for public stances which are hostile to Pretoria' (Graaff, 1990: 56). This became increasingly the case as the contradictions of apartheid mounted in the 1980s.

With a homeland's 'independence', the conduit for Pretoria's influence shifted from the verkrampte (conservative) Department of Rural Affairs, to the verligte (enlightened) Department of Foreign Affairs and its Development Bank of Southern Africa (DBSA). This amounted to a move from the influence of the right wing of the NP to that of the left wing and, in the late 1970s and early 1980s, it brought much greater access to private-sector funds for the independent homeland governments. But the crucial drawback to autonomy, even for the independent homelands, proved to be their continuing economic dependence on 'white South Africa', primarily a result of overpopulation of the restricted areas provided and of a lack of internal agricultural and industrial capital. The fact that homeland 'commuters' were able to cross supposedly national borders into white space to work, and that metropolitan districts of white space therefore continued to be functionally linked to areas politically outside of that space, persistently undermined the cultivated image of homeland independence (see Chapter 6).

The overcrowding of reserve land was evident even in the 1920s. Far from being eased over time, with the political development of the homelands, overcrowding was exacerbated by the removal of Africans from 'white South Africa'. In 1960, the reserve population was 4.5 million. By 1980, it had increased to 11 million (Wilson and Ramphele, 1989). Apart from natural increase, between these two dates, the homelands had to accommodate one million Africans removed from white farms, 600,000 from 'black spots' (African-owned land in 'white South Africa') and 750,000 from the cities. From 1918 to 1950, the population density of the reserves had varied between fifty and sixty people per square mile. By 1970 the figure was 125 per square mile.

However, the backward state of homeland agriculture was not primarily to do with overcrowding. In fact, much of the homelands'

territory was under- or unutilized – in Nkandla, Kwazulu 50 per cent
of the area was unused, constituting 16.3 per cent of the possible
arable total according to Wilson and Ramphele (1989) and one-third
of this potential according to Halbach (1988). The main causes of this
neglect were the absence of adequate labour, with males seeking work
in the cities, and the lack of capital (seeds, oxen, implements) to work
the available land. The former difficulty is illustrated, again by
Nkandla. Here, in 1989, 81 per cent of the twenty- to fifty-year-old
population were women and a quarter of the household heads were
pensioners (Wilson and Ramphele, 1989). In the Transkei, the sources
of cash for rural households earning under R125 per month were
found to be 68 per cent remittances from urban workers, 16 per cent
from pensions, 13 per cent from local jobs and only 3 per cent from
home production. The most significant contribution to Nkandla's cash
economy was from the pensions of the over-65s (Wilson and Ramphele,
1989).

To the problem of inadequate labour, Halbach (1988) adds the
shortage of agricultural credit, deriving from a lack of lending
institutions and the absence of assets to secure loans. Where capital
was available, there were often inadequate advisory extension services
and a dearth of information. Apart from these structural constraints,
localized overgrazing, property fragmentation originating in traditional
land laws, and opposition to modern farming methods made local
contributions to the generally dire state of homeland agriculture –
although the late nineteenth-century response of African peasant
producers like those of Herschel indicates that, in many areas, the
limitations of 'tradition' could have been readily overcome if it were
not for the colonial government's direct and indirect suppression of
African commercial production (Bundy, 1972; Marks and Atmore,
1980b). Despite their predominantly rural nature and the fact that
they lay mostly in adequate rainfall zones, the homelands taken together
produced only one-third of their own food requirements (Halbach,
1988). (The shortages have recently been exacerbated by the severe
drought which, over the last few years, has plagued southern Africa.)

There was no compensatory level of homeland industrial development. The context for a lack of agricultural development was a
shortage of labour and capital; for the lack of industrial growth, it has
been the deficiency of urban infrastructure. In 1960, there were only
three homeland towns, containing a combined population of 33,486.
Smit et al. (1982) cite two reasons for this: the lack of a widespread
African urban tradition and the inhibition placed on homeland urban
development by the draining of labour to cities in South Africa proper.
Once the South African government had embarked on a programme

of the decentralization of industry, partly in order to stem further urbanization in 'white South Africa', it was more willing to subsidize urban development in the homelands. Sixty-six per cent of the budget for homeland physical development was awarded to urban infrastructure from 1961 to 1966. With a target of 80,000 houses, 38,500 were built and, from 1961 to 1978, over R520 million was spent by the South African Development Trust, homeland governments and development corporations on the establishment of homeland towns. In 1986, there were eighty-eight such towns, but the increase since 1960 was not primarily because of the increasing attractiveness of urban homeland life. Rather, it was the consequence of the removal of 68,144 Africans from white areas to homeland towns between 1960 and 1970, and the freeze on African house-building in white cities, implemented from 1968 and further contributing to the already extensive backlog. The limited decentralization of industry that the South African government succeeded in promoting, also encouraged homeland urban growth.

The number of Africans employed in manufacturing and commerce in 'white South Africa' had increased by 50 per cent from 1951 to 1960, fuelling an urban African population expansion from 2.4 million to 3.5 million (Giliomee and Schlemmer, 1989). The planned decentralization of this industrial magnet to the borders of the homelands would, it was thought, allow employers to continue to meet their labour requirements, while preventing the further growth of a politicized urban African population in white space. The 1967 Environment Planning Act introduced the first statutory controls to accelerate decentralization. New industrial developments or extensions envisaged in South Africa's urban areas now had to receive central permission, and firms in the proscribed areas found their African workforce limited in size (Natal was excluded from this provision), until employers' protests brought about a fixed ratio of African:white employees instead. Disincentives to expand in the cities were complemented by incentives to move to the homeland and border regions. They included grants and loans, plus the indirect advantages of lower wages and poor worker safeguards (less holiday and sick leave and a longer working week) in the homelands. From 1970, minimum-wage legislation was scrapped altogether inside the homelands (Rogerson, 1982). However, neither the incentives nor the disincentives addressed the fundamental locational disadvantages of a 'border' area deprived of infrastructure (Lemon, 1987). From 1960 to 1972, a total of only 85,544 jobs emerged from the government's scheme in the homeland and border areas (Giliomee and Schlemmer, 1989).

Without an independent economic base, the homeland governments remained, to various extents, dependent on Pretoria, Bophuthatswana coming closest to self-sufficiency with its own platinum mines. The dependence was manifested through a reliance on both Pretoria's aid budget – constituting 70–80 per cent of Kwazulu's income and from 50–70 per cent of Transkei's and Bophuthatswana's in the early 1960s (Giliomee and Schlemmer, 1989) – and on the earnings of migrants employed in white South Africa. Even with the remittances of these workers taken into account, 50–85 per cent of the homelands' purchasing power leaked back into white South Africa, where the major services and centres of employment were concentrated (Halbach, 1988). When assessing the degree of homeland autonomy, Lelyveld (1987) noted that the homeland of Lebowa's GDP was exceeded by the subsidy that the South African government provided to bus its workers across the border.

2 The pressures on apartheid, 1960–76

Economic contradictions

Clearly, the homelands failed as separate economic entities. It was probably never the South African government's intention that they should succeed as such. It did intend, however, to create in the homelands an outlet for African employment and urbanization outside white South Africa. Although the methods by which it would be achieved were the subject of dispute, since 1948 the government had always perceived limitations on further African urbanization as being one of the central goals of apartheid.

Apart from the incentives for industrial decentralization and the assistance with homeland industrial development, during the 1960s the government employed other, more insidious measures to prevent further African urbanization outside the homelands. The administration of the urban townships was transferred from the white local authorities to the Department of Bantu Administration and Development. This centralization of control enabled tighter supervision and the implementation of further restraints on African movement, labour, housing, education and social welfare in South Africa's urban areas. 'No dictator in history has exercised more power over human beings than the South African Minister of Bantu Administration' (Douglas Brown, cited in Giliomee and Schlemmer, 1989: 69).

In order to combat the increasing numbers of Africans becoming legally resident in the cities by working for the same employer continuously for ten years, from 1968 migrants were compelled to return to their homelands at least once a year, so that the continuity of their employment would be broken. Such 'Catch 22' urban residence rights were to continue to be a feature of the adaptations of urban apartheid legislation. Through the late 1960s and the 1970s, the Labour Bureaux joined the struggle to hold back further African urbanization by dictating legal job choices and destinations to those seeking work from the homelands.

By the 1980s, though, the situation in the homelands had become sufficiently desperate for hundreds of thousands to by-pass the bureaux and illegally squat or rent in the cities. Strategies to evade the system of influx control included a flourishing trade in forged passbooks and time-consuming applications for new passbooks once the 'lost' original had already been stamped as 'endorsed out'. Although, in this instance, the 'offender' would ultimately be caught out, due to the cumbersome nature of the urban African administration a reprieve of months could be gained (Posel, 1991).

The Western Cape's Coloured Labour Preference Policy was a regionally specific attempt to stem further African urbanization. Between 1957 and 1962, 30,000 Africans were endorsed out of Cape Town, but economic growth and the demand for labour continually attracted Africans willing to defy influx control. In particular, the boom of 1968–74 brought increasing numbers of contract workers, while the government froze township house construction and battled to bring the rate of evictions up to the rate of influx. The Crossroads informal settlement emerged spontaneously, as 'illegals' clustered their makeshift shelters together, and it continued to grow. After innumerable evictions, clearances and illegal rebuildings, the settlement finally won official acknowledgement in 1976, but state and vigilante harassment continued into the 1980s (see Chapter 7). By the late 1970s, the application of the Coloured Labour Preference Policy had crumbled under the weight of popular flouting by employers and workers. Nevertheless, the combined effect of the state's disparate influx-control measures through the 1960s and 1970s has been estimated as the prevention of a further urban growth of 1.5 to 3 million Africans (Giliomee and Schlemmer, 1989). The growth rate of the black urban population slowed from 6.4 per cent from 1946–50, to 3.9 per cent in the 1960s (Cilliers and Groenwald, 1982, cited in Terreblanche and Nattrass, 1990).

While this slowdown partially fulfilled one of the government's key political aims, it had more negative long-term economic implications. Despite influx control, by the end of the 1960s there was still an urban oversupply of illegal unskilled labour, but there was simultaneously a shortage of skilled African labour which was required in increasingly mechanized production processes (see below). Giliomee and Schlemmer (1989) believe that mechanization itself was a response to the restrictions on the influx of labour, but it probably had more to do with the structural imperatives of South Africa's integration with the world economy and the inflow of capital following the reversal of Sharpeville. In any case, its result was to create, on the one hand, an enduring legacy of high unemployment among unskilled Africans and, on the other hand, an increasingly serious shortage of skilled urban workers. Through the 1960s, the more skilled employment of some blacks in the cities prompted a general increase in black wages, co-existing with rising urban black unemployment.

From the seventeenth century to the early twentieth century, the ideological motivation behind spatial segregation and black political exclusion in South Africa was broadly compatible with white economic activity. Agriculture was served by the retention of a large, unskilled, black workforce and assisted by that workforce's exclusion from the white towns. In those towns, mining and early industrial enterprises could meet most of their labour requirements with the skilled, urban white population and a semi- or unskilled, black migrant labour work-force supplemented by those workers permanently present in the urban townships. However, the modernization of the economy – its increasing reliance on commerce and the updated methods of manufacturing in particular – nurtured a fundamental contradiction between apartheid's modified form of segregation and South Africa's late twentieth-century economic performance. The contradiction had started to emerge in most sectors by the end of the 1960s; by the end of the 1970s, it was becoming apparent to a wider cross-section of South African society.

In the late 1960s, the gold-mining houses, in spite of white-worker protection and the job colour bar, could still maintain profitability through the use of cheap African labour from South Africa and neigh-bouring states. But coal and copper mines, in fiercer competition with overseas suppliers, were already taking on an increasingly mechanized form. Their requirement for a more skilled African workforce rose correspondingly. While it took slightly longer for the gold mines to share their concern for a more skilled black workforce, when they did so, they brought far more muscle to the campaign.

In the gold-mining sector, once the gold price had started to rise dramatically, from $35 to $800 in the early 1970s (Giliomee and Schlem-mer, 1989: 76), the owners were able to escape their white workers' stranglehold. The mining houses' new profitability encouraged a commitment to modernization that would no longer tolerate skilled labour shortages for the sake of racial privilege. They were assisted in their determination by the convenient fact that white miners had also become relatively less politically important: in the early 1970s, the miners' political affiliation partially shifted away from the NP, to the new and relatively powerless, conservative Afrikaans Herstigte Nasionale Party

(HNP) (Adam and Moodley, 1986). By the end of the 1970s, the gold mines had, by and large, 'finally succeeded after a century in thwarting the job colour bar on the mines' (Giliomee and Schlemmer, 1989: 76), and some important mining concerns, notably Anglo-American, were stressing the cost advantages of a smaller, stable African family labour force to work increasingly sophisticated technology, rather than traditional unskilled migrants (Freund, 1991).

In the farming sector there was a longer tradition of racial labour domination and support for the NP to be overcome. Through the 1950s and early 1960s, large-scale state support for agriculture continued, and the farming sector remained a key supporter of racial policy. By 1970, state aid constituted one-fifth of the average white farmer's income (Nattrass, 1981, cited in Giliomee and Schlemmer, 1989). As long as production remained based on the use of relatively large quantities of unskilled African labour, the government could expect white farmer support for the key apartheid policy of influx control, and for the suppression of skilled and highly paid black employment. Yet, by the end of the 1960s, the very support provided by the state, by helping to remove African tenants from the white farms, had facilitated a transformation of white farming, to a capitalistic sector employing fewer and more skilled wage labourers (Marcus, 1989). The needs of large farmers were converging with those of manufacturers as mechanization reduced the importance of securing a large quantity of cheap labour, and therefore rendered influx control partially redundant. Instead, they required skills of their remaining black workers, which apartheid was not suited to provide. Cheap, untrained labour, they found, could ultimately be very expensive when dealing with delicate and costly equipment (Davenport, 1991). In the 1970s, the South African Agricultural Union began to press for higher wages, improved working conditions, better training and increased mobility for black agricultural workers. However, the less efficient, more marginal white farmers, who still furnished the numerical bulk of the sector, tended to remain implacably opposed to these innovations.

While apartheid's labour restrictions were gradually becoming outmoded for the mining and much of the farming sector, they were proving to be much greater obstacles to manufacturing growth, and that growth assumed increasing significance as the manufacturing sector overtook the primary sector's contribution to the national economy in 1965 (Davenport, 1991). The tensions between manufacturing interests and racial economic restrictions had been manifest as early as the 1940s, but Malan, Strijdom and, to a greater extent, Verwoerd, in turn, had determined to reinforce racial separation, even at the cost of manufacturing growth. The shortage of skilled labour became increasingly evident in manufacturing in the early 1960s, when there was virtually full white employment, and whites were moving into the tertiary sector. Among those remaining in the secondary sector, it was remarked that the absence of skilled competition from cheaper blacks was leading to slackness, absenteeism and high staff turnovers (Giliomee and Schlemmer, 1989).

By the end of the 1960s, despite apartheid's regulations, more skilled work was being given to blacks in the cities, especially Coloureds and Indians. In 1970 the government legislated that the employment of an African in any position might be prohibited, but, by this time, informal flouting of the colour bar was well established (although many employers maintained, by agreement with white trade unions, a 'floating colour bar', by which the racial pay differential would be maintained. In the gold mines, the benefits of increasing black productivity were passed on in the form of wage increases for the white workers.) Manufacturing industry had found before the mines, though, that with the modernization of techniques, 'low wages are not the *sine qua non* of profitability' (Price, 1991: 33).

While apartheid's limitations on the production side were becoming apparent, its restraints on consumption were also causing more concern. Even in the 1940s, it was remarked by some observers (for example, Blackwell and May, 1947) that, by holding down black incomes, South Africa's racial system was denying a large potential market to its industrial producers. While white domestic markets were still expanding and South Africa still had unimpeded access to external markets, the costs of the racial market restriction could be borne. But, by the late 1960s, wealthier farmers, gearing up for capital-intensive production for the home market, had come to share the concern expressed by manufacturers over the preceding two decades: apartheid was helping to restrict black consumption and therefore hindering profitability.

For the manufacturers themselves, the white market for many consumer items was by now becoming saturated, with further sales mainly on a replacement basis. For example, by the end of the 1970s the domestic car industry, in response to government encouragement for import substitution, had developed a production capacity of 400,000 cars *per annum*. But white sales were now only 200,000 cars *per annum* and the numerically dominant black population was still generally too poor to provide a significant market for new cars (Price, 1991: 33).

Even some of those producers who were not reliant on domestic markets had cause for concern by the late 1970s, as exporters found their links with external markets being severed by trading partners made hostile by apartheid. Industrialists came particularly to regret the Organization of African Unity's (OAU) boycott of South African goods, with its denial of access to the natural African market to their north. As the 1970s progressed, manufacturers came to perceive further contradictions between apartheid and other, more subtle requirements for economic growth: internal political stability, external credit-worthiness and investor confidence (Giliomee and Schlemmer, 1989).

This account of apartheid's emerging impediments to economic growth contradicts a commonly held opinion about South Africa's economic performance and its relationship with apartheid. Marxist scholars have traditionally emphasized the rapid rates of economic growth that South Africa achieved in the 1960s, and stressed their coincidence with the period of the strictest application of apartheid. The inference that has frequently been drawn from these observations is that apartheid must have been conducive to, rather than restrictive of, economic growth. Indeed, the 1960s decade has often been used as the Marxists' most effective weapon in combating liberal assertions of apartheid's economic contradictions. The fact that the economy was flourishing just when black labour was most repressed by apartheid suggests that it was apartheid's function of cheap labour repression that facilitated economic growth. Thus, the Marxist view of the symbiotic relationship between capitalism and apartheid is confirmed.

However, the mechanism by which the economy was seen to prosper from apartheid in the 1960s – the maintenance of cheap black labour – is illusory. As more skilled employment and trade union gains (see below) became available through the 1960s, black product wages were actually rising, rather than being held at extremely low levels. In the meantime, apartheid allowed white wages to maintain their advantage over black, despite the absence of a compensatory advance in white productivity. Thus the 1960s saw gradually declining profit rates and rising black wages (Nattrass, 1990) – the reverse of what radical Marxians had believed.

Moll (1990) has gone furthest in challenging the received wisdom of a 1960s 'apartheid boom'. Growth over the period, although impressive, was in fact slower than that in many middle-income developing countries (5–6 per cent, compared to a 7.6 per cent average for Brazil, Mexico, South Korea and Taiwan), and poor when South Africa's resource endowments and advantageous connections are borne in mind. After Sharpeville, South Africa had a relatively stable political system, a competent administration, a suppressed working class, a skilled white population, good infrastructure and financial systems, easy access to overseas markets and relatively cheap local labour; yet its share of world manufacturing exports fell from 0.8 to 0.3 per cent from 1955 to

1985 (trade sanctions being a limitation only from the late 1970s). This relative failure was 'partly because the apartheid superstructure impeded economic development and partly because of the constraining effects of a range of short-sighted and ill-directed state economic policies' (Moll, 1990: 271).

Instead of encouraging exports, economic policy was directed at import substitution, which proved to contribute to a balance of payments deficit. Although local suppliers were able to displace imported consumer goods, the restricted size of the domestic market denied them the economies of scale needed to produce their own capital goods. As they expanded local production, then, they also swelled the imports of expensive capital machinery, nullifying the exercise of import substitution. Moll suggests two reasons for the reticence in pursuing export growth: the Afrikaner nationalist desire for autonomy from external links (especially to Britain) and the urge to limit the black urbanization and proletarianization that a flourishing export sector would encourage. Even during the 1960s 'golden age' of South African capital, then, apartheid's limitations combined with those of government economic policy to hamper 'efficient resource allocation' and prevent 'firms from making full use of black workers' (Moll, 1990: 290). Bunting, writing in 1967, believed that the government itself was aware of its limitations: 'if there is one sphere in which the Nats (NP) have not yet been able to triumph as they would wish it is that of the South African economy' (Bunting, 1969: 369).

The NP had minimal representation in manufacturing concerns in the late 1960s (Bunting, 1969). From an early lack of political affinity, by the mid-1970s more concrete opposition to the government's economic interference had emerged. Adam and Moodley (1986) trace the growth of an industrial 'reform lobby' to concerns over the skill shortages, the restricted domestic market, the blocking of international market expansion and capital inflows and the undermining of confidence caused by South Africa's negative image overseas. Industrial concern was deepened by the failure of the government's attempts to accommodate manufacturing interests through decentralization.

Even in the mid-1960s, Anglo American's Harry Oppenheimer was a prominent supporter of the opposition Progressive Party (PP). He was joined by a wider group of industrialists in the 1970s. Hackland believes that Oppenheimer simultaneously gave support to both the NP and the PP as a form of insurance in case the NP failed to protect capitalist growth (Hackland, 1980, cited in Lemon, 1987: 94). Nevertheless, Oppenheimer was vocal in his belief that 'rapid economic development of South Africa would in the long run prove incompatible with the government's racial policies' (Lemon, 1987: 94).

Bantu Education, purposefully stifling the accumulation of black skills, was a prime candidate for reform in the interests of the economy. In 1953, only 1,064 Africans graduated from university. The Bantu Education Act had since accomplished a deterioration, by killing the spirit of those mission schools that did offer quality education and by ensuring that the number of technical colleges for blacks fell from fifty-four in 1953 to twenty-one in 1954 (Giliomee and Schlemmer, 1989). In the 1970s, as large companies diversified into manufacturing and commerce, the concentration of ownership increased. As a result, there was a more co-ordinated call from industry for a more skilled mass workforce. With 45 per cent of a sample of large manufacturers stating that they had difficulties acquiring adequate skilled labour in 1977, and 80 per cent by 1980, the government had little choice but to commit more of its resources to black education. In 1960, 54,598 Africans were at school and 1,871 at university. By 1980 the respective figures were 1,192,932 and 49,164 (Giliomee and Schlemmer, 1989: 117–18).

This is not to say that, merely by being opposed to some aspects of apartheid, capital would bring about its downfall (along the lines of the Anglo American executive O'Dowd's thesis that economic growth would in itself be an irrepressible force for greater racial integration). Capital is an adaptive creature: when conditions are imperfect, profits can still be made, and 'the notion that the interests of maturing capitalism would dictate the shape of South African government policy is a rather crude form of economic determinism' (Price, 1991: 35). Within 'capital', the interests of the farming, mining, manufacturing and commercial sectors were internally and externally differentiated. Similarly, for capitalists, apartheid represented more than just labour repression and control. The individuals comprising the capitalist class in South Africa may have been inclined, for instance, to oppose job reservation and the denial of skills to black workers, while supporting apartheid's social precepts and African spatial segregation and political exclusion.

Nevertheless, the general trend in employers' thinking in the 1970s was marked by the Federated Chamber of Industry joining the Associated Chamber of Commerce and some members of the Afrikaans Handelsinstituut to protest the cost and impracticability of Separate Development. 'The previously separate interests of capital were now converging' (Lipton, 1988: 62).

As the liaison of the main English- and Afrikaans-speaking capitalist bodies indicates, crucial changes had also occurred within the body of the Afrikaner volk. The 1930s Afrikaans economic movement had presaged a post-1948 strategy of state intervention to 'uplift' the volk, especially through the utilization and protection of its manufacturing, commercial and farming capital. Apartheid's nurturing of these capital concerns to the point, in the 1970s, where they were established and flourishing, paradoxically brought their desire to remove the restraints on future growth that the apartheid system now represented. Politically influential Afrikaans capitalists had, by the 1970s, come to share economic concerns and interests with their established English counterparts, as they found themselves drawing level with them in terms of size and diversification. Afrikaans and English capitalists were, by the late 1970s, beginning to merge into a single, economically dominant class. With their accession to economic prominence, Afrikaner capitalists became more committed to a market economy and less dependent on the political patronage and rigid racial and labour stratification of apartheid (Thompson, 1985).

The NP had already lost the support of many small Afrikaans farmers, forced off the land by its backing of modernization and denied increasingly expensive subsidies. To some extent, the shedding of this more conservative Afrikaans constituency to more extreme Afrikaans political parties, released the NP to cater more for the newer Afrikaans commercial and industrial classes. By the late 1970s, then, the restructuring of Afrikaans manufacturing, commercial and agricultural capital had helped clear the road for apartheid's economic reform.

In the 1970s, not only important members of the state's core constituency, but the state itself began to suffer more from the costs of apartheid. In 1970, Johannesburg's state-run bus service was 30 per cent short of drivers and conductors due to the resistance of the white Municipal Transport Workers Union to Coloured crews (Lipton, 1985). Even in 1953, the General Manager of the same bus department had estimated that, if apartheid transport was abandoned, half a million pounds profit could be made *per annum*, instead of running at a loss (Bunting, 1986). Within the central state, the managers of ISCOR, SAR (railways) and the Post Office were calling, in the 1970s, for labour reform, including abolition of the colour bar. From 1974, the South African Defence Force (SADF) had to recruit black soldiers, and the increasing costs of apartheid were becoming manifest in a steadily increasing defence budget. The concerns of a growing group of capitalists were not sufficient in themselves to alter the course of government policy, but when combined with apartheid's more significant economic costs to the state itself and the material threat that the current political system posed to traditional NP constituencies, by the end of the 1970s, enough momentum was generated to initiate serious consideration of a reform of apartheid, in so far as it affected the economy.

Security contradictions

By the mid-1970s, internal contradictions were encouraging a reconsideration of the economic aspects of apartheid. But the government only shifted decisively into a change of mood when a severe escalation of the external and internal security threat was superimposed on political and economic problems within the country.

South Africa's external relations were under threat fundamentally because by the 1970s the country was a 'unique phenomenon: a pigmentocratic industrialised state' (Thompson, 1985: 191). Through most of South Africa's history, its racial system of government had had its counterparts in other European colonies, but with the onset of independence for most of these territories, only South Africa and a neighbouring buffer zone to its north remained of racially discriminatory rule. In the 1970s, even this cushioning belt was to be removed, as Angola, Mozambique and, finally, Zimbabwe attained independence.

South Africa was progressively isolated in world politics, and its economy correspondingly suffered from a severing of external links. However, the loss of South Africa's northern 'cordon sanitaire' meant more than just a new status as a uniquely, explicitly and relatively isolated racist state. It also exposed South Africa's borders to incursions of ANC guerrillas from the sympathetic new black states to the north, and assisted the South-West Africa People's Organization (SWAPO) in its challenge to the SADF occupation of Namibia. In the 1970s and 1980s, Cuban aid to the recently established Marxist government in Angola allowed it to resist a South African invasion in support of Pretoria's favourite candidate for Angolan government.

Within South Africa, the Soweto uprising, often seen as a dramatic and sudden revival of black resistance, had its prelude in the form of the unexpected strikes launched by Durban workers in 1973. Their actions highlighted the economic dimension of black resistance, which also fed into the more ideologically influenced Soweto uprising.

The year 1973 marked the birth of a trade unionism fundamentally different from that repressed in the 1960s. Whereas in the former era of trade union revival, never more than 2,000 workers were involved in strike action in one year, in 1973, 100,000 participated, and since that year, the figure has never fallen below 14,000 (Mitchell and Russell, 1989a: 232). The difference was primarily to do with a change in union structure from formal, and easily repressed, leadership representation to a 'vibrant system of factory committees that provide for the democratic involvement of the rank and file membership in day-to-day union affairs at the place of work' (Mitchell and Russell, 1989a: 233).

The resurgence of strike activity and its new organizational structure must be sited in the broad economic context of the early 1970s oil-price shocks. African unemployment was increasing as both the government and the private sector retrenched, but the primary incentive to strike was provided by inflation. Between 1971 and 1973 the price of essential commodities for black workers rose by 40 per cent (Hemson, 1978, cited in Terreblanche and Nattrass, 1990). It had taken from 1910 to 1959 for the general level of prices in South Africa to treble, but they did so again between 1978 and 1986 (Wilson and Ramphele, 1989: 250). Wage bargaining – the normal recourse of workers – was a luxury denied to many blacks, so they were hard hit by a decline in real income (Khan, cited in Wilson and Ramphele, 1989: 250). The poor were particularly affected by the rising price of paraffin – in the Transkei over 10 per cent of income was already spent on fuel. Between 1973 and 1980 the nationwide level of real wages fell by 16 per cent (Wilson and Ramphele, 1989: 250).

While falling real wages were of general concern, in Durban the economic burden of the worker was further loaded. Economic consciousness and resentment had recently been nurtured in the region by local press coverage of the extent of the black population which fell below the poverty datum line, and a 16 per cent increase in bus fares between townships and the city was in the offing, generating talk of a boycott. As elsewhere and at other times, a mixture of traditional and 'progressive' forms of action was taken. The Zulu paramount chief, to whom many workers in the city still felt they owed their first allegiance, made it clear that he would support workers' action.

The strikes were led by workers from the France Textile Group, notorious for its low wages and poor labour relations (Lodge, 1983). Once the first strike had resulted in a wage rise, striking spread to other sectors and other parts of the region. The strikes tended to be apparently leaderless and of short duration. The absence of a negotiating body among the workers protected them from victimization or co-option by the management or the state (Lodge, 1983). In the context of the shortage of skilled and semi-skilled workers – the category to which many of the strikers belonged – real economic gains were often forthcoming and general moves towards a non-racial 'rate for the job' and the erosion of the 'civilized labour' policy followed from the outbreak of industrial action (Terreblanche and Nattrass, 1990).

For the unions, the success of the strikes encouraged the wider adoption of a workerist, 'grassroots' form of agitation (Lodge, 1983), which irreversibly shifted the balance of power in Africans' favour. No longer was the most significant African power base largely restricted to the relatively small middle-class group of teachers, ministers, clerks and their followers (Adam, 1987); it was now centred at the core of South Africa's economy. In the long run, the shift contributed to the phasing out of job reservation and to the increasing power of black political movements with trade union associates. The greater influence of even unregistered black trade unions would force negotiations from employers and precipitate a repressive state response. In the late 1970s and early 1980s, police detentions reflected the trend of the increasing trade union threat: there was a rising number of arrests and beatings of trade union leaders, culminating in 1982 in the death in detention of the white trade unionist, Dr Neil Aggett (Davenport, 1991).

While the general trend after 1973 was towards increased wages, the stabilization of labour and recognition of trade union viability, the behaviour of workers and employers remained greatly differentiated. Even within the mining sector, employers' attitudes varied significantly, with the Afrikaans Gencor and Goldfields resisting wage and trade union recognition advances, and the Anglo American Corporation adopting a 'progressive' line. Throughout the sector, the migrant labour system remained intact (Lipton, 1988). The workers' position was similarly incohesive. Seemingly progressive strike action continued to be accompanied by traditional ethnic ritual and factional politics, which often flared into inter-ethnic violence within the workplace. The adoption of new forms of struggle against economic oppression had not excluded older traits of enmity among the workers (see Malan, 1990: 245–63 for one example from a 1985 mine strike).

If the industrial scenario with which the state had to deal in the 1970s was confused, it is not surprising that its own response was ambiguous. The increasingly evident economic contradictions facing the state inhibited it from unmitigated repression of the organized African workforce, while the conservatism of its own white political constituency imposed limits on the extent to which it could reform racial economic relations. 'This strategic indecisiveness on the part of the state' was 'one of the most significant factors which ... distinguished the development of black resistance movements in the 1970s from those of the preceding two decades' (Lodge, 1983: 326).

But the context of rejuvenated black opposition in the 1970s also included the increasingly rapid rate of African urbanization. The material deprivation of the new, urban-born African generation was in all too apparent contrast to white urban affluence. Through the 1960s and 1970s, economic forces encouraging agglomeration of the factors of production in the cities had gained ascendancy over the ideological and political forces attempting to restrain African urbanization (Smit et al., 1982). The most evident manifestation of this urban growth was the proliferation of informal African settlements on the urban fringe –

another development which, particularly around Pretoria, blurred the political distinction between white space and neighbouring homelands. A survey of such a settlement, Vlakfontein on the Witwatersrand, indicated that most rural immigrants had moved to the urban area in the 1970s as a result of agricultural restructuring and rural tenant eviction, flouting the influx-control regulations. But of greatest significance is the fact that a sizeable proportion of the inhabitants of these shacks had been born, and lived all their lives, in the urban area. This population's membership of a poorly paid, unskilled working class and the shortage of formal township housing had conspired to restrict it to informal accommodation, and nearly a quarter of the population were employed only casually or in the informal sector (Crankshaw and Hart, 1990). The government estimated in 1981 that in Cape Town 42.8 per cent of blacks were 'illegals' (Dewar and Watson, 1982).

For the young African generation born in the urban areas, these material conditions, in the face of white urban privilege, were increasingly resented. Exhilarated by the defeat of white regimes in Mozambique and Angola, this generation entered the mid-1970s with a receptive attitude to any ideology or organization that offered a renewal of mass opposition to apartheid after the post-Sharpeville years of quietude. 'The generational shift was marked by a change in the demeanour of Africans towards whites: a change from deference to defiance' (Thompson, 1985: 192).

The urban African population, however, did not cohesively shift to a new pattern of radical political action. Traditional forms of consciousness, carried to the cities by rural migrants, were handed down to succeeding urban generations too. Older ideals coexisted with the new in the townships, in much the same way as they did in the workplace. For instance, inyangas and sangomas (traditional healers and diviners) retained a powerful influence in the urban settlements and traditional herbal medicine was transplanted to the townships, though it became wrapped in a Western, commercialized form as it competed with Western medicine for urban patients (Malan, 1990; Dauskaardt, 1990).

The Black Consciousness (BC) movement contained this blend of traditional and modern forms of expression. As a political ideology, mobilizing and regenerating unprecedentedly vehement opposition to the state, it was novel, but its self-image rested upon a more traditional appraisal of African history and identity. In the cities of the 1970s, the roots of budding political resistance partially lay in a distant, older, rural African culture.

The Black Consciousness movement's influence was greatest on the young, emergent black middle class. The growth, during the 1950s and 1960s, of an African white-collar class, cultivated on increased African education provision, facilitated a more politically conscious urban population. The BC philosophy originated among students dissatisfied with the white liberal National Union of Students (NUSAS) monopoly of anti-apartheid student protest. The South African Students Organization (SASO) was formed as an assertive black alternative. Within SASO a philosophic and introspective movement developed, its activism being largely restricted to black community projects. The strategic and tactical questions addressed by the Africanists of the preceding two decades were largely neglected (Lodge, 1983). A precondition for future, successful resistance was identified as being the removal of the psychological sense of inferiority to which black people had been reduced, under the influence of three centuries of white domination and liberal white paternalism like that of NUSAS. Indigenous cultural traditions would have to be tapped to allow the bonds of negative self-imagery to be shaken off.

The movement developed as more than just an extension of the 1950s Africanist ideology in two respects. First, its ideologues recognized the reality of class divisions within the African community, and thus the absence of racial solidarity. Secondly, it opened its structures and its sense of affinity to Coloureds and Indians as well as Africans. Its more inclusive approach was based upon an appreciation of common treatment under the white power structures. 'More acutely than their predecessors, Biko and his colleagues understood the complexity of feelings engendered through subservience' (Lodge, 1983: 325).

By rejecting the hegemony that white, Western ideology had assumed over blacks as they were incorporated in the white urban economy, the movement 'enabled the masses of the people to detach themselves from their unthinking respect for white culture' (Magubane, 1989: 11). This was reflected in the development by black writers of a new style of literary expression. The early 1970s saw a revival of traditional African oral poetry. Township gatherings heard poems like Oswald Mtshali's *Sounds of a Cowhide Drum* read aloud. This poem, in particular, reawakened a sense of a distant African cultural tradition, with Mtshali embracing 'rural consciousness into his picture of dispossession' (Gunner, 1988: 228). However, traditional African poetry was extended to include direct, warlike invective against the modern South African state.

Even within the structures of the Western prose form, a new group of black writers manipulated and subverted hegemonic interpretations. Miriam Tlali, Ahmed Essop, Sipho Sepamala, Mbulelo Mzamane and Mongane Serote were all overtly urban-centred and BC-oriented. They wrote explicitly in order to 'conscientize' their black readers. All their novels of the period refer to a complex of injustices perpetrated by the cohesive system of white repression: Bantu Education, the pass laws, the homelands, the urban housing backlog and urban deprivation, the violent and socially disintegrative behaviour inherent in township life and the overwhelming saturation of hopelessness. All saw the white response to black assertion as being a blend of fear, brutality and vacillation, and all incited the youth to demonstrate to their passive elders how the 'white man's machine' of technological capitalism could be overthrown (Sole, 1991).

Despite BC's appeal to the township youth, it never induced a mass-based organization to implement the resistance it encouraged. Its effect was more to galvanize the imagination and the belief that resistance could be fruitful after the lull of the 1960s. Its set of catchphrases, for instance, filtered down to a wider following (Grundy, 1991), while an appreciation of the ideology itself was restricted to a more select stratum of the urban African population. The thinking behind BC diffused successfully among schoolteachers, priests and journalists, and its themes were taken up in the press, in township cultural events and in black educational establishments. But, while this allowed the wider diffusion of its slogans and of its motivational power, it did not necessarily engender a widespread understanding of the ideological principles upon which they rested. The influence of BC on the Soweto revolt was mediated and diffused through a filter of popular interpretation, modification and simplification.

The student originators of the movement were never able to enrol fully the wider community in their own attempts to defy the system, neither conceptually nor practically. The students of Soweto did not take on the wider grievances of rents, unemployment, inflation and working conditions as much as they were portrayed as doing by BC-oriented writers. Even these writers, agitating for concerted and cohesive township action, pictured workers as 'sheeplike, easily frightened, under-politicized and more susceptible to the lure of homeland governments' (Sole, 1991: 195). There was not necessarily a clear articulation between the proponents of BC theory and the mass of participants in township revolt.

Black Consciousness ideals were partially extended into the 1980s with the Azanian People's Organization (AZAPO), which allowed for more of a 'workerist' perspective, but in the 1970s, the BC movement's adherents often conveyed the impression that, if only the masses would follow the lead of the intellectuals and students, drastic change would ensue. In fact, many of the schoolchildren who initiated the Soweto revolt were probably not acting directly under the influence of BC's ideological imperatives, but according to an initiative conditioned partly by the more tangible influence of BC slogans, but largely by the specific conditions in which they found themselves in their schools and homes in 1976.

Soweto's situation in 1976 was determined partly by economic and political forces affecting the whole of South Africa in the mid-1970s, and partly by the specific conditions of life in South Africa's largest, sprawling township. South Africa's deteriorating economic performance was felt by township residents in an immediate and harsh way. The recessions of 1976 and 1982 were both accompanied by a resurgence of township activism (Brewer, 1989b). The widening gulf between black economic expectations and reality was generating an increasingly aggrieved sense of material deprivation in all of South Africa's townships, and in Soweto food and transport price rises were felt particularly harshly (Price, 1991).

Wider administrative changes also had a particular impact in Soweto. By 1971 the government had decided to ensure that municipal authorities, subject to the demands of local employers, would no longer vacillate in imposing influx control and encouraging decentralization. Township administration was taken out of municipal control and handed over to Regional Administration Boards. Soweto's West Rand Administration Board (WRAB) received R2 million less in subsidy than was currently required to make the township self-financing. In response, the WRAB increased rents and cut spending on housing. It also recouped some of the revenue by charging lodgers' fees to those aged over eighteen years living with their parents in municipal houses (Lodge, 1983). Yet, the WRAB managed to build only 2,734 new municipal houses between 1973 and 1978 (Urban Foundation, 1988, cited in Lea, 1982: 200). The informal housing initiative taken by Africans themselves was being met with bulldozers and evictions. By 1976, Soweto had an average of fourteen people per house. When such housing inadequacies were accompanied by a 25 per cent rent increase in the first year of the WRAB's control, and further increases in the next, there were 'ideal conditions for mass rebellion' (Price, 1991: 56).

If macro-economic and administrative changes provided the powder for the Soweto rebellion, educational issues provided the spark. The state's expansion of urban secondary education had provided new terrain for political mobilization in black communities. While the townships themselves were under close supervision in the 1970s, the schools within them became some of the few relatively open arenas for the development of a new, oppositional momentum (Wolpe, 1988). Bantu Education had brought increasing numbers of pupils into already over-crowded schools which lacked adequate facilities and qualified teachers.

Racist History syllabi and an absence of Maths and Science teaching contributed to disenchantment among pupils. The ideology of resistance that BC represented, in popular form, found a fertile recruiting ground (Hyslop, 1991).

While BC provided, in the background, an ideological basis for resistance, its organizational complement was absent over most of the country. In Soweto, the organizational vacuum was filled by the Soweto Student Representatives Council (SSRC). Eleven of its members were subsequently tried for their role in the Soweto revolt. Whereas educational protest in the 1960s had been led by parents and conducted with ANC guidance, in 1976 it was the students themselves, particularly the SSRC, who took the initiative, while parents and the externally based ANC were swept along by events (Wolpe, 1988).

The deeper economic concerns and tension of the community fed into the township's educational establishments, but it was the decision to make Afrikaans a language of instruction in the schools that prodded deep dissatisfaction into open rebellion. Hyslop (1991) sees the Afrikaans language issue as a symbol of the underlying grievances, drawing an analogy with Freud's connection between conscious symbols and their inaccessible root in the unconscious. An attack on Afrikaans school instruction manifested more than a detestation of the oppressor's language and the difficulty of learning through it; it symbolized an assault on the very structures of oppression. Continuing the Freudian analogy, 'as students themselves moved from a symbolic to a conscious understanding of their society, what had been repressed was no longer' (Hyslop, 1991: 111).

What had started as a demonstration of revolt by Soweto students spread through 1976 into a conflagration in many of South Africa's townships. Police brutality in dealing with localized instances of rebellion in Soweto removed the inhibitions restraining sympathizers in other locations, and helped unleash the seething, repressed anger that was fairly universal. In Cape Town, the 1976 uprising contained the first large-scale Coloured rioting in South Africa's history (Western, 1982). Here, Soweto's conditions – poor housing, overcrowding and unemployment – were replicated. Before 1976 many whites had seen Coloureds as being more akin to themselves in their political outlook than to Africans. The rapid spread of rebellion from Soweto to Cape Africans, and thence to Cape Coloureds proved disillusioning. As in Soweto, the targets of youth attack spiralled from specific educational structures to the symbols of apartheid in general: Bantu Administration offices, African beer halls (implicated in the slogan 'Drink Keeps Us Down'), housing offices, civic centres, police stations and the houses of policemen and suspected informers, as well as their persons.

The government's Cillie Commission of Inquiry reported the causes of the 1976 unrest as being the introduction of Afrikaans as a medium of instruction and the lack of competence of police and educational officials both in anticipating the effect of this innovation and in taking countermeasures. Brookes and Brickhill (1980) also focus on the impact of the educational changes. Unsatisfactory schools and the anger provoked by the obligatory use of the economically redundant and ideologically unacceptable Afrikaans language are cited as the major causes of the revolt. Hirson (1979) stresses the role of the precedent set by the 1973 strikes in galvanizing working-class militancy. For him, the BC movement only acted to divert energies created by this class, and dissipate them in a non-workerist struggle. But this is probably to conceive a direct connection where none exists. The strikes were over three years before the Soweto revolt, and Durban had a very different local context (Lodge, 1983). Soweto's large African petty bourgeoisie and an incident in which hostel-dwelling workers attacked the protesting students, militated against a strong link between workerist revival and the township's spirit of resistance.

Kane Berman (1978) goes to another extreme in placing the initiative for the revolt in the hands of BC activists. However, while their ideals were probably familiar in outline to the participants, and provided legitimacy for their actions, it was more the material, or as Price (1991) puts it, the 'situational' conditions in which they found themselves that provided the spur to action in 1976. This situation contained certain critical elements: structural economic hardship, both directly for workers and indirectly for township residents, due to the requirement for self-financing local authorities; an oppressive educational context being made a significant degree more intolerable; and an expectation of political action and change to end the 1960s hiatus in resistance.

The young, urban, black generation of the 1970s contributed by its resistance to the economic and political contradictions which were already pressurizing apartheid, and directly provoked the government's reappraisal of the system. The Soweto uprising was a dramatic departure from previously localized and momentary instances of resistance. It marked the beginning of significant and coherent challenges to state structures (Lodge, 1983). The state's immediate response to the crisis was to leave 575 dead and 2,389 wounded (not exclusively due to police action). The resistance, and the repression with which it was met, further deepened South Africa's sense of economic insecurity and facilitated the re-emergence of the ANC as the primary focus of township political aspiration. The state's repression provided an impetus for hundreds of township youths to leave South Africa for training in the external ANC's armed wing, and it was this hardened core of exiled, rebellious youth which, in the 1980s, would provide the personnel for the ANC's sabotage campaigns.

In the remainder of the 1970s, repression dampened but did not smother unrest in the townships. In the 1980s South Africa became locked in a violent equilibrium between a government that could not possibly be overthrown and a spirit of mass resistance that could be temporarily repressed, but could not be extinguished (Sparks, 1990; and see Chapter 7). The community-based insurrectionist tactics of the 1980s were presaged in the formation in Soweto of the first Civic Association under Nthatho Motlana. Its organization of a rent boycott, after a further 100 per cent rent rise in 1979, marked the transition to a form of resistance which would ultimately cripple apartheid's black urban control structures.

The Soweto uprising's repercussions extended beyond South Africa's borders. It added further external pressures to the internal contradictions of apartheid. Immediately after Soweto, there was capital flight, talk of sanctions and disinvestment, a slowing of white immigration and a deepening of the balance of payments crisis. For South Africa's trading partners, Soweto 'revived the whole issue of international acceptability that Prime Minister Verwoerd had sought to lay to rest through the policy of Separate Development' (Price, 1991: 62). In November 1977, when the security threat was near its peak, the UN arms embargo became mandatory. By 1978 South Africa was cut off from new long-term loans and foreign-owned firms based in South Africa had begun to repatriate more of the revenue they earned there. A net inflow of $660 million in 1976 had, by 1978, become an outflow of $1,073 million (Price, 1991: 68), and in 1977 GDP rose by only 0.1 per cent (Moll, 1989). Apart from the institutional response, South Africa suffered from a consumer boycott in the West, when the repression following Soweto made alternatives more acceptable than 'Made in South Africa' items. In turn, the government's efforts to overcome mounting Western hostility played a crucial role in instigating the 'Muldergate' affair – the misappropriation of public funds intended for overseas propaganda – which eventually forced Prime Minister Vorster's resignation and his replacement by P.W. Botha.

Conclusion

By the end of the 1970s, despite extensive ideological adjustments in the guise of Separate Development and the pragmatic development of impoverished separate homeland administrations, a fundamental paradox had emerged within the apartheid system. The set of laws accumulated over the last thirty years to guarantee white prosperity and security were in themselves contributing to the undermining of these very goals. The modernization of key economic sectors was being impeded by discriminatory laws adopted for white protection in an earlier economic context, and government attempts to encourage industrial decentralization had done little to remove the constraints. Internal economic contradictions were reinforced by the damaging effect that South Africa's political *modus operandi*, and black resistance to it, had on external investor confidence, first after Sharpeville, and then after Soweto.

Apartheid's economic and political contradictions were manifested most clearly in its unstable spatial form. The state's two overarching geographical constructs – reserved white (particularly urban) space and the homelands as corrals for blacks – were both being consistently undermined as economic reproduction pulled black workers and white employers together in an uneven urban interaction. Despite the government's attempt to conceptualize them as discrete phenomena, along with the integration of the factors of production in the cities, came the bodies and the politics of a significant black workforce.

The rising sense of black political strength in the 1970s was commensurate with an increasingly vital black role in the economy. Black workers had realized their collective power from the 1950s, and in the 1960s they initiated an unprecedented level of trade-union activity. The 1973 Durban strikes and the Soweto revolt both reflected and catalysed further militancy. The fact that black resistance, rather than being progressively eliminated, was increasing in its scale and intensity with each discrete period of rebellion, made a secure economic and political future for apartheid unlikely. Nevertheless, the state could possibly have legitimated entrenched apartheid for longer if the support of its own Afrikaans constituency had not simultaneously begun to fragment.

6

The Reformulation of
a Structure

Introduction

Botha came to the premiership in 1978 with the conviction that apartheid could be coherently reformed so as to ameliorate its economic and spatial contradictions, to pacify black urban resistance and to ensure continued white political and economic hegemony. In order to force through the reforms he envisaged, he first altered the nature of government in such a way as to strengthen his own position relative to the other elements involved in the formulation of state policy. With unprecedented individual power within the state, he began to take some of the directions for reform indicated by post-Soweto commissions set up by his predecessor, Vorster, and by his own advisory bodies.

Botha's background in the Ministry of Defence had helped inform his perception of a South Africa undergoing a Total Onslaught. An ideology based upon this perception emerged within the higher echelons of government. An onslaught, ultimately orchestrated by communist elements within and outside the country, could only be met by a Total Strategy, involving a set of new alliances with the classes and groups who would defend the type of stability favoured by the state. Capital was one of these groups and it was envisaged that Coloureds, Indians and even urban Africans could be encompassed in a struggle to fend off radical change. Many of Botha's initiatives during the 1980s were directed at forging such an alliance.

While Botha's premiership was guided in its early stages by more of a blueprint for change than Vorster's was, the implementation of reform was still vacillatory and sometimes contradictory. The government was still, to a large extent, reactive rather than proactive in its reform measures. Elements in the reform package that seem, with hindsight, to have been components of a grand and long-term strategy were not necessarily devised in such a light. They were often the result of the unintended consequences of earlier initiatives, or of developments beyond the government's control.

This chapter is divided into three sections which are broadly chronological in order but have frequent temporal overlaps. The first section is an account of the adaptations which were made to government thinking and practice under Vorster, in the light of the Soweto uprising. Botha's preparations for reform and the development of reform ideology within the government are the subject of the second section. The third section recounts the policy measures which comprised Botha's reform package. African, and particularly, township responses to these reforms, their unintended consequences and the forceful resistance with which the state was met in the mid-1980s, plus concluding comments on the period, are left for Chapter 8.

1 Post-Soweto realizations and adaptations

In the wake of the Soweto uprising, government commissions were appointed by Vorster to investigate the problems and to try to negotiate a way through the economic contradictions of urban apartheid. Soweto had thrown a spotlight on the difficulties of maintaining white political and economic privilege, but the problems were of a structural nature, inherent within the system of government. Urban administrative chaos was the necessary outcome of so many territorial and racial structures of government – forty-four in the Durban metropolitan region alone (Lemon, 1991b). A deplorable housing shortage, accompanied by mushrooming squatter settlements and the dislocation between workplace and home for most of the city's population, were commensurate with the attempt to keep the city core white. Periodic upsurges in black resistance and a further deepening of economic contradictions stemmed from the conditions in which most of the city's population lived. Hence there was an underlying 'conflict threshold evident from the mid-1970s' (Davies, 1991: 85), upon which the dramatic events of Soweto were superimposed.

Four major developments were responsible for the government's perception that South Africa was at a threshold in the late 1970s: apartheid's internal economic/spatial contradictions; the changing class interests of apartheid's core white constituency; the economic impact of mounting international condemnation; and the stresses and costs imposed on administration by bouts of heightened black resistance. In fact, in Habermas's phraseology, apartheid was facing both an economic and a legitimation crisis.

The perceived economic basis of the state's difficulties resulted in a shift in government ideology over the next decade. 'The ruling [groups] are ... now increasingly concerned with securing their material advantages ... rather than preserving their collective identity ... when 70% of the group are considered to be middle class, avoiding jeopardizing this position vies with ideological relics' (Adam, 1990: 236). Adam and Moodley (1986) also detect a shift in the source of legitimacy, from nationalist identity and racist doctrines towards bureaucratic notions of law and order. The shift may represent more than a simple re-evaluation; it may mark the descent into mere 'survival ideology' (Adam and Moodley, 1986: 72) of a government in disarray over defeat in Angola, the Soweto uprising and the Muldergate affair, in which Vorster's government and the Cabinet member Mulder were revealed to have misappropriated funds.

Whether as re-evaluation or last resort, Professor Viljoen, head of the vanguard of ruling-group ideology – the Broederbond – asked after Soweto, 'must we not think again in our inner circle about Dr. Eiselen's idea of a neutral or grey area with political power shared by white and non-white alongside a smaller, exclusive, white state?' (Williams and Strydom, 1979, cited in Kuper, 1988: 43).

In the late 1970s, government rethinking coincided with the advent of a broader split in Afrikaans ranks, facilitating moves in a reformist direction. A verligte, or enlightened, tendency characterized the political outlook of some influential Afrikaners under Vorster's premiership. In the forefront of the movement, and adopting the most radical position, was an intellectual elite which had been nourished on the revival of Afrikaans education since the mid-century and which both broadened the horizons of Afrikaans literature and followed a more humanistic approach to ethnic politics (Sparks, 1990). In particular, the 1960s and 1970s produced a generation of radical writers like André Brink, known as the sestigers (Sixty-ers), who had studied abroad and absorbed something of the revolutionary campus politics of the times. The verligte group in general, though, was more cautious in its departure from orthodox Afrikaans political belief, and it remained bound by a racially fragmented view of politics.

Bunting (1986) traces the divide within the polity between verligte and conservative verkrampte to Vorster's attempts from 1968 to meet black leaders of other African nations and to allow black athletes to represent South Africa abroad. Apart from opposing these specific endeavours, the verkrampte wing of the NP was critical of Vorster's emphasis on overall white unity and dominance, rather than on the traditional concern for the exclusive safeguarding of Afrikaners. Integration between the two dominant white groups was only marginally less feared than the first signs of apartheid's relaxation, heralded by the diplomatic and sports ventures. It was thought that such innovations, seemingly innocuous in immediate conditions, by abrogating the principle of maximum segregation, contained the seeds for a long-term undermining of white, and particularly Afrikaans, supremacy.

The verligte members of the NP were well aware of the power of a verkrampte reaction, and their 'main objective ... was to reformulate the apartheid ideology within the party without forcing a split' (Giliomee, 1987: 376). While the party would, after all, split, the growth of a verligte outlook in the NP, despite the verkrampte reaction, prepared the ground within the wider Afrikaans community for the reforms contemplated in the late 1970s. The movement also attracted some new electoral support to the NP from more liberal English-speakers, and was influential in persuading Western leaders that structural change was contemplated, thereby delaying economic sanctions.

While, within the state, certain ideological shifts were occurring, and opening avenues for reform, they did not extend to a reconsideration of the racial basis of policy. The implicit aim of late 1970s and the early 1980s reformism was to preserve white political and economic superiority under new conditions, even if its retention involved suboptimal economic performance, rather than to jettison it entirely. Under Vorster, the prejudicial legal measures to protect separate identities – the Mixed Marriages and Immorality Acts and the various pieces of geographically segregationist legislation – continued unchallenged.

Thompson (1985) attempts to rationalize the fundamental lack of ideological progression and the continuation of an academically outmoded conception of identity within the wider white society. By 1980, scientists had generally abandoned the racial paradigm, but the general public in South Africa, as in North America and Europe, lagged behind. It is, after all, easier to understand an immutable division of the human species into distinctive physical and, coincidentally, cultural entities, than it is to comprehend the concept of fluid populations, defined genetically and subject to continuous cultural and even, in the long run, physical change. The findings of late twentieth-century physical and social anthropology were less readily filtered through white society than were those of the late nineteenth century. Apart from the simple index of understandability, the fixed racial paradigm also satisfied a white sense of superiority and helped uphold white self-esteem, while complementing neatly white material self-interest.

In Europe and North America, the real structures of society were overtaking such racially based conceptions of them, but in South Africa the racial paradigm continued to be legitimated by reference to empirical observation. There were (and are) still great differences between rural African and white Western cultures. 'Tribalistic' faction fights, the tension between migrant and urban workers and the endemic violence of township life, while all having conditions of impoverishment and oppression as their context, still provoked white fears of the unreliability and underlying barbarism of Africans. That ability and aptitude were commensurate with race could be demonstrated, as long as the background conditions were not investigated too closely, by the fact that blacks continued to do worse in their schools than whites in theirs. And in South Africa, cultural and attitudinal gulfs were deliberately perpetuated as an explicit policy goal. With school textbooks continuing to reinforce the notion of a fundamentally divided human group, for example, classifying 'the African physical and cultural type' into distinct and timeless tribes (Muller, 1969, cited in Thompson, 1985), it is not surprising that fixed ideological points of reference remained generally unshaken.

Views of history have played an important role in perpetuating racial fears in South Africa. With most popular, established interpretations of South African history being largely the history of racial and 'tribal' conflict, a racial conception of contemporary political and social division became natural. 'Most white South Africans have been able to ignore many of the new intellectual findings (recovering the historical flux of African polities) ... because they have represented changes from relatively simple to relatively complex explanations of human taxonomy and historical processes' (Thompson, 1985: 205). An extreme example of resistance to the academic undermining of established historical interpretation was provided in 1979, when Afrikaner Weerstandbeweging (AWB) members tarred and feathered the Afrikaner historian, F. Van Jaarsveld, as he was about to deliver a lecture questioning the myth of the Blood River covenant. Even the introduction of television into South Africa in 1976 did not allow a non-racial message to be communicated, since the South African Broadcasting Corporation (SABC) was under tight government control. The late introduction of television indicated the government's fear that the new medium would bring Anglicization and non-racialism. There was consequently a heavy pro-government slant in domestic current affairs coverage and 'its news services and commentaries, like those on radio, are thinly disguised government propaganda' (Thompson, 1985: 48).

Ideological constants would not allow the transformation of South Africa's system of white rule, but the system had at least to be relaxed if future economic well-being was to be secured. The state's response consisted of a partial return to the rights of which urban Africans had been deprived over the last three decades (Lea, 1982). The government's philosophy can be reduced to the principle of making more rational economic use of those Africans who were already in the cities.

It was anticipated that this would be commensurate with the removal of the major black urban grievances and stabilization of the political system.

The housing shortage was the most visible urban problem. In the late 1970s a reappraisal of African housing policy was encouraged by increasing international hostility to well-publicized removals and 'rustications', and by the particular politicization of the housing issue in the townships (Dewar and Watson, 1982). A change of direction was also required on economic grounds: the state clearly would not be able to bear the cost of formally housing all legal urban residents.

Some township tenurial security was introduced with a ninety-nine-year lease scheme, although, in 1978, building society mortgage finance rules still barred the vast majority from taking advantage of the scheme. Within the Department of Co-operation and Development, a gradual acceptance of self-help housing emerged, to stabilize the accommodation of those outside formally built structures. In some areas, the pre-Soweto pattern of squatter removals and clearances was reversed.

A more tolerant attitude towards informal economic activity accompanied the recognition of informal housing. Activities such as brewing, the running of shebeens and street trading, previously regarded as an unwelcome African intrusion into white urban space, were increasingly seen as part of a stabilization programme for those Africans irreversibly present in the cities (Beavon and Rogerson, 1982). The incorporation of such activities under official patronage also facilitated a much-needed extension of the urban tax base (McGrath, 1990).

The state was not alone in initiating new housing projects. It was joined by the private sector in the form of the Urban Foundation (UF), backed by Anglo American among others. Lea (1982) argues that the UF had 'more to do with the imperatives of the accumulation process than it has to do with welfare', being a 'direct and rapid response by capital to the urban unrest' (Lea, 1982: 206). Its leading lights aimed not only to defend capital from unrest, but also to spread the free-enterprise ethic to an emergent black middle class, thus engendering both political and economic stability in the townships. Its programme, then, is interpreted as being similar to the state's own under Botha. However, an unadulterated conspiracy theory of the UF needs modifying to take into account some genuine philanthropic impulses among its backers. In terms of its practical impact, the UF has financed and organized the building of formal housing and assisted in informal upgrading. Smith points out that its command of significant financial resources enabled it to wield disproportionate influence in development debates. In effect, it was able to establish a new reformist orthodoxy (David Smith, personal correspondence). Even relatively minor improvements in housing represent significant advances in the lives of many, and they can also contribute to the political mobilization of those whose material insecurity previously mitigated such activity.

Apart from the promotion of housing improvement, a further area of post-Soweto state reform was township administration. The 1977 Community Councils Act allowed for a limited measure of black control over local affairs in the townships, implicitly confirming the permanency of the African presence in the white cities. For the first time, those with Section 10 rights were also allowed to change jobs within their Administration Board District without recourse to Labour Bureaux (Lemon, 1991b).

More flexibility in the implementation of the Group Areas Act was another response to the urban problems generated by apartheid. A 1966 amendment to the Act had allowed areas to be proclaimed according to their use rather than the occupation of any one racial group. In the late 1970s, the clause was more frequently implemented, so that, by 1983, there were twenty-six mixed-race, free-trading areas; Durban, Port Elizabeth and Kimberley having two each. Where racial occupation remained the criterion for zoning, blacks increasingly used white nominees to run concerns on their behalf within white group areas. Eventually, these changes in business areas were accompanied by a partial erosion of 'petty apartheid' as the Separate Amenities Act was undermined, but throughout the 1980s, *de jure* alterations recognizing these developments lagged behind the rate of *de facto* change (Lemon, 1991b).

Beyond the commercial use of white land, in the late 1970s, black employees in large corporations were the first to join the black foreign dignitaries and churchmen already living in white group areas. Gradually, they were joined by blacks using nominees or front companies to occupy more luxurious houses in the white suburbs. This very restricted movement of an economic elite preceded the larger-scale black occupation of the flats in inner-city areas like Johannesburg's Hillbrow and Joubert Park during the 1980s. While still extremely limited when put in perspective with the scale of black urban residence, the moves displayed the government's toleration of an erosion of Verwoerdian, fundamentalist spatial apartheid.

With a partial relaxation of control over urban black residential and economic strategies, came limited concessions in the black urban workplace. The 1973 Durban strikes had revealed how the absence of organized negotiating partners within the workforce could render strike prevention and control hazardous and costly. In the late 1970s, the government began to offer recognition to black trade unions in order to incorporate them within official structures and channel their activities along supervised lines (Price, 1991). The move sparked a debate among black trade unionists as to the alternative strategies open to them. Ultimately, the government's attempt at containment would largely fail, as trade unions became enmeshed in the wider township community struggle against the state.

In a number of discrete moves in the late 1970s, the state relaxed its own rules over black urban living and working. If there was a philosophy behind these moves, that philosophy can be said to have been one of containment. The Soweto uprising had revealed that the living conditions of most urban blacks under apartheid would never engender the stability needed for economic growth. With influential elements of the private sector already discarding apartheid labour practices and agitating for a more stable black urban workforce, attempts were made to ameliorate the conditions of this workforce. The majority of Africans would still be kept outside the core economic regions through influx control, but for those blacks already inside white urban economic space, concessions could be made to contain future instability. While the philosophy of containment was implicit in the series of discrete actions that the state took after Soweto, it was not explicitly revealed until the publication of two influential Commissions' reports at the end of the decade. The Riekert and Wiehahn Reports would provide the basis for Botha's attempts at reform in the 1980s. Initially, those attempts were a continuation of the ameliorative measures, directed at the urban black 'insiders', pursued under Vorster.

2 Preparations for, and the ideology of, reform under Botha

The procedures by which the South African state was run began to change on Botha's accession to power. Botha immediately set about centralizing NP policy within the Cabinet. His dogmatic style of leadership ensured that, throughout his premiership, the government would take the initiatives, and only subsequently would the party be brought into line. Within the party, 'no one dared challenge him, and this far reaching change was accepted with little overt resistance' (Schrire, 1992b: 37). These developments justify a rather personal account of the Botha government's strategies. Botha himself was far more the initiator of a mentally preconceived strategy than previous Prime Ministers had been, and, as an individual, he was more responsible for his government's actions than his predecessors were for theirs.

It was not just force of personality which effected the change. The structures of government were themselves modified to strengthen the Prime Minister's position. A Cabinet Secretariat and four permanent committees advised the Prime Minister, replacing twenty *ad hoc* committees set up under Vorster. One of Vorster's innovations, the State Security Council (SSC), became the most important of these committees under Botha. It developed as the key decision-making body in the fields of security and foreign policy. To some extent, the SSC displaced even the Cabinet as the forum for determining government strategy. Under its supervision, a political/military apparatus was built to co-ordinate counter-insurgency. It was known as the National Security Management System (NSMS). The NSMS co-ordinated Joint Management Committees (JMCs), the territorial boundaries of which were those of South Africa's military districts (later becoming those of nine economic development regions). The JMCs were staffed by regional security officials and politicians. Their sub-regional offshoots were known as mini-JMCs and they marshalled influential officials and security officers at the municipal level. The whole structure was devised so as to co-ordinate 'on the ground' top-down initiatives from the SSC, for example, implementing plans for black community assistance, and to relay local security-related information back up the chain so that the SSC could devise policy in the light of accurate intelligence from across the country.

With power within the executive shifting to a more restricted, security-conscious body, the civil service had to be streamlined so as to ensure that initiatives would not be diluted in their implementation. For instance, the Bantu Administration 'empire' was dismantled, and its functions distributed to other departments, effectively transferring power from civil servants to politicians (Schrire, 1992b). Nevertheless, one-third of white workers and two-thirds of Afrikaners remained employed by the state, and central initiatives could still be thwarted by the minor officials who were the local interpreters of the daunting morass of new legislation.

The direction that central reform initiatives should take was suggested by the Riekert and Wiehahn Commissions. Each was concerned with different aspects of the economic utilization of urban blacks. The Wiehahn Commission was set up to investigate industrial labour relations, while Riekert led a Commission advising on efficient labour supplies and productivity.

The Riekert Commission was established in 1977 and headed by Vorster's economic adviser. Riekert's enquiries began with the observation that apartheid's spatial framework was being undermined by social and economic pressures which could not be indefinitely resisted. These pressures consisted of internal and international opposition to the homelands and their continued economic decline; rapidly increasing rural to urban migration, with the early 1980s drought, in particular, overcoming the defences of influx control; mounting opposition to the pass laws in the cities; and the increased political and economic power of urban blacks. The report was influenced by the dominant Western free-market approach to economic systems. The fundamental flaw in the present system was perceived as being its failure to accommodate market forces. 'Market failures' included uneconomic racial discrimination, the coexistence of skilled labour shortages and unskilled labour surpluses, the legally constrained mobility of labour and the inhibitions on domestic economic growth (Pickles, 1988).

The report called for simplification and rationalization of the laws controlling the labour market, but the white paper based on the report made it clear that 'the question to which the commission and the government had to find an answer was not whether there should be influx control, but what the right mechanism for influx control would be in South Africa's circumstances' (quoted in Pickles, 1988: 234). It was argued that influx control could still be achieved with non-racially discriminatory legislation, by limiting the lawful, urban black presence according to the availability of housing and employment. Section 10 rights would be extended to more, currently 'illegal', urban blacks, but the exclusion of further blacks from the cities would be effected by limiting the housing available and enforcing the ejection of 'illegals' by fining their employers (Adam and Moodley, 1986). Thus, the distinction between black 'insiders', to whom legal urban employment and housing opportunities were available, and rural 'outsiders', to whom they were closed, was reinforced (Terreblanche and Nattrass, 1990). Those who qualified for Section 10 rights would be stabilized and given a stake in the *status quo* through the option (already in place) of taking a ninety-nine-year lease on their municipal properties. Further, the report recommended that they be no longer subject to a legal job colour bar and that the 'petty apartheid' discrimination of the Separate Amenities Act should be removed. Finally, the industrial decentralization programme should be injected with new vigour in order to slow the rate of black urbanization, without overtly racist influx control.

The Wiehahn Report complemented Riekert's vision of a more privileged black urban, working class. Investigation into labour relations in the cities yielded the finding that greater economic stability could follow from the recognition of black trade unions, and their co-option into a formalized negotiating structure. Wiehahn advised that legally recognized trade unions exclude migrant workers, but the government's implementation of this restriction soon gave way in the face of trade union antagonism. Wiehahn shared Riekert's view that job colour bar legislation should be abolished (Horowitz, 1991).

Both reports were striving for an urban economy run along more efficient allocative lines than existing legislation would allow. Economic efficiency lay at their heart – Ashforth (1990), noting that these government reports, unlike preceding ones (excepting the Fagan Report), spoke of urban Africans as units of labour first. Their 'African-ness' was only a secondary quality. Both sought to give capital a freer rein in its use of black labour by removing the unnecessarily discriminatory aspects of labour legislation that hemmed it in.

Economic efficiency was a salient influence on Botha's overall policy direction, as his government appreciated more the difficulties of South Africa's economic context. The country had experienced a brief period of economic recovery in the early 1980s, buoyed up partly by the revived fortunes of gold in the international economy. But, by 1983, it was becoming increasingly clear that the phenomenon would be short-lived. South African capitalists had not escaped the constraints of their own particular political economy: 'they worry about calm labour relations and they dislike operating in a siege economy, cut off from technology, innovation, easy capital flows and access to markets abroad' (Adam and Moodley, 1986: 22).

With the established restrictions on labour utilization and market size and, after 1983, a deterioration in external terms of trade, the extent of capital's professed reformism increased. In 1984, the Associated Chamber of Commerce (ASSOCOM) and the Federated Chambers of Industry (FCI) both made representations to the government against the detention of black trade unionists and, in 1985, they produced a *Manifesto on Reform* which called for 'a universal citizenship' and 'meaningful political participation' for all blacks. In September 1985, several prominent businessmen visited ANC representatives in Lusaka to sound out their attitude towards South African capital. While the representatives of capital remained diverse in their political attitudes and in their relationship to the state, a clear trend in favour of reform became more evident in the mid-1980s, a trend which was implicitly predicted in the Riekert and Wiehahn Reports.

Elements of South African capital had experienced the economic constraints of apartheid legislation since the 1960s, but the government showed a greater willingness to listen in the 1980s, as South Africa's economic position became more evidently jeopardized. After 1982, the government itself was forced to borrow from abroad, in short-term, uncovered loans (Lipton, 1985), and the onset of severe drought increased the need to draw on external finance for disaster relief and homeland grain imports.

Foreign capital was not only required for rural relief; it was also needed to cover spiralling security costs, as black resistance mounted again. However, the increasing violence and televised police brutality which resulted from security measures (see Chapter 7), brought domestic pressure to bear on South Africa's creditors, to deny renewal of the loans. In 1985, South Africa found itself confronted with a comprehensive package of US sanctions and the refusal of lending institutions to renew short-term loans of $14 billion, which were due for repayment. The subsequent debt crisis precipitated a drastic fall in the value of the rand and the closure of the Johannesburg Stock Exchange, with the declaration of a moratorium on many of South Africa's foreign debts.

'Market sanctions', like those of the banks, pursued out of economic self-interest, were probably more damaging to the South African economy than foreign government-imposed, politically guided sanctions, but 'both Finance Minister Barend du Plessis and the South African Broadcasting Corporation (often regarded as a government mouthpiece) have credited sanctions with pushing the government toward social reform' (Grundy, 1991: 71). Nevertheless, groups within the government continued to take a contemptuous view of sanctions, particularly in the light of the state arms corporation, ARMSCOR's success in building a domestic weapons industry once denied open access to external trade.

Botha's government paid more attention to the desires of capital than preceding ones, realizing that some degree of economic vitality was required for political stability. But the government did not see radical reform in the interests of capital as being necessary. Instead, the political strategy developed in the late stages of Vorster's prime ministership and elaborated under Botha, would be sufficient to generate economic improvement. By stabilizing a black urban group, and incorporating it within economic structures to a greater degree through trade union rights, the removal of some discriminatory labour legislation, improved education and home ownership, it was thought that capital's requirements could be met within the general racial structures which the government sought to maintain as part of its political strategy.

Nolutshungu (1982) argues, from a Marxist perspective, that the crucial goal at the centre of Botha's initial strategy was the co-option of the black petty bourgeoisie. It seems more likely that it was the geographically defined, multi-class, urban black group which was singled out for co-option (Adam and Moodley, 1986). The key government agencies hoped that this group would prefer the benefits of immediate material gains in wages and services, to agitation for improved status within the racial state. A memorandum to the Prime Minister from the Transvaal Chamber of Mines claimed that such a preference was already being expressed in the cities: 'The emergence of a "middle class" with Western type materialistic needs and ambitions has already occurred in these areas. The mature, family-orientated urban black already places the stability of his household uppermost and is more interested in his pay-packet than in politics' (quoted in Kane Berman, 1979: 156). Despite the reference to a 'middle class', the primary division that such a development would foster is urban-rural, rather than class-defined.

The extension of privilege to urban blacks was justified by influential figures drawn from within the administrative establishment. In 1979, the economic adviser to Botha, S. Brand, wrote in the *Rand Daily Mail* that the government had to 'open the system in order to save it and build upon it' (cited in Lipton, 1985: 59). A 1986 Broederbond publication emphasized that 'the abolition of statutory discrimination measures must not be seen as concessions but as prerequisite for survival' (quoted in Horowitz, 1991: 80).

The decision to advance the material cause of urban blacks so as to bring them 'on side' encouraged a perception that white, and particularly Afrikaner racial ideology, already fragmented under Vorster, was being abandoned under Botha in the interests of pragmatism. Sparks (1991) wrote, 'The Afrikaner revolution is over and all that is left of it is the politics of survivalism. The fortress of the volk is to be defended, but there is no faith within its walls' (1991: 328). The South African novelist, Christopher Hope, expressed the same theme metaphorically:

> Pragmatism was the spur. And desperation. Those who ran the factory found they just didn't have enough hands to go round. To work the machine, once upon a time you had to be white, over 21, dedicated to the party and to the preservation of Western Christian civilization and believe that the Afrikaners were God's anointed. Nowadays anyone could mind the machine, as long as they were willing to keep shooting. This policy of desperation went by the name of progress. (Hope, 1986: 150–1).

There was certainly no abandonment of a racially conceived view of societal order though, and what black incorporation was envisaged was to be firmly on the government's terms and only for the purpose of continued white supremacy. This would involve the jettisoning of some redundant, ideologically inspired racial legislation, but no fundamental re-evaluation of the racial paradigm. However, in government circles, there was a significant ideological shift within this paradigm.

Malan and Verwoerd's ideological drive to segregate was gone. It was replaced by the resolution that what most whites now had would be protected by a Total Strategy, designed to combat the Total Onslaught to which white supremacy was now being subjected.

These concepts – of a Total Onslaught and a Total Strategy – were first enunciated by Botha, as Minister of Defence, in response to the increasingly hostile environment of 1975. With neighbouring states falling to socialist black governments, the exiled ANC in close collaboration with the Communist Party, and internal black workerist mobilization gaining sympathy from communist states, South Africa's security establishment perceived the various threats to white superiority to be co-ordinated by communist-inspired activists. The Total Strategy was designed to counter this complex of opposition by mustering 'all activities – political, economic, diplomatic and military'. By 1977, the Defence White Paper had added 'psychological' to the list of spheres in which counter-attack would occur (Price, 1991: 85).

The outline of the Total Strategy was based on French counter-guerrilla activity in Algeria, explicated by Beaufre (Sparks, 1991). Price (1991) identifies its elements as being simultaneous reform, repression and wider, regional initiatives. Reform was required to ease apartheid's economic bottlenecks and to create a black urban grouping sympathetic to the *status quo*. This would guard the political stability required for renewed international investment. In this reform initiative, the involvement of private capital would be crucial. With capital made more amenable by the removal of apartheid's hindering labour legislation and increased resources for black education and training, it was hoped that the rewards that capital growth would bestow on urban blacks would contribute to their co-option.

It would have been naïve of the government to assume, though, that sufficient material inducements to stability could be distributed to urban blacks in the short term. The masses of the urban poor would have to be rendered quiescent, in the face of unequal structures of power and privilege, by other means, while the amelioration of their deprivation progressed gradually. While firm repression would not ease their grievances, it would prevent them from bursting forth in spectacular and economically damaging outbursts like that of the Soweto uprising.

Security analysts within the government were aware of the fact that the level of repression required would depend on the extent of perceived deprivation and the degree of expectation for future change. Security-force repression, using detentions, bannings and, later, surrogate vigilante violence, would help lower political expectations by demonstrating the power of the white state and its determination to control events. It also served to reassure the ruling party's white constituency – in the 1987 whites' general election, the NP slogan 'Reform – yes! Surrender – no!' was convincing on the evidence of repression under a State of Emergency, and it helped prevent wholesale defection to the Conservative Party, formed from the extreme verkrampte wing of the NP in 1982 (Schrire, 1992b). In the early period of Botha's premiership, the contradiction between a path of internationally publicized repression (despite media censorship) and the goal of presenting a reformist and stable image to the world was not yet appreciated.

In order to neutralize the external threat posed by Marxist and ANC-sympathizing governments across South Africa's borders, a third dimension was added to the reform-repress package. This was a regional policy to establish a 'constellation' of client states within the region, economically dependent on, and therefore politically amenable to, the South African government. With South African economic and political hegemony over the entire southern African region, the government could not only enlarge markets for its own capitalists, but also demand that the ANC be denied the opportunity to organize its external opposition and internal guerrilla activities from anywhere near South Africa's borders. The government hoped that the dependence of proximate states on South Africa's economy would simultaneously prevent their advocation of further international sanctions against South Africa.

The destabilization of independent economic and political progress, which would ensure these states' dependence on South African patronage, began with the collapse of their white regimes. The long catalogue of South African intervention in the region included repeated SADF incursions into Angola in support of Jonas Savimbi's opposition Uniao Nacional para a Independencia Total de Angola (UNITA) movement, support for Muzorewa against Mugabe in Zimbabwe, the sponsorship of the Democratic Turnhalle Alliance (DTA) as an alternative to SWAPO in South African-occupied Namibia, and a litany of violent, destructive acts performed by South African-backed Mozambique National Resistance (RENAMO) in Mozambique (see Hanlon, 1986; Johnson and Martin, 1989; Barber and Barratt, 1990). While these actions did not necessarily ensure fully compliant regimes in the region, they did, by and large, help effect the non-functioning of the least stable, hostile neighbouring governments, particularly Mozambique and Angola. Nevertheless, South Africa's economic hegemony was resisted by surrounding states, its threat prompting the formation of the Southern African Development Coordination Conference (SADCC) by southern African states determined to forge a degree of economic independence from their aggressively dominant neighbour. The initi-ative was aided by Western recognition and some material assistance.

As part of its Total Strategy, in the early 1980s, the state, as we have seen, tried to involve capital in a more strategic role within the power bloc. A complementary goal, which gained more momentum as the decade wore on, was the withdrawal of the state from the extent of economic intervention which it had assumed under the NP. Price (1991) argues that central state intervention was what distinguished apartheid from colonial segregation. It was the central state which had become the target of rebellion over the last three decades. Its partial withdrawal from economic and administrative intervention would both remove a focus for resistance and effect a much-needed reduction in government expenditure. A privatization of the state's role could also dovetail with the strategy of co-opting a black urban group to support government and business. An early example was the 1983 decision to sell off a part of the state's black housing stock. The goal of a home-owning, stabilized, black urban group was furthered in the Cape by the new Coloured area of Mitchell's Plain being made available only for purchase and not for rent (Mabin and Parnell, 1983).

Municipal house sales to occupants progressed slowly at first, but gathered pace towards the end of the 1980s, particularly in Soweto where over 40 per cent of the formal housing stock is now owner-occupied, and elite areas like Beverley Hills have developed (Lemon, 1991b). The privatization of public utilities was extended from 1985, becoming the 'greatest structural change in the development of South African commercial history since the establishment of ISCOR in 1927' (Davenport, 1991: 493). A 1987 white paper laid guidelines for further state withdrawal and ISCOR itself was placed on the Johannesburg Stock Exchange in 1989, with South African Transport Services and the Post Office to follow. Towards the end of the 1980s, a further motive was attached to this progression by some observers – that of leaving a future black-run government with fewer economic assets under its direct control and thus, less potential for the redistribution of resources to blacks in the way that the NP had used the state for Afrikaners.

Government economic policy in the 1980s extended beyond the privatization of key assets in line with current Western thinking to include encouragement of more general restructuring of the economy. By the early 1980s, South Africa had encountered, along with many other states, the classic limits to an import substitution policy, following from restricted internal markets and the need to import capital goods. The government recognized that an initiative needed to be taken in finding new international markets. A 1985 white paper stressed the need to develop the manufacturing of a balanced set of exports (Wellings and Black, 1986). Consequently, export incentives were revamped and government assistance given to restructure certain targeted industries. To stimulate internal restructuring, tariffs and quotas on certain competing imports were lifted. Once again, the specific economic aim of the government slotted into its wider strategic and political goals. With closer links to world markets, there should follow an improvement in international relations and more sympathy for the reform package being implemented within the country.

Through the combined components of the Total Strategy, Botha sought the same goal as his predecessor – the maintenance of the white political and economic supremacy that had been forged over three centuries and consolidated under Afrikaner patronage in the Nationalist Party's apartheid years. Now though, the mechanisms of supremacy would have to change to accommodate new global and domestic circumstances. The reforms of Botha's administration were often criticized as being 'cosmetic'. To the extent that they reflected no other goal than the established one, that view is accurate, but, as Botha found to his cost, 'the political, social and economic dynamics into which reforms are introduced may produce a significant erosion of white power nonetheless' (Price, 1991: 83).

3 Reform initiatives

The new constitution, announced in 1983 and effected from 1984, was the first significant legislative step away from rigid, racial separate development and, tentatively, towards a fuller image of nationhood. Coloured and Indian political representatives were to join the business community and sections of the black urban classes in a co-opted amalgam with vested interests in the new system (Terreblanche and Nattrass, 1990). As a strategic initiative, the new constitution was a perfect example of the problem-solving, 'technocratic' image that Botha's government wished to project (Marks and Trapido, 1987b).

Under the new political dispensation, two parallel houses were added to the House of Assembly (the white parliament). The House of Delegates would represent South Africa's Indian population, while the House of Representatives would accommodate Coloured MPs. Each house was empowered to legislate on its 'own affairs', but these would be defined by the State President. What he defined as 'general affairs' would be the province of the Cabinet, but legislation in general affairs would normally be passed by all three Houses. The office of State President itself would replace the office of Prime Minister, and the President would be emplaced by an electoral college of fifty white, twenty-five Coloured and thirteen Indian MPs, drawn from their respective Houses. A President's Council, comprising ten Coloured, five Indian and twenty white MPs, plus twenty-five appointed by the President, would advise the President on controversial legislation.

The complexity of the Tricameral Parliament system was largely due to the fact that it was 'designed to ensure that policy could be made and implemented regardless of the behaviour of the Coloured and Indian chambers' (Schrire, 1992b: 65). Several inbuilt mechanisms would ensure this. First, the President's Council, with a guaranteed majority of whites, would break deadlocks between the parliamentary chambers, and could therefore force through legislation opposed by the two black Houses. Secondly, the white House of Assembly was given the capacity to act as Parliament if the other two chambers failed to function. Thirdly, there was a fixed 4:2:1 numerical ratio of white:Coloured:Indian representation in the system, reflecting the population sizes of the three legally defined groups and entrenching white hegemony. Finally, the separation of these groups into discrete Houses made it 'impossible for genuine cross-racial coalitions to develop' (Schrire, 1992b: 65).

Apart from the incorporation of Coloured and Indian representatives, however ineffectually, into the system of government, the new constitution had two other effects, one deliberate, the other unintended. The former was the formal consolidation of Botha's grip on the reins of government. From being a Prime Minister alongside a non-executive State President, he was now executive State President – like that of the US. With the transition, Botha's closest security advisers won greater influence over policy, while the influence of the Cabinet, the NP parliamentary caucus, Parliament and the civil service correspondingly diminished (Schrire, 1992b: 42).

The second effect turned out, in the long run, to be very costly for the new executive elite. This was the African reaction to being completely left out of the new central government dispensation (see Chapter 7). The only clauses in the Act relating to this majority were that '[t]he control and administration of Black affairs shall rest with the State President', and that consideration of 'Black affairs' would be the common concern of the Tricameral Parliament, since they are included in the definition of 'general affairs' (Wolpe, 1988: 93).

The government's concessions to Africans were still only those which fitted the strategy of co-opting the economically and politically crucial urban group. Initiatives at the level of local township representation complemented the strategy, but the national representation in Parliament of a numerically superior African population went far beyond it. While this could be envisaged for Coloured and Indian populations smaller than the white population, not even a precedent-setting toehold in Parliament could be accorded to Africans.

Botha's 'securocrat' government believed that the crucial African classes – those already performing a vital economic function in white cities – could be co-opted by the amelioration of their political and economic position at the metropolitan level, thus preserving central political power for the white population and its Coloured and Indian 'allies'. The proposed changes in urban African administration were based on two principles suggested by Riekert's recommendations. The first was that influx control would be maintained, but in a less patently racist guise. Limits on urban housing and services, instead of the racially based legal code that was currently used, would ensure that few more Africans would migrate to the cities. Stadler (1987) describes this development as a revival of 'liberal' methods of segregation, eschewed by Stallard in the 1920s and Verwoerd in the 1950s and 1960s, but adopted in the light of late twentieth-century conditions of incorporation in a world economy.

But plans to limit the expansion of the relatively privileged urban 'insider' group were soon seen by the government to have been overly optimistic. The post-1982 recession and the consequent breakdown in rural labour recruitment, plus the economic state of the homelands, made access to the urban economy essential for many rural poor. Despite limits on housing and job availability, by 1989 there were an estimated seven million informal settlers around city peripheries and an average of fifteen people to a four-roomed house in the formal townships (Lemon, 1991b: 20).

With the failure of market forces to halt African urbanization, an alternative component of government spatial intervention assumed more emphasis. The government once again turned to the decentralization of industry as a force to deflect urban growth. In the 1980s, decentralization was also pursued for an additional, non-political reason. This was the PWV (Pretoria–Witwatersrand–Vereeniging) metropolitan region's shortage of water supplies – the result of intensified industrial agglomeration in a relatively arid environment.

During the 1980s, Botha's government recast Vorster's policy of decentralization into a more regional and functional framework. Botha's aim was no longer purely to decentralize to growth points in or near each homeland, but to establish eight (later nine) Development Regions. The new regions cut across homeland borders and, for planning purposes, integrated sections of the homelands with the metropolitan centres to which they were already functionally linked (Lipton, 1985). The system represented a step towards a more pragmatic planning of South Africa's economic relations: economically defined regions, containing both the metropolitan centres and their labour source regions, regardless of homeland boundaries, were to replace the Verwoerdian racial-come-spatial administrative divisions. For example, Durban's labour source region in the northern Transkei was included in the white city's metropolitan region.

Within the nine regions, four types of industrial development areas were identified. From 1982, incentives were offered to processing and assembly industries to locate at Deconcentration Points (mostly near homeland borders) and Industrial Development Points. The Development Bank of Southern Africa (DBSA) was established to facilitate private investment away from the Metropolitan Areas, and direct controls were placed on further industrial expansion in these areas to replace the existing indirect fiscal controls.

There is no consensus over the result of the policy. Some decentralization followed its implementation (the decentralized areas' share of employment increased from 12.9 per cent in 1972 to 19.3 per cent in 1984), but the significance of, and motivation for, this outcome are debatable. One viewpoint is that it was market forces rather than the government's intervention which enticed industries to the target areas. The movement of labour-intensive processes to homeland and border areas, where labour is cheap enough to improve competitiveness with imports, reflects concepts elucidated by Harvey (1982) and Massey (1984) on the increasing geographical mobility of capital and its changing technology (see also Gregory and Urry, 1985). The industries which have taken advantage of the decentralization package do tend to be light and labour-intensive – clothing and metal products in particular.

However, generally, 'efforts to redistribute population and economic activity are consistently undermined by the primate city and core region biases inherent in many sectoral policies – import substitution, subsidised urban services, international terms of trade distortions etc.' (Richardson, 1987, cited in Tomlinson, 1990: 137). Before the new decentralization package was announced, many small labour-intensive industries had relocated from Johannesburg, to Durban and Cape Town for instance, but not to the areas favoured under the government scheme. Industrial relocation was largely deconcentration to 'border areas' already integrated with the metropolitan cores rather than wider decentralization (Wellings and Black, 1986).

The fact that, after 1982, firms moved to the decentralization points like Isithebe and Dambuza is best explained by the government's employment subsidies, making labour free, or even allowing for excess revenue to be made on it, rather than as a local reflection of the global restructuring of capital. Many of those firms that did relocate under the government's patronage were eventually to see metropolitan labour as ultimately cheaper, given the drawbacks associated with their new location. Once the government's monetary incentives are withdrawn, it is quite possible that these companies may move back to core regions.

For Botha's immediate strategy of containing urban African population growth, if the industry could not be moved to homeland borders on a large scale, an alternative was to encourage the growth of homeland towns near those borders, so that workers could service the metropolitan economy but reside outside its administrative boundaries. By 1982, there were already over 700,000 of these 'frontier commuters', many making excessively long journeys to and from work each day (Lemon, 1982). To some extent these workers assumed the function of the migrant workers who had traditionally serviced the metropolitan economies (Tomlinson, 1990). Where homeland borders were too far away for the growth of white South African cities to be deflected within them, informal settlements inside 'white South Africa' were often planned at unnecessarily great distances from urban workplaces, while anti-squatting controls were enforced over land nearer the cities.

The remaining racially based influx-control legislation was finally repealed in 1986, but in a climate of black insurrection which made its repeal alone insufficient to meet expectations. Despite the state's pursuit of continued influx control by other 'liberal' means, the fact of massive and continued informal settlement growth suggests that the state had in fact lost control of the black housing situation. In consequence, a central support of urban apartheid was being undermined (Maylam, 1990). However, informal, 'liberal' influx control may have partially achieved its aims. Given that there is already extensive peri-urbanization in the non-agricultural homeland fringes – a development actively encouraged by 'liberal' apartheid – the removal of restraints on urbanization may not result in rapid urban growth, and the 'rush to the cities' once urban apartheid crumbled, predicted by some, may turn out to be illusory in the long term.

The second principle of urban African administration was that some African political autonomy would be granted, beyond the functions of the existing community councils in the townships. African residents in the cities were to have their own Black Local Authorities (BLAs). The Black Local Authorities Act of 1982 set up village and town councils, resembling white local authorities, for the townships. They would have more powers and autonomy than the community councils they were to replace. Black Local Authorities were devised partially as an unofficial *quid pro quo* for African exclusion from the Tricameral Parliament system, despite the official government line that African representation was already provided for in the homelands. The Regional Administration Boards, which had held responsibility for township control, were abolished and their supervision of the Black Local Authorities passed on to the provinces.

However, the main source of the Administration Boards' independent revenue – sorghum beer sales – had dried up by the mid-1980s, with shebeens destroyed in the 1976 revolt and many Africans switching their consumption to commercial lagers. As the BLAs assumed administrative responsibility for the townships (including the unpopular tasks of influx control and the removal of 'illegals'), they found themselves unable to become, as the government intended, self-financing. Their response to fiscal difficulty was a series of rent and service levy hikes – an important factor in the next, deepest and most violent phase of black resistance (see Chapter 7).

The Regional Services Councils (RSCs) were a later element in the Botha government's adjustment of apartheid's spatial forms. The BLAs had, by the mid-1980s, become virtually unworkable across large swathes of the country. The 1980s township insurrection (detailed in Chapter 7), accomplished their failure as legitimate, or even functioning institutions. By 1985, a more radical gesture towards urban African service provision and administration was required from an internally and externally beleaguered government. The RSCs were intended to fulfil this role.

Despite the evident rejection of the BLAs in the townships, the government still saw their fundamental weakness not so much in terms of their racially defined constitution, but in terms of their fiscal limitations (Lemon, 1991b). The RSCs would encompass the BLAs alongside white, Indian and Coloured local authorities, and co-ordinate redistribution of financial resources between these authorities. This would allow the upgrading of black townships using finance partially and indirectly drawn from local white areas, thus providing a more positive image for the BLAs. The administrative functions, lost in some townships to the informal civic and street structures of the mid-1980s insurrection, could also be reclaimed by local authorities with enhanced fiscal clout. The RSCs can be seen as part of the 'hearts and minds' component of the government's Total Strategy, their provision of urban services and utilities buying calm in the townships.

By 1987, eight RSCs were established. In Natal, at KwaZulu leader Buthelezi's insistence, Metropolitan Joint Service Boards, linking the province and homeland administrations, were set up instead. Regional Services Council members were nominated by the white, Coloured, Indian and African local authorities within their administrative boundaries, but voting power was proportional to the level of services consumed by each local authority, invariably leaving the white local authority's representatives with a controlling interest. In 1990, the voting power of Soweto, by far the largest settlement in its central Witwatersrand Region, was only 17.27 per cent on its RSC (Lemon, 1991b). However, consensus was often achieved on the boards of the RSCs without recourse to voting. Their finance came from taxes on employment and turnover of local business, including state concerns, which contributed about half of the total budget (Lemon, 1991b). Since one of the functions of the RSCs was to redistribute spending from white to black areas within the regions, it was thought too politically sensitive to finance them entirely from white rates.

Money indirectly raised in white areas was nevertheless used for the upgrading of township services. Yet there was no noticeable improvement in the efficiency of the BLAs benefiting from the finance, and 'there [was] little evidence that RSCs have won greater legitimacy for official local government structures' (Lemon, 1991b: 25). This is largely because, to urban Africans as well as academic observers, 'it [seemed] clear that their prime objective [was] indirect promotion of the legitimacy of official local government structures by means of their redistributive function' (Lemon, 1991b: 25). Their imposition, without consultation, by the state, and their reliance on the same racially based local authorities that had been rejected by black communities, rendered the RSCs similarly politically unacceptable.

The government was finally forced to concede *de jure* recognition to some racially integrated local government structures in 1988. The Free Settlement Areas (FSA) Act recognized pre-existing 'grey areas' of inter-racial settlement in certain cities, and provision was made for the election by residents of their non-racial management committees. Only whites could continue to vote on a separate roll for the local authority administrating the FSA. Even in August 1989, the government was continuing to encourage whites to report on black neighbours contravening the Group Areas Act outside of the FSAs, but the fact that little subsequent action was taken against these illegal residents, and that in many cases, their residence was then formally recognized, suggests that the government encouragement was motivated more by a desire to retain the conservative vote in the forthcoming election than by a continuing pursuit of residential segregation. Meanwhile, the NP and Democratic Party (DP) council in Johannesburg was requesting that the whole city be declared an FSA, thus by-passing the Group Areas Act, while Cape Town's council was calling instead for complete exemption from the Act (Lemon: 1991).

Conclusion

While the overall conclusion on Botha's reforms will be left to the next chapter, once the reaction to them has also been described, something of their 'performance' in relation to the government's aims has been implicit throughout this chapter. Botha had inherited a set of economic recommendations from Vorster's premiership, and had tried to implement them as part of a wider, political Total Strategy. But even a Total Strategy could not predict and accommodate the events which were to ensue when a continuing struggle against apartheid was combined with the partial reform of the system.

7

Policy and Reality

Introduction

Many of the Botha administration's reform initiatives either had repercussions which were unintended, or simply failed in their implementation. Rather than being determined solely by government policy, the course of South Africa's economic and political development in the 1980s was dictated by a complex welter of dynamic and unpredictable factors. Both in broad outline and in local implementation, central state aims were rarely achieved before they were undermined or overcome by unpredicted, violent events. In the 1980s, South Africa fulfilled the vision that Fanon held of Algeria some twenty years before: 'The violence of the colonial regime and counter-violence of the native balance each other and respond to each other in an extraordinary reciprocal homogeneity' (Fanon, 1963: 58).

The single most important reason why Botha's technocratic reformulation of apartheid failed to engender stability was that state policy was met in the mid-1980s by widespread township-based insurrection. The grievances behind black anti-apartheid mobilization on an unprecedented scale and the agencies and structures which helped mobilize black counter-state power, are the subject of the first section of this chapter. The second attempts to delineate the structural conflicts, between state and activists and between black organizations and tendencies, which combined to create the conditions of violence characterizing South African townships in the 1980s and early 1990s. The state's repressive response to insurrection, recent political developments in the homelands, and shifts in white attitudes resulting from the insurrection, are traced in the third section, providing the context for De Klerk's abandonment of apartheid structures.

1 Grievances and mobilization

In the 1980s, Botha's reformist government encountered vehement resistance to its very authority. While the structures of government could not possibly be overthrown, and outright armed rebellion was unlikely to develop in the South African context, from the mid-1980s, in specific places and for specific periods, the organs of the state were by-passed and displaced by popular township organizations. The events of August–November 1984, in the East Rand (Vaal triangle) townships of South Africa's industrial heartland are seen as a 'watershed in contemporary South African history' (Price, 1991: 184). These events, which, with hindsight, presaged the dismantling of apartheid (Terreblanche and Nattrass, 1990), manifested a fundamental shift in the balance of power away from the state and towards the black resistance movements.

Giliomee and Schlemmer (1989) have cited the government's own political initiatives as the partial cause of the rebellion. Botha's government embarked on reform just when the economy was beginning to resume its deterioration after the brief early-1980s reprieve. In the early 1980s, township inhabitants had been led to anticipate significant material improvements. Consequently, the sense of deprivation was relatively greater when significant material gains failed to materialize from the reform programme. In common with Louis XVI, Botha found that '[t]he most dangerous moment for a bad government is usually that when it enters upon the work of reform' (De Tocqueville, *The Ancien Regime*, Everyman Classics Edition, 1988).

The government expected to cover the costs of township upgrading from economic growth. Instead, the 1980s became a period of economic stagnation as OPEC oil-price rises, an Arab anti-apartheid oil embargo, international recession, a falling gold price and apartheid's own structural economic impediments took their toll on South Africa's economic vitality. From 1980 to 1986 GNP rose by under 4 per cent, while the population increased by over 12 per cent (Price, 1991: 159). It was therefore not only impossible to make good earlier material promises, but difficult to stop black living standards in general from falling. With rising inflation, leading to increased administration costs, Pretoria felt that it had no option but to make its township reforms self-financing. Many township councils in the late 1970s were already on the verge of bankruptcy and the BLAs would have to raise rents and service levies to cover their costs. In the early 1980s, greater and greater chunks of income being appropriated in rent became a salient feature of township life. In 1982 the situation was exacerbated as an International Monetary Fund (IMF) freeze on consumer subsidies led to a sales-tax increase which shifted the fiscal burden on to the poor (Lodge, 1992). Through the 1980s, the state progressively abandoned its housing provision for the poor. Allowing self-build shack schemes, like that of Khayelitsha outside Cape Town, as a substitute was effectively to privatize the poor housing market (David Smith, personal correspondence). The fact that the population of the townships was swollen by prolonged rural drought in the early 1980s, contributed to the groundswell of discontent (Lodge, 1992).

The Botha government's initial overtures to the wider world proved just as unreliable as its economic strategy. The 'organizational effervescence' (Price, 1991: 171) of the early 1980s was insignificantly hindered by the state as it sought to discard its repressive image and present a reformist image to international investors and foreign governments. Consequently, an 'organizational foundation for a sustainable multi-class nationwide movement of liberation' (Price, 1991: 160) was laid during the early years of Botha's premiership. Even when the state did react to black mobilization with repression, it was precisely those black leaders who could, and probably would have moderated developing forms of resistance, who were detained and restricted (Giliomee and Schlemmer, 1989).

Within the black communities, the earliest manifestation of a resurgence of defiance after 1976 came in township schools. For many, school was the primary point of contact with state restrictions and direct authority and, as in 1976, educational issues could not be isolated from the wider social and economic concerns of the township. With unemployment levels reaching 40 per cent among the African population by the late 1980s and 55 per cent of the African population being under twenty years old (Lodge, 1992), educational grievances became linked to wider mobilizational factors. The deteriorating conditions of education prompted the formation of the charterist Congress of South African Students (COSAS) and the BC-oriented Azanian Students Organization (AZASO) in 1979. The two organizations launched a schools boycott, beginning in Cape Town and, by 1981, spreading nationwide.

The most obvious grievances of the Cape Town students were a lack of books, broken windows, a lack of electricity and the summary removal of three popular teachers. Their discontent was exacerbated with the refusal to readmit pupils who had failed their matriculation exams and the use of SADF veterans in teaching roles. With such grievances widespread, the boycott developed into a popular response. In Cape Town, student placards had initially proclaimed 'Rights not Riots' (Western, 1982) and for the first month of protest there were no casualties. Then two Coloured children were shot dead as they stoned white vehicles at Elsies. The shootings served to polarize sentiments and, two weeks later, on the anniversary of the Soweto uprising, there was an almost total work stayaway in Cape Town, followed by large-scale civil unrest.

Wolpe (1988) charts the subsequent course of the schools boycott in the Pretoria area. It began in 1983 with the demand for free textbooks to be provided in class, better-qualified teachers, an end to corporal punishment and sexual harassment, and the recognition of elected Student Representative Councils (SRCs). In a climate of general township unrest, the movement spread and the SRCs extended their aspirations from reform to control over the education that Africans received.

By 1985, in South Africa as a whole, 650,000 students were receiving no education. The government's Department of Education and Training began closing schools, while the boycott's leaders were detained, harassed and, frequently, killed. In August 1985 COSAS was banned and the SADF began to move not only into the townships, but into the schools as well (for a local instance of the conflict this caused, see Kentridge, 1991: 104–9). What had begun as a boycott over specific educational grievances had mutated under the slogan 'Liberation First, Education Later', into a key component of insurrection. 'The boycott was no longer a tactic, it was a strategy' (Wolpe, 1988: 207).

This evolution was by no means wholly welcomed by the leaders of wider black resistance. The debate over the appropriateness of the schools boycott as a strategy to achieve a more balanced and equal education was a significant component of 1980s resistance politics, with many concerned at the prospect of a future generation of totally uneducated urban youth, and, more immediately, the perception that the boycott was a goal in itself, which meant that no benefit could be derived from its negotiated end. In the light of these concerns, a National Education Crisis Committee (NECC) was established by concerned parents. 'To the students' cry of "Liberation before Education" the NECC counterpoised the slogan "Education for Liberation"' (Price, 1991: 212). The NECC began writing new History and English curricula in 1986, and in Soweto and parts of the Eastern Cape, two days were set aside in some schools for an alternative education, the teachers being paid by the community. The envisaged education would be generally anti-capitalist in outlook. With this substitution of state structures by community ones, educational resistance entered the phase of insurrection. By the late 1980s, in the absence of state measures to conciliate, thousands of pupils remained outside school.

The causes of the schools boycott fed into wider township organization and resistance early on, and the wider insurrection had already started before the founding of the NECC. In the Western Cape, boycotting students directly helped to organize a community boycott of meat in support of striking workers. Soon after its inception, COSAS began to mobilize young workers and the unemployed as well as students. The boycott strategy itself was adopted in a wider range of actions, with a revival of the bus boycott in Durban and East London forcing capitulation over increased fares in 1982–83.

Within urban African communities, though, the most obvious generators of grievances in the mid-1980s were the BLAs. It was the experience of their administration which townships all over the country had in common and which served to mobilize a nationwide response to local grievances. The civic associations (civics) which articulated these grievances began as geographically limited, single- or few-issue organizations, but they developed as the skeleton of a national movement in black society. At first, in Soweto, local residents were organized informally in neighbourhood associations which petitioned the authorities over specific local grievances – rents, fares and removals in particular (Price, 1991). Such organizations extended into broad popular associations, initially in the Eastern Cape, Port Elizabeth and the Cape Peninsula (particularly in the Coloured areas). In addition to tackling local problems like transport, rents and poor recreational and child-care facilities, 'alternative' newspapers were published. The movements were frequently successful in fulfilling immediate community aspirations, for instance wielding local pressure to get shelters for commuter bus stops (Lodge, 1992). Wider political participation followed these immediate gains, but the shift to a popular mass base often occurred even where local organizations were less successful, as the government's rejection of their petitions prompted the formation of a more organized, formal civic group.

Police repression of the civic structures precipitated an extension of local grievances into anti-state politics in general. Continued local organization and alliance with parallel groups in other locations and other oppositional groups in the same locality allowed the civics, as an amalgam, to become a new mass political force, infusing a 'politics of refusal' among township activists and co-ordinating school, consumer, bus and rent boycotts as well as political stayaways.

The organizational cohesion for an alliance of such locally based structures of defiance had emerged in 1983, with the founding of the United Democratic Front (UDF) in response to Africans' exclusion from the new constitution. The UDF was an umbrella body which incorporated community organizations as affiliates in the immediate anti-constitution struggle. The state-sponsored election campaign for the BLAs allowed it space to campaign against their very existence as a substitute for national representation, but its longer-term objective was the development of a non-racial, unitary state. From its inception the movement was vaguely Charterist in philosophy and it adopted the Freedom Charter overtly in 1985.

The UDF's strength was derived from its interweaving of the various strands of resistance that township communities across the country had developed. Its founding conference included eighty-two civic, thirty-three student, 338 youth (many local branches of Congresses), eighteen worker, thirty-two women's, sixteen religious, twenty-seven political and twenty-nine other organizations (Price, 1991). 'From the vantage point of the state, the UDF was like a weed with deep roots' (Price, 1991: 179), and under UDF leadership, local and national political struggles became conceptually indistinguishable in the minds of many activists. Norval points out that 'it is only this form of [purposefully inclusive] politics which creates the conditions of possibility for the disarticulation of the dominant [exclusive, apartheid] discourse, and which can act as a "fermenting agent" for the dissemination of democratic demands into all areas of the social' (1990: 153).

By its very nature, as a front comprising many diverse units of organization, the UDF's membership contained competing perceptions and prescriptions. Brewer (1989b) identifies three main ideological tendencies within the Front. 'Nationalists' mobilized around the figure of Nelson Mandela – almost as a folk hero while imprisoned – and accorded the Freedom Charter a central place in the philosophy of the struggle. 'National Democrats' were more socialist oriented. For them, the Charter was a first step in a progression towards a socialist state, and the UDF's populism was a means to that end. The workers would be in the vanguard of this advance. This tendency was taken to an extreme by the 'Socialists' themselves, who interpreted apartheid as a particular form of Western-backed imperialism: 'Leninism may be dead in Eastern Europe but it is not dead in the townships' (Horowitz, 1991: 20). Many of the unemployed youth who supported the UDF adopted a political position towards this extreme. 'For them the millennial alternative held out by the ANC/South African Communist Party's "vulgar Marxism" [a phrase of Johnson, 1977] may be all the more compelling, removed as they are from the compromises and limited rewards of conducting their everyday existence within the labour process of a capitalist firm' (Brewer, 1989b: 227).

From outside the UDF, other influences penetrated the movement. While Africanists and BC sympathizers, who were philosophically opposed to the UDF's non-racial Charterism, remained separately organized, they had a significant ideological impact on the UDF's membership. Examples include the use of the word 'Black' to include all who are oppressed by race in South Africa, the preference for the term non-racialism over multi-racialism and the Africanist application of the word 'settler' to whites other than those who shifted their attitudes to become Africans too (Horowitz, 1991). These appellations

indicate more than just an influence over nomenclature; they represent
the infusion of a Black Consciousness/Africanist ideological stance
into mainstream Charterist politics.

To a greater extent than the ANC of the 1950s, the UDF of the
1980s incorporated specifically women's struggles in its agenda.
Membership of UDF-affiliated women's organizations, like the Federation of Transvaal Women, grew as women leaders emphasized the
overlapping of three spheres of oppression: race, class and gender.
South African social structure, it was pointed out, is organized so as to
inflict particular penalties on black working-class women: with racial
laws being applied to keep women and their reproductive potential out
of the urban areas and in the homelands, where paternalistic social
structures prevail; with women concentrated in the lower-paid sectors
of the economy – domestic service, agricultural and industrial shift
work – and clustering in the low-paying 'border' industries; with a lack
of maternity leave or benefit for many workers and with an almost
complete absence of child-care provision. Such pressures accounted
for the unprecedented success in the number of women mobilized and
integrated with wider political resistance. Nevertheless, a disproportionate number of women, compared with men, remained unpoliticized
during the insurrection, wishing merely to remain detached from
political strife.

The partial mobilization of a women's constituency was accompanied by that of an Indian constituency within the UDF. The Natal
Indian Congress was revived after its post-1960s decline, to help
organize a boycott of the elections for an advisory South African Indian
Council in 1981. An 8 per cent participation rate in the polls represented the first significant funnelling of local Indian anger into national
politics since the 1950s (Lodge, 1992). However, while the Natal and
Transvaal Indian Congresses aligned with the UDF, most Indians
preferred to remain apolitical, and 'the serious Durban anti-Indian
riots of 1949 and some much milder but threatening episodes in 1974,
1985 and 1990 have served to remind many Indians of the dangers
that have befallen Asian communities elsewhere in Africa' (Horowitz,
1991: 82). Many Indians went towards the opposite extreme of those
affiliating with the UDF, by withdrawing into political conservatism,
especially those who had accumulated significant material possessions.

In comparison, a greater proportion of Coloureds took part in
UDF-orchestrated insurrectionary acts. Horowitz puts this down to a
feeling of betrayal felt by Coloureds as a result of the injustices
imposed upon them by a state dominated by fellow Afrikaans-speakers,
in particular the massive forced removals they were subjected to in the
1960s. Yet, there was still a large proportion of the Coloured population

that could be considered apolitical, even in the midst of an insurrection.

Despite the variations in political mobilization, both within and between apartheid's racial groups, the UDF's campaign for Coloureds and Indians to boycott the national polls and for Africans to boycott those for the BLAs was largely successful. From November to December 1983, 21 per cent of registered voters participated in the BLA elections, while 18 per cent of Coloured and 20 per cent of Indian eligible voters took part in the Tricameral elections (Price, 1991: 183). These results encouraged the civics to extend their ambit so as to by-pass BLAs in as many respects as possible by developing alternative and informal systems of township management, extending even to informal courts. (However, as the level of township violence rose during the mid-1980s, the extent of national leaders' restraint over the activities of such bodies became questionable.)

More than the partial racial alliance (also including an unprecedented level of white anti-apartheid commitment) that the UDF represented, it was its potential for economic disruption that made it powerful. In the 1980s, black trade unions co-ordinated skilled and economically vital manufacturing workers, in addition to the unskilled and plentiful workers, that they had marshalled in the 1950s. '"Amandla ngawethu!" ("Power is Ours!") was a slogan inherited from the 1950s. Then it voiced an aspiration; in the 1980s it became an assertion' (Lodge, 1992: 30). The Federation of South African Trades Unions (FOSATU) was closely involved in the Vaal triangle rent boycott even before the more overtly political Congress of South African Trades Unions (COSATU) was formed. On a national scale, it was partially due to the formation of COSATU in 1985 that a record number of working days were lost in strikes between 1985 and 1987.

The progression of trade unions to a position of strength in the 1980s was also partly the result of the government's own reforms. The legalization and recognition of black trade unions, as advocated in the Riekert and Wiehahn Reports, were intended to bring their activities under control. In fact the trade union movement swelled as a result, from thirty-nine non-racial unions with 206,000 members in 1978 to 109 unions with 900,000 members in 1986, and strike activity doubled by 1980 and doubled again by 1982 (Price, 1991: 163–4). Far from restricting themselves to workplace issues, as the government anticipated, the unions became increasingly involved in the material and political concerns of the wider black community. 'Since race, not class has been the primary basis for social discrimination and economic deprivation in South Africa, the political appeal of multi-class coalitions seeking liberation from racial oppression is very powerful'

(Price, 1991: 164). Hence, many of the black trade unions could not help but become involved in struggles defined by the workers' and their community's race, as well as those on the shopfloor (see Lambert and Webster, 1988). In Uitenhage, for instance, from 1979 to 1981, Volkswagen shop stewards led the township civic association in a boycott of local suppliers.

With the formation of COSATU, the main body of black industrial trades unions joined the political struggle as affiliates of the UDF. Through the unions, not only permanently resident workers but migrants too, were mobilized, especially in the East Rand townships, over housing, removals, unemployment benefit and family rights. Brewer went so far as to say that 'today it is the black trades unions who present apartheid with its most serious political challenge' (1989b: 249), but it must be remembered that the unions' potential to wield power was increased through the economic impact of wider political turmoil and instability and the state's financial crisis. Apartheid's structural economic weaknesses rendered the government more susceptible to the pressure that black trades unions could bring to bear in the 1980s.

The UDF and its separate affiliates' organized political and economic opposition to the state went through a series of stages as campaigns were initiated, state countermeasures were responded to, and setbacks were suffered through the mid-1980s. The high-profile campaign against the Tricameral and BLA elections from November 1983 to August 1984 was met by the security forces with the detention of UDF leaders (see section three of this chapter). A shift towards more covert and locally based organization was thus forced upon the Front.

As it was driven 'underground', the movement's initiative was supplied more from below, particularly as its members were incorporated in the Vaal uprising in September 1984. It was 'the centrality of the issue of rents, and the perception of councillors as sellouts' that 'helps to explain why the first major violent confrontation occurred in the Vaal triangle' (Seekings, 1988: 71). Rents here had increased over 400 per cent from 1978 to 1983, the greatest increases in South Africa (Price, 1991: 159). The gap between the government's reformist-induced expectations and material reality was widening in these townships into an unbridgeable gulf, and into this highly charged atmosphere, the new constitution, excluding Africans from participating in central government indefinitely, was introduced. The revolt began with schoolchildren's attacks on official buildings and developed into a general rent boycott and a violent stayaway from work. By the end of the period of insurrectionist struggle (the story of which is continued when the state's response is considered below), the ANC was in a position to claim leadership of the anti-apartheid forces in negotiations with the government. That an externally based and banned organization was able formally to re-enter internal South African politics at the end of the decade on such advantageous terms was largely due to the ANC's popularity among those responsible for the insurrection, since 1983, inside South Africa.

Even in 1979, a shift away from the more racially exclusive institutions and ideology of the Black Consciousness movement (BC) and back towards the non-racial, inclusive ideology of the ANC was noticeable within South Africa (Lodge, 1992). The Freedom Charter was adopted by many of the organizations which proliferated in the early 1980s, and two prominent BC exiles – Barney Pityana and Tenjiwe Mtintso – joined the ANC in 1979. During the insurrection, slogans, songs, flags and the rhetoric of the ANC were all revived at popular meetings, and allegiance to the organization was expressed in various polls and surveys (Lodge, 1992: 43).

The causes of this allegiance were diverse. The fact that only the ANC's armed wing, Umkhonto we Sizwe (MK), offered significant guerrilla opposition to the state's security forces was a crucial factor: in 1979–80 a series of attacks on government buildings, police stations and infrastructure, forming the ANC's strategy of 'armed propaganda', culminated in the sabotage of the Sasolburg plant, which was of prime importance in converting coal to oil, of which South Africa was in relatively short supply; the execution of the ANC guerrilla Solomon Mahlangu in 1979 provided MK with a martyr; a generation of BC exiles from 1976 received training from MK due to the lack of a well-organized alternative, and the infiltration of these guerrillas back into the townships in the 1980s gave the ANC a widespread legitimacy denied to the other resistance organizations.

The non-racial philosophy also gained ground during the 1980s. What had been an unpopular ANC principle among many young Africans in the past, now became more legitimate. Adam and Moodley (1993) argue that, in the late 1980s, the ANC's tradition of non-racialism was one of its most attractive features. However, while non-racialism may have been influential in attracting the support of an intellectual and academic group, the ANC's real strength lay in mass township support. That support was not based on its enlightened non-racial philosophy; if anything, the natural predilection of township activists and youth was towards more exclusive and militant Africanism or socialism. What secured their support for the ANC was its role, via MK, as the only *effective* black opposition to apartheid, and indirectly its relatively successful diplomacy in exile.

Nevertheless, the inclusion of whites in the black trade union hierarchy helped to establish a greater perceived viability for class rather than racially based resistance, and thus legitimized non-racialism for a number of black activists. The publication, by white revisionist historians, of studies of the 1950s resistance campaigns contributed to the respectability of white involvement in the 'struggle', as, to a much greater extent, did the sacrifices of many whites actively involved in UDF opposition. The easing off of state repression in the post-Soweto climate of the late 1970s allowed the reappearance of a 'pantheon of ANC notables' (Lodge, 1992) in resistance politics, including the white Helen Joseph, Albertina Sisulu, Florence Mkhize of the 1950s anti-pass campaign, Steve Tshwete, Edgar Ngoyi and Henry Fazzie from Robben Island prison. All, on their return to public life, became involved in UDF-orchestrated resistance, consolidating perceptions of a continuity of resistance from the ANC heyday of the 1950s to the insurrection of the 1980s.

2 Conflicts and targets

The township insurrection of the 1980s was far more chaotic and less orchestrated than any linear account can convey. Townships have always been seemingly randomly violent places, with inhabitants afraid to travel alone at night due to the depredations of the tsotsis (local gangsters) and periodic bouts of faction fighting, in the context of material and psychological deprivation. But in the 1980s, the scale of the violence increased significantly, and it became endemic. Townships are still suffering from the round of violence associated with insurrectionary opposition to apartheid. While certain lines delineating conflicting parties can be drawn, the insurrection was marked by innumerable violent incidents which were only partially or had nothing to do with the major structural antagonisms in black society. The most evident structural conflict – that between the state and the black organizations which opposed it – is described first.

A picture of the pattern of 'unrest', as defined by the security forces, can be constructed from the police unrest report published by the *Cape Times* for four days in January 1986 (cited in Smith, 1987). The townships provided the focal points for unrest (twenty-five out of the thirty-four incidents reported). Two incidents were in homeland locations and only one in a white residential area. The targets of violence were overwhelmingly the property or persons of perceived 'sell-outs'. A typical police report is:

At Nyanga a councillor was killed when a group of people stopped his vehicle and set it on fire. ... At Soweto a policeman, who was injured when a hand-grenade was thrown at him, fired shots at the group and it is believed that one man was injured, but was taken away by the rest of the group (quoted in Smith, 1987: 82).

In December 1985, the Minister of Law and Order reported that twenty-seven policemen had been killed since September and the homes of 500 black police destroyed (Smith, 1987: 157). In total, 175 people were killed in 1984 and 800 in 1985.

From 1976 to the 1980s, there was an underlying shift in the targets of violence, from the physical structures of apartheid to the people who represented the 'system' (*The Times*, 27 May 1992). The influence of the co-optive strategy of Botha's government can be seen here, particularly the resentment generated by the workings of the state's representatives in the townships – the BLAs. The councillors on these authorities became the most visible and accessible components of the repressive 'system', and therefore the prime targets for acts of violence. The ostentatious spending on homes and cars of some councillors aggravated the community's hostility more than simply being a symbol of the state could. The councillors' perceived responsibility for the rent and levy hikes of the BLAs and their image as 'sellouts', 'traitors' or 'collaborators' ensured a level of antagonism sufficient for violent reprisals to be enacted by some, and condoned by many, in the townships. Attacks on 'collaborators' tripled between 1981–83 and 1984–86 (Price, 1991: 193). By July 1985, only five out of the thirty-eight BLAs were still functioning (Price, 1991: 197).

Apart from attacks on state symbols and representatives within the townships, two other salient aspects of insurrectionary activity stand out: the role of public transport and that of funerals. Given the structure of the apartheid city, public transport, servicing the white city centre with workers from the peripheral and externalized townships, 'symbolised oppression and subservience' (Pirie, 1992: 172). For millions of black South Africans, commuting to work is an 'everyday encounter with one of the most palpable creatures of apartheid' (Pirie, 1992: 172). The deplorable conditions on African trains and buses (particularly the long-distance carriers ferrying 'commuters' from the homelands) deepens the perception of public transport as an aspect of enforced inferiority. Public transport had always, like the townships themselves, been vulnerable to 'criminal' violence, including theft and organized gang muggings, murders and rapes. During the insurrection, though, commuter trains in particular became important and politicized meeting places, when other forums were closed off by the security forces. Carriages were used *inter alia* as churches, strike committee rooms and boycott organization centres.

In the private transport sector, the informal organization of minivan taxis (kombis or 'Zola Budds') became the focal point for independent African economic participation on the one hand (see Khosa, 1990), and for further conflict in the townships between rival operators on the other. The kombis were less prone to the orchestrated violence of the trains, but subject instead to the violently dangerous manoeuverings of their own unlicensed drivers. They became more popular, during the early 1990s transition, as commuter trains became the sites of massacres, largely by Inkatha and/or security 'third force' elements.

Much of the energy which drove forward the acts of outright resistance and rebellion in the townships during the mid-1980s was generated at township funerals. Funerals lay at the heart of a cycle of violence which seemed to take on a momentum of its own. The killing of an activist by the security forces or vigilantes aroused a determination to perpetrate further acts of rebellion in the dead comrade's name. These acts often resulted in further killings, perpetuating the cycle. The toyi-toyi – a chanting, rhythmic trot performed at funerals and at virtually all township gatherings – reinforced the solidarity and spirit of resistance of its participants and elevated the courage of the individual, who felt him- or herself as part of a formidable mass. The mass singing of the ANC's adopted anthem, *Nkosi Sikelel i' Afrika*, as part of a wider repertoire of resistance songs, gave a sense of bonding with the struggles of that organization's guerrillas against the state and helped reaffirm allegiance to the ANC itself.

Even in the general insurrectionary climate of the 1980s, older regional variations in the spirit of resistance remained:

> The continuities of Eastern Cape radicalism and the traditions of African nationalism have been symbolised by the banners of the banned ANC and CP of South Africa flying at the funerals of Matthew Goniwe and his associates in Craddock, an old nationalist centre; the strength of working class consciousness on the East Rand and also its ethnic division and violence have been equally demonstrated in recent events; while once again Natal after a period of relative quiescence has seen the backlash of conservative forces against vulnerable groups, in part a product of the politics of cultural nationalism. ... Deep rooted political traditions have been re-worked to meet the demands of a dramatically changing present. (Marks and Trapido, 1987b: 61–2)

The Vaal triangle, for reasons outlined above, became the arena for particularly intense conflict between police and other state symbols on the one hand, and UDF/ANC supporting 'comrades' on the other.

After state refusals to compromise on raised rents and levies, the Vaal civic association called for a strike which involved 60 per cent of workers and 93,000 students. A harsh police reaction initiated a month-long battle in which thousands of local activists were detained, sixty people killed, including four councillors and 30 million rand in property destroyed (Price, 1991: 184).

The Vaal uprising set the scene for a nationwide, low-intensity civil war, characterized by the varying regional expressions described by Marks and Trapido (1987b). J.M. Coetzee's novel, *Life and Times of Michael K* (1983) portrays particularly well the alienation felt by an individual in the strife-torn context of the eve of insurrection. As the insurrection developed, to nullify state power and create its *de facto* replacement by mass mobilization in certain portions of *de jure* state territory, it had some parallels with the Paris commune of 1871, Russia in 1905 and Hungary in 1956 (Price, 1991). But the areas in which the state momentarily lost control were restricted to townships outside the mainstream life of the most powerful white constituency. Within these areas the ANC's call to make the townships ungovernable was more reactive than proactive, since it was local inhabitants themselves who had displaced state control. Nevertheless, even Pretoria was admitting the existence of some 'no-go areas'.

Direct conflict between representatives of the state and black activists was, however, offset to an unprecedented degree by violence between different black movements and tendencies. The state attempted to divert as much attention as possible to these conflicts, and away from those between activists and the security forces. But they existed independently of the state's spotlight, and some developed, with apartheid laws revoked, into destabilizing fault lines which characterize South Africa in the early 1990s.

During the mid-1980s, horrific acts of violence were not just directed against 'sellouts' within the community, but also against followers of the 'wrong' line of resistance, and the divisions became more clearly delineated and etched into the fabric of township life in the insurrectionary climate. There were not only the old divisions of Africanist–non-racialist, national populist–'workerist', but also a heightening of disagreement over the acceptable degree of compromise with a government deliberately setting out to co-opt a strategic black social group. This disagreement flared between 'collaborationist' organizations like Inkatha, the 'Coloured' and Indian parliamentary parties and Sofasonke (the Soweto municipal party), as well as between them and the wider resistance movements. Within the unions there was disagreement over the mixture of plant and community struggles in which they should be engaged (see Lambert and Webster, 1988). Within the non-collaborationist organizations divisions continued over long-term goals, notably AZAPO's socialist Azania or the UDF/ANC's liberal-democratic state, and over the political and economic position of the white population in a post-apartheid order (Brewer, 1989b).

Behind these evident political differences lay other influences which pushed the expression of some of them towards violent conflict. In order to explain the translation of political differences into violence, one has to be aware of a context of local struggles over scarce resources, particularly land, the presence of a deprived, unemployed and politicized youth comprising a large segment of township populations, the prevalence of poor housing and the exploitation felt on an everyday basis by blacks in the workplace. These factors, combined with the social dislocation brought about by urbanization and, particularly, the breakdown of traditional family structure, are considered by Schlemmer (1991b) to be 'background conditions', shifting the likely expression of political or other difference further towards a violent extreme and eroding the normative restraints on murder. Superimposed on these conditions are 'predisposing factors' such as the social dislocation of rural migrants in the urban youth subculture (Adam and Moodley, 1993).

In this climate, professed political differences undoubtedly provided a pretext for some acts of violence which had more to do with the settling of personal scores and participation in crime (Lemon, 1991b). Overt political differences were often similarly superimposed on differences of ethnicity or of material status (particularly between formal township residents and informal squatters or migrant hostel residents). Once established, the violence often became self-perpetuating. While innumerable incidents of such violent conflict took place in all of South Africa's townships through the 1980s, two divisions stand out as being long-running and responsible for particularly heavy casualties: the conflict in and around Crossroads in the Western Cape in 1986 and that between Inkatha and the UDF/ANC in Natal from 1985 to the present, which had (and has) the most serious impact.

Xhosa migrants to the Western Cape, who were denied access to the formal housing of the townships, tended to form their squatter camps under 'chairmen' of squatter communities. In many cases these men were the literal descendants of traditional rural headmen and they exercised a similar kind of relatively autocratic rule over their communities. They were generally respected and feared and are often brutal in their implementation of authority. Despite a common profession of allegiance to the ANC, in line with most formal township activists, there were sharp differences between these activists and the squatters on the peripheries of the Langa, Nyanga and Guguletu townships (see Figure 4). Whereas the township residents were relatively literate, largely employed, and occupied basic, but at least formal housing, the adjacent squatters lacked these attributes and were often tenants of the formal residents. Similar differences delineated many of the conflicts between blacks in South Africa, but in Crossroads it was the influx of new squatters rather than the presence of a more privileged township population which triggered large-scale violence.

The government's response to the increasing incidence of squatting at Crossroads was the establishment of a new formal township at Khayelitsha and the extension of Section 10 rights to the inhabitants of the squatter camps with schemes to upgrade their conditions. However, greater numbers continued to arrive and settle, particularly in the KTC area. Those who had been granted Section 10 rights in Crossroads, and who were therefore being allowed to stay and consolidate their housing with government aid, became antagonistic to the influx of newcomers who threatened their new-found stability and their prospects of receiving housing assistance. The established residents were mobilized under the headman, Johnson Ngxobongwana. Ngxobongwana was soon recruited by the state to attack and destroy the new settlements around KTC so as to prevent further squatter-camp growth in the area. He pursued this goal with a 'vigilante' force known as the 'witdoeke' after the white scarves they wore. From May to June 1986, a small-scale war was fought between witdoeke and 'comrades' from KTC (Davenport, 1991). During the conflict, the comrades often found themselves opposed not only by Ngxobongwana's followers, but also by the state's security forces.

Ngxobongwana eventually founded a new camp at Drift Sands, which became his personal fiefdom. But his adherents were soon in conflict again with his successor as chairman in Crossroads, Jeffrey Nongwe, and the local ANC Youth Congress. The complex and dangerous situation descended further into chaotic instability with the emergence, in the late 1980s, of a taxi war between a squatters' Western Cape Black Taxi Association and the formal township's Lagunya Taxi Association, which was patronized by the local civic association. The conflict, involving petrol-bomb attacks and over seventy deaths, was waged over the disputed control of taxi routes crucial to urban African life. Since all the organizations involved in the Crossroads violence professed ANC sympathy, 'one begins to glimpse how little meaning political labels [could] have beside the more fundamental laws of squatter life' (R.W. Johnson, *Independent Magazine*, 10 August 1991).

Of all the individual conflicts that can be delineated in the 1980s, the conflict between Inkatha and the UDF in Natal was the most costly in terms of human life, being responsible for over 4,000 deaths.

In the 1990s the conflict became transplanted and diffused, as part of a wider struggle, in the Transvaal as well as Natal (see below). This most prominent, continuing conflict between black groupings in South Africa is more clearly defined by formally organized political structures, but even here the material conditions dividing peri-urban from urban residents, inter-generational cleavages and disparities in privilege and access to scarce resources have a strong motivational effect.

In the KwaZulu homeland, which is inter-digitated with Natal province, Mangosutho Buthelezi had, by the 1980s, established firm political control through the Inkatha organization. Inkatha's patronage was necessary for many of the requirements of everyday life in KwaZulu, particularly land, so most inhabitants of the homeland found it expedient to belong to the organization. But, crucially, Inkatha was also mobilized through a Zulu nationalist rhetoric, by which Buthelezi succeeded in instilling pride and dignity among many, mostly rural and peri-urban based, conservative Zulus (see Maré, 1992). The movement encountered its limitations more in the formal townships around Durban and Pietermaritzburg. Inkatha's unwillingness to let these urban areas fall under the influence of the increasingly popular UDF in the mid-1980s was the background cause of the conflict, which became endemic, between supporters of the two organizations.

To some extent, there was an earlier parallel to Buthelezi's conception of the political activity in these townships. From the 1840s to the 1870s, the Zulu kings Dingaane, Mpande and Cetshwayo had sought to prevent their subjects from crossing into the Natal Colony to the south where they would be outside their control. Many Zulus, though, had made the crossing, in an assertion of their freedom to marry the person of their choice, or simply in an attempt to set up as independent head of household (Brookes and Webb, 1987; Atkins, 1993). Just as Buthelezi saw himself as the inheritor of the traditions of these kings, so he resented the loss of authority that independent political organization by Zulu-speakers in the Natal or KwaZulu townships entailed. In the mid-1980s, as the township insurrection spread, the UDF's civic structures found themselves increasingly arrayed against the township councils and BLAs, over which Buthelezi's Inkatha exercised a regional monopoly. Buthelezi's 'moderate' resistance to apartheid, and his identification with the ANC, had ensured his popularity with most black South Africans during the 1970s, when he seemed capable of filling the vacuum left by the crushing of the BCM. His participation in the homeland structures was justified as opposition from within the system, and his refusal to accept 'independence' for KwaZulu could be interpreted in this light. But a dispute with the external ANC and his increasingly obvious, totalitarian grip on power within the homeland began to undermine his popularity with students and politicized youth in the late 1970s and early 1980s.

Flashpoints in the long and convoluted history of the war in Natal included the following: an early fight at the University of Zululand, where students opposing Buthelezi's participation in state structures were attacked, and Inkatha attacks on UDF-supporting, boycotting school pupils in 1980; the incorporation of the main Durban townships of KwaMashu and Umlazi into KwaZulu, and the initiation of the COSATU-backed SARMCOL strike, which was met by violence from Inkatha's rival United Workers Union of South Africa (UWUSA) in 1985; the suppression of the UDF civic organization in the Pietermaritzburg township of Imbali, also in 1985; and the forced recruitment campaign of Inkatha in 1987. But in between these specific instances of political conflict, violent encounters between Inkatha and UDF members were being perpetuated with attack and counter-attack, driven by a never-ending series of retributive raids. In many areas the political labels of Inkatha and UDF were superimposed on other divides between the warring parties: squatters versus formal residents, or older, more traditionally-oriented men versus township youth. Throughout, the conflict was characterized by the security forces' active or passive support for Inkatha. The KwaZulu homeland police (ZP), in particular, were very much identified with Inkatha.

Buthelezi's personal character has often been cited as an important factor in the continuance of the conflict: 'Chief Buthelezi does not appear to take the objectives of the various UDF and COSATU campaigns at face value ... [he] frequently claims that the actions of the progressive organisations are planned as a direct challenge to his political control over the region' (Kentridge, 1991: 221). He has often displayed his sensitive pride in the number of libel cases he has brought against such commentators.

The conflict in Natal grew from relatively discernible political cleavages through the 1980s into a chaotic and continuous series of seemingly indecipherable acts of terror. 'Every incident makes some sense at the micro level, but at the macro level matters are less clear ... [it is] not a case of normal life plus some fighting, but that "some fighting" [has] become normal life' (Kentridge, 1991: 14). The majority of the inhabitants in the region were non-participants in the fighting, but they were inexorably involved as intended or accidental targets on both sides of the conflict. The numbers of refugees seeking to flee the area was testament to the pain and disruption that the conflict caused. Tens of thousands were rendered homeless, and their ranks swollen by thousands simply seeking relief from the fighting and hoping to return to their homes shortly. An element in the interpretation of the conflict, always suspected, emerged more clearly during 1991, as the scale and content of the state's assistance to Inkatha, extending, it is likely, even to military training, was revealed with the 'Inkathagate' scandal.

Some clear parallels exist between the conflicts of the Western Cape and Natal, which cast light on the general conditions of strife in the black areas of South Africa. In both cases, the conditions in which the peripheral squatters found themselves, having to compete for scarce resources with a materially advantaged, established, 'insider' urban population, played a role in defining the parties to the conflict. In Natal, the 'insider' township group was, since the 1950s, associated with ANC urban resistance, and in the 1980s with the UDF civics. Inkatha, on the other hand, voiced Zulu migrant and squatter interests. Thus, political overtones developed to characterize a more universal socio-economic conflict (Adam and Moodley, 1993).

The form of social organization of relatively recent arrivals to the urban areas also differentiated them. In Crossroads, conflict with formal township residents was not the prime issue, but both here and in Natal squatters tended to be led by chiefs transplanted from quasi-traditional rural practice, while the comrades of the townships were of an entirely different political character, being urban, socialistic and radical. These lines of division were reinforced by a generational gulf. The older male squatters saw in the youth mobilization and politicization of the urban areas something of a defiance of the traditional paternalistic authority of the rural areas.

During the 1980s, the number of squatters near the major urban centres of employment rose inexorably. In the homelands a combination of severe drought, a decline in real migrant wages succeeding the 1970s increase, and large-scale unemployment following farm capitalization in the platteland, threw both single men and women and whole families off the land (Beinart, 1987). Where recently arrived squatters have their ethnicity, too, to set them apart from established residents, conflict over resources is all the more likely. 'The fighting between those identifying as Zulu and Mpondo just south of Durban in early 1986, in which over 150 died – the largest death toll in any single incident in the last couple of years – is one grim example' (Beinart, 1988: 145).

Apart from the distinction between newcomers and established urban residents, another clear dimension to both the Crossroads and the Natal conflicts was the role of the police. Police logistical and active military support was given, in both cases, to the traditionalist, anti-ANC/UDF party. This reflects a prominent security force view that such parties could be extremely valuable as surrogate forces in counter-insurgency action. 'The vigilantes were powerful allies of the South African state and could cripple or root out radical opposition

groups more effectively than could the police'; while Inkatha had a
genuine support base, generally the vigilante leaders 'lacked a compelling ideology and were unable to mobilize a popular and loyal social
base. Nevertheless the vigilante phenomenon in the 1980s demonstrated
the surprising extent to which the South African state was able to
enlist, at least intermittently, powerful allies from within the black
community' (Lodge, 1992: 169).

Active security force support for one side in the conflict was usually
complemented by inactivity on the part of the prosecution services
and the courts in charging and convicting known killers. In Natal,
several Inkatha 'warlords', many with relatively high positions in the
organization's hierarchy, were generally known to be responsible for
acts of intimidation and murder, and were permitted to remain at
large. On the other hand, no effort was spared by the police in hunting
down and detaining or killing members of the movements opposing
the vigilantes. But perhaps the most profound parallel between the
conflicts of Natal and the Western Cape was the fact that most residents in both areas simply wished to stay out of the firing line, wherever
their sympathies lay.

The government placed particular emphasis on the role of ethnicity
in the late 1980s. The obvious implication was that, in the absence of
continued white political supervision, a feuding, ethnically divided
African population could not be expected to elect a stable and sound
unitary government. Partly because of its association with state propaganda, the role of ethnicity in the violence of the 1980s has been by-
passed by many analysts who wished to preserve their anti-apartheid
credentials. Nevertheless, it has become more evident that there is an
important ethnic dimension to some of the recent conflicts.

While the commonly applied epithet of 'tribal violence' is eminently
unsuitable for conflict between politically, spatially and economically
divided modern groups, an ethnic cleavage can often become the most
clearly visible division between warring parties. The eruption of Zulu
migrant workers on to the streets of Soweto, attacking youths, particularly in the 1976 revolt, and the Zulu attacks on Mpondo migrants,
had a variety of causes associated with the alienation of rural migrants
in an urban context, but in the minds of the attackers, the alien
ethnicity of the victims was a most apparent characteristic of the
'enemy'.

In the Natal war, many of Inkatha's Zulu 'foot-soldiers' have been
galvanized more by the perception of the UDF/ANC as a Xhosa-
dominated organization (even though it is Zulu adherents that they
are fighting), than by the political motivations of their leaders. In
1985, Shangaan and Pedi fought over the boundary between their

respective homelands, Gazankulu and Lebowa. Then in 1986, Ndebeli fought Pedi over a plan to incorporate the Pedi Moutse area, outside Pretoria, into the KwaNdebele homeland (Horowitz, 1991). The 1990s extension of the Inkatha–UDF/ANC war from Natal into the Transvaal brought a clear ethnic dimension to the conflict which was absent in the overwhelmingly Zulu Natal, as Zulu migrant workers carried Inkatha's offensive into the Xhosa-, Sotho- and Tswana- (as well as Zulu)-speaking communities of the Vaal region.

All of these conflicts involve political, social, economic and geographical differences as well as ethnic distinctions. Many have also involved security force fomentation, but 'the fact that ethnic affiliations were available for manipulation or encouragement suggests that ethnic violence is not just the product of the state's action in setting one group against another, but reflects the continuing importance of ethnicity' (Horowitz, 1991: 74).

3 State repression, homeland coups and white responses

In 1985, the year after the insurrection had begun in the Vaal triangle, Botha hinted that announcements introducing common citizenship and a relaxation of the pass laws would be made in a forthcoming speech to the Natal Provincial Congress of the NP. Such was the level of anticipation that the speech was transmitted live on television in the US, the UK and Germany. It turned out to be not only an anticlimax, but the guarantor of deep international disillusionment with Botha's reformism. His tone throughout the speech was defiant and defensive, and no concrete new initiatives were introduced. He pointedly refused to 'lead white South Africans and other minority groups on a road to alienation and suicide' (quoted in Barber and Barratt, 1990: 322). Western opinion was struck by his insensitivity at a time of severe crisis for South Africa's internal and external political relations. It appeared that Botha had drawn back from his promised 'crossing of the Rubicon' due to fear of an internal conservative reaction and personal resentment at external advice (Barber and Barratt, 1990: 323).

Botha's Rubicon speech, provoking rather than deterring international sanctions, was significant for the state's response to the township rebellion. It revealed a change in government thinking. In the light of domestic instability, which would preclude economic recovery anyway, the government partially forsook its previous policy of mollifying international investors and governments, and oriented itself more towards internal repression. Its subsequent restrictions on the reporting of the unrest were intended to limit the damage by hindering a full overseas awareness of the domestic situation, but they could not prevent a knowledge of the repressive measures that existed. The day following the speech, South African share prices plummeted and the rand fell 44.5 US cents. The Stock Exchange was closed and restrictions were placed on outward capital flow. The speech provided the cue for Chase Manhattan's precedent in refusing to roll over maturing short-term loans (prompted by shareholder, client and public interest group pressure in the USA). A Commonwealth Eminent Persons Group recommended government sanctions in 1986, having been alienated, while still on its visit to South Africa, by SADF raids on Gabarone, Harare and Lusaka ANC bases (see *Mission to South Africa: The Commonwealth Report*, Penguin, 1986), and the US Comprehensive Anti-Apartheid Act, forced through President Reagan's opposition by Congress, provided for further government-imposed economic sanctions.

In the wake of the speech and its indirect international reaction, the South African state threw its full weight behind domestic repression. Botha's National Security Management System (NSMS) was used as the primary vehicle for crushing the insurrection. An integrated strategy was pursued with, on the one hand, security forces seeking, detaining or 'destroying' the enemy (establishing a pattern that the recent NP leadership found it hard to curtail), and, on the other hand, a continuation of some material improvements to remove the socio-economic basis for black alienation. 'Hearts and Minds' propaganda, borrowed from the military, and 'counter-organization' at the local level to displace the civics completed the strategy (Price, 1991).

As an example of the 'positive' wing of counter-strategy, the Atlantis Coloured township in the Western Cape received food parcels and soccer tours for its children from the local Joint Management Committee (JMC). Pamphlets and newspapers publicized such benign state activities and accorded the credit to local 'Coloured' politicians who worked within state structures. In Alexandra, new homes and utilities were constructed in 1989, and BLA councillors were given the credit.

Meanwhile, the 'negative' aspects of the state's reaction involved the use of treason and subversion laws against UDF members and the outlawing of the NECC and its alternative schools courses (Price, 1991). In the townships, the police had their ambit of repressive measures excessively widened to enable them to conduct war against the UDF. The 1986 State of Emergency Regulations allowed first police commissioners, then non-commissioned officers, in all branches of the police to restrict the movements and access of people, or confine or remove them, and to control services, protect installations and distribute or withhold information. There was no public right to seek court interdicts restraining police personnel from such measures, and such acts were carried out with blanket indemnity (Davenport, 1991).

Police intervention in the townships was supported by the SADF (who were often preferred by the residents for their relative moderation, many being conscripts rather than volunteers for such duties). To assist further in rooting out activists, black municipal police were recruited with brief training. Labelled 'kitskonstabels' or 'instant constables', they were put at the disposal of the black councillors. The kitskonstabels were often recruited rurally so that they lacked affinity with the township communities, and they rapidly established a reputation for extreme brutality.

In 1985, 8,000 UDF leaders were detained. The state's action resulted in the removal of most of the organization's national and regional executives, if not directly, then indirectly through assassinations or emigration. The intelligence which enabled such measures was gathered by Botha's JMC surveillance and filtered upwards through the NSMS. In 1986, a further 9,000 were detained in eight months. This figure was twelve times that of the Soweto period. Of the detainees, 40 per cent were under eighteen years old, most being members of street or area committees. The second largest category was that of members of the 'people's courts' (Price, 1991: 258). As well as being detained, UDF members were banned or restricted and COSATU was prevented from engaging in 'external political activities'.

Behind the overt clamping down on township political activity lay a shady and nebulous network of state structures responsible for a campaign of harassment, disruption and assassination. The most notable of these bodies was the Orwellian-named Civil Co-operation Bureau (CCB), set up to direct hit squads against civilian targets. At the start of 1989 there had been 113 attacks, including bombs, arson and burglaries, against opposition organizations, with not one arrest following. Another aspect of the covert war was the use of the surrogate or 'vigilante' forces whose role has been examined in the Western Cape and Natal contexts. Other than the witdoeke and Inkatha 'warriors', smaller bands of vigilantes like the Ama-Afrika in Kwanobuhle, near Uitenhage, were recruited from ranks of township groups that lost out in the insurrection. Such groups included black policemen, gangsters, small businessmen, traditional headmen and disaffected UDF members (the numbers of which grew as the UDF punished those responsible for the loss of community support through bullying), as well as squatters denied formal township privileges. A number of township residents were also disillusioned when their perceived right not to participate in political action was abrogated by militant activist pressure, applied to ensure conformity in 'the struggle'.

By mid-1987, a veneer of order had been returned to the townships. Yet, while overt insurrectionary activity had largely been halted, the UDF's grassroots substructure remained latently powerful. A liberatory, rather than co-opted political atmosphere could still be sensed in the townships, where there was 'utter hostility and cynicism toward the government and its overtures' (Price, 1991: 266). The 1988 township elections were effectively boycotted (only 10 per cent of eligible voters cast ballots), with over half the council seats going uncontested and no candidates at all offering themselves for 138 seats. While the state had prevented a loss of official political power to the UDF, it had failed to secure its own legitimacy or consent for, or even the functionality of, its own structures.

Rent strikes continued and trade unions could not be repressed with the vehemence directed against the UDF, given their role in the fragile economy. In June 1988, COSATU launched the biggest stayaway in South African history in commemoration of the Soweto revolt. A three-day general strike was 70 per cent effective in the manufacturing sector, and cost 500 million rand (Price, 1991: 267). In spite of the unions being made legally accountable for illegal strikes in February 1988, the government was still unable either to destroy or co-opt them.

It was also difficult for the government to stem the growing swell of church opposition, as ministers like Desmond Tutu, Allan Boesak and Frank Chikane stepped into the gap created by UDF suppression and spoke out against the government. Even the most conservative of the three Dutch Reformed Churches admitted the sin of apartheid. Meanwhile, a detainees' hunger strike was launched with 600 participants. As 100 were taken to hospital in a serious condition, international attention intensified and fear of their deaths prompted the government to withdraw from the use of large-scale detention without trial. The year 1988 saw more guerrilla activity than any preceding year and the schools boycott was perpetuated with over 90 per cent of pupils absent in the Western Cape (Price, 1991). The state's own black councillors began to demand the unbanning of resistance organizations and the release of political prisoners, in order to offer some sense of identity with the township communities and to avoid the continued dangers of a 'collaborationist' tag (Price, 1991). Finally, a new resistance front – the Mass Democratic Movement (MDM) – was formed in the late 1980s, backed prominently by church and trade-union figures, to take over where the UDF had left off – with a fresh mass defiance campaign.

The scale and cost of the repression required to restore even surface calm in the townships was a significant incentive for the new NP leadership to open negotiations with the ANC. The bureaucracy developed to implement Botha's Total Strategy was in itself enormously costly. In East London, central-government policy was being filtered through twenty-seven Working Committees, three Regional Advisory Committees, nine Joint Working Committees, one Regional Liaison Committee, several *ad hoc* task teams and an Eastern Cape Strategic Team (Lemon, 1991b). Under these multitudinous structures,

> order has been restored, but with the probable deployment of one-third to one-half the standing army in the townships it is likely that the fiscal strain of sustaining white supremacy is to be much greater than in the past ... it is very unlikely that the republic will ever again, under its present rulers, restore its outward façade of political confidence and economic vigour. (Lodge, 1989: 226–7)

With the continuance of almost complete township non-co-operation, the late 1980s were marked by unprecedented local negotiations between township resistance organization representatives and local white government officials and businesspeople. Representatives of Soweto's rent boycotters, for instance, went through arduous and complicated negotiations with the Johannesburg municipality and local businesses, which resulted, by 1991, in a *modus operandi* for their future co-operation (for details, see Young, 1989 and Swilling and Shubane, 1991).

Around the end of the decade, though, the government had to respond not only to the state of insurrection in the townships, but also to significant changes in the political composition of the homeland governments. Overall, these changes comprised a loss of the state's firm grip over the political process in rural areas to complement the outcome in urban areas.

In the Transkei, a coup led by General Bantu Holomisa in 1987 ended the rampantly corrupt rule of the Matanzima brothers. Bell (1988) suggests that Pretoria approved of the intervention, since it soon recognized the new government. However, Holomisa's overt ANC sympathies soon brought him into dispute with the South African government. In October 1989 he raised the issue of Transkei's reincorporation into South Africa and in October 1991 his government became part of a brief, ANC–PAC-led 'Patriotic Alliance' (Humphries and Shubane, 1991).

A coup also took place in Bophuthatswana in February 1988. This time, though, Pretoria swiftly intervened to restore 'Life President' Mangope to power. The South African government's response was provoked by possible ANC involvement in the coup and the fact that Mangope's regime controlled the most economically successful of the homeland states. Even with the later unbanning of the ANC, the

Bophuthatswana administration continued to ban pro-ANC demonstrations in the homeland and, in alliance with Inkatha and right-wing whites, it sought a regional role under a new constitution.

The Ciskei coup of 1990 displaced Lennox Sebe, who had assumed the title of President upon 'independence'. As with the Transkei coup, it was led by young army officers opposed to corruption, and it went unopposed by Pretoria. Initially, the new leadership's rhetoric followed Holomisa's, being critical of the homelands' continued existence as separate entities. However, once the new president, Brigadier Oupa Gqozo, was established, he began to reveal a hostility to the ANC and to enthuse over a new constitution and Bill of Rights for his 'subjects' – developments which somewhat contradicted his earlier professed desire for reincorporation. October 1992 saw Ciskeian armed forces open fire on pro-ANC demonstrators at the border of the territory, and revealed the administration's final conversion to a desire to hold on to the reins of power within the homeland. Yet another military coup installed General Gabriel Ramushwana as the new head of the Venda state for the beginning of the decade. He too, professed a desire for reincorporation.

Even in the 'self-governing' states, which were under more direct South African government control, unrest developed in the second half of the 1980s as inhabitants pressed for reincorporation. Incidents occurred in Gazankulu, KwaNdebele and Lebowa, where the local ANC was critical of Ramodike's presidency despite his expression of support for the movement (see Lodge, 1992). By the early 1990s, the Kangwane leadership had already started preparations for reincorporation and Qwa Qwa seemed favourably inclined to it (Humphries and Shubane, 1991). Only Buthelezi among the self-governing homeland leaders claimed a place in post-apartheid national politics, but while he was certainly able to ensure instability in the event of his exclusion, his position had been undermined, both internally and internationally, by Inkatha's increasingly evident use of violence, the resignation of Oscar Dhlomo, Inkatha's respected Secretary General and the Inkatha-gate scandal of 1990–91.

The general shift of homeland leaderships away from a position supportive of Pretoria and towards a profession of sympathy for the ANC represented a recognition of the wider shift in the balance of power. That homeland leaders first should want to proclaim support for the ANC and reincorporation and secondly, should be allowed by Pretoria to do so, indicates the extent to which the South African government's systems of managing political, economic and social developments had become ineffective by the end of the 1980s. Indeed, while there was no possibility of the state being overthrown, it seemed that the government had given up hope of maintaining internal order without a state of emergency.

The state's own white constituency was not as aware of the sea change that had taken place in the balance of power, both in the homelands and in the townships, as some politicians in the NP were. It is a remarkable feature of the insurrection that the sector of the population in whose interests the systems under attack had been formulated, generally knew little of the nature of the attack or of the detailed state of affairs in nearby black areas. This phenomenon is testimony to the remarkable degree of spatial structuring which lay at the core of South Africa's political system. Whites were relatively politically insulated because they were spatially cocooned. However, despite a general lack of first-hand experience of the insurrection (other than among security force personnel, including conscripts), developments in the townships did have a more subtle impact on the white population's sense of security. By the late 1980s, a general psychology of fear could be discerned in the white areas, and it was exacerbated by the increasing incidence of 'non-political' violent crime directed at whites by blacks.

On the one hand, 'concentrated in the incompletely controlled distant periphery and African formal townships the conflict plays itself out beyond the experience and out of sight of the white metropolitan core' (Lemon, 1991b). In Pietermaritzburg, while pitched battles took place between residents of the formal Imbali and the informal Slangspruit settlements, culminating in SADF intervention, white residents less than a kilometre away, separated by a Group Areas Act buffer strip, went about their daily lives with only the presence of African women and children refugees in the streets and garden shelters of sympathetic households as indicators of the strife nearby (Wills, 1991: 102). J.M. Coetzee's novel, *Age of Iron* (1990) portrays the average level of white awareness:

> ... of trouble in the schools the radio says nothing, the television says nothing, the newspapers say nothing. In the world they project all the children of the land are sitting happily at their desks learning about the square on the hypotenuse and the parrots of the Amazonian jungle. What I know about events in Guguletu depends solely on what Florence [the African maid] tells me and on what I can learn by standing on the balcony and peering northeast: namely that Guguletu is not burning today, or if it is burning, is burning with a low flame. (1990: 36)

On the other hand, literary descriptions like this have in themselves provided 'another challenge to the bland assurance of the state' (Gunner, 1988: 231), and no matter how stringently the government censored news reports of the townships, an awareness of the political and economic instability into which South Africa was descending could not help but filter through to the white population. Despite their geographical separation, and their media insulation from the insurrection, the white sense of physical well-being and security was gradually undermined, especially when ANC bombings increased the rate of white civilian casualties from three in 1982–84, to 118 in 1984–86. '"White" South Africa began to take on the trappings of a society under siege: public buildings were sandbagged and barricaded, metal detectors were installed at the entrance to supermarkets and periodic bomb blasts shattered windows in busy downtown streets or crowded suburban shopping centres' (Price, 1991: 236).

The growing white sense of insecurity was manifested in the emigration figures: 8,500 *per annum* up to 1984, in 1985, 11,401 and in 1986, 13,711. In 1987, 57 per cent of the white male students of Rhodes University had either decided to leave South Africa or were contemplating it, largely due to its political instability and conscription for township duty. In 1989, one-quarter of the draft applied for deferment of service and 15 per cent failed to report. Thirty-eight per cent requested exemption from township duty (Price, 1991: 238). The End Conscription Campaign became a growing force among disaffected whites, until it was denounced by Defence Minister Magnus Malan as a national threat.

The threat that the insurrection posed to white security undoubtedly contributed to a long-term shift in white political outlook. In 1970, 70 per cent of MPs and 60 per cent of voters had supported a 'pure' apartheid line (that is, the NP or HNP). The remainder (UP) favoured a move away from apartheid, but with continued white political control. By 1989, the NP had itself moved to this position and it now commanded 57 per cent of parliamentary seats and 48 per cent of the vote. But a further 20 per cent of seats and votes went to the Democratic Party (DP), which adopted a position further towards 'majority rule'. This gave the 'reformist' parties combined 77 per cent of the seats and 68 per cent of votes. The 'pure' apartheid line which had been dominant in 1970 was now upheld only by the CP and, insignificantly, by the HNP, the CP having 23 per cent of MPs and 30 per cent of voters (Price, 1991: 224). Even so, a 1988 survey showed that 80 per cent of white urbanites still associated majority rule with physical threat and impoverishment (Price, 1991: 244). Therefore, what seems to have underlain the white electorate's shift towards a more reformist stance was not the desire for a transformed socio-political future, but that for a return to stability. In this context, the NP's tough security policy proved an attraction for voters in the 1987 general election. Even the most 'radical' of the white parliamentary parties – the DP – proposed that a future black-dominated central government should have its power to transform wealth distribution limited under a federal system.

Conclusion

Botha inherited the recommendations of the Riekert and Wiehahn Commissions set up by his predecessor to deal with the increasingly apparent economic/spatial contradictions of apartheid. Out of their reports arose a strategy of co-option, by which white economic and political superiority would be maintained within white space as apartheid was adjusted to modern economic reality. In alliance with capital, the state would ameliorate conditions for black urban 'insiders' to ensure smoother economic development, while securing their gains from competition by effecting new 'market' forms of influx control (Stadler, 1987). Industrial decentralization would also help to limit further growth of the urban African group.

Wider political reforms would ease South Africa's international isolation and establish greater internal stability. But the Tricameral Parliament and Black Local Authorities proved largely politically unacceptable, and when they were superimposed on an economic situation which was deteriorating despite decentralization and urban reform, the result was far from co-option. The rhetoric of reform had, in itself, raised expectations which a deteriorating economic situation rendered it impossible to fulfil. Instead, the experience of impoverishment became all the more acute as the gulf between expectations and reality widened. Popular mobilization ensued. With a powerful economic and political role being played by the black trade unions, and with black urban communities refusing to pay the costs of their own administration, the state's initiatives were met with insurrection. A new ideology of resistance had emerged, linking local and national political and economic grievances, and, with UDF direction, a coherent challenge was offered to the state's very presence in the townships (Price, 1991).

The extent of the challenge was sufficient to cause concern even to its initiators and beneficiaries. In achieving the ungovernability of the townships, a 'brutal anarchy' (*The Times*, 27 May 1992) became established. United Democratic Front and ANC leaders were aware of how the insurrection not only destabilized the South African state, but precipitated capital flight which could last longer than white minority rule. Political and economic instability did not just help bring the government to the negotiating table – it also rendered millions of young blacks brutalized and, perhaps, unemployable.

As UDF-orchestrated internal resistance mounted, Botha's administration was increasingly influenced by the security establishment, with its perception of Total Onslaught. A dual reform–repress strategy was formulated to counter the insurrection, and the shift of government thinking became evident in Botha's Rubicon speech. In the mid to late 1980s, repression became the dominant theme, interspersed with periodic reforms which helped only further to undermine the coherence of apartheid.

In an unstable political and economic environment, De Klerk assumed the presidential office as leader of a reformist bloc within the party. He was more genuinely aware of business interests than Botha had been and he recognized the need for negotiations with legitimate black representatives, notably the revived ANC, to break international isolation, particularly as the MDM launched its new defiance campaign, and as white psychological security continued to decline.

8

The Changing South African State

Negotiations and elections

This chapter narrates the developments in South African politics since De Klerk's assumption of the presidency. Particular attention is paid to the reasons why the South African executive departed from established policy conceptions and initiated negotiations with the ANC. There follows a guide to the course of those negotiations and the historic elections with which they culminated. Finally, the current extent of social and spatial inequality and the prospects for their diminution are discussed.

Botha resigned as party leader after a heart attack in 1989, but with the intention of retaining the presidential position. However, De Klerk, as the new leader of the party, began to accumulate support for this position too. 'Once De Klerk became party leader, the government was largely paralysed by the simmering conflict between Botha and De Klerk and by the need to prepare for the white election that was to be held in September 1989' (Schrire, 1992b: 112). Pressures mounted on Botha's presidency, including the nationwide campaign for the release of detainees, the Mass Democratic Movement's (MDM) defiance campaign and the formation of a new, reformist Democratic Party. These developments alone conspired against Botha's continuation as president, but when they were accompanied by the retirement of key Botha supporters and NP 'thinkers', including Chris Heunis, he realized that he had no option but to resign, which he did, with ill-concealed bitterness, in August 1989. He retired from the party altogether in May 1990.

His successor almost immediately presented a dramatically different and reformist image to the world. His personal transformation was no less remarkable than that which he proposed for the country as a whole. In the mid-1980s, De Klerk had been considered a conservative within the NP and he had certainly declared publicly his support for the maintenance of apartheid institutions. Nevertheless, the release from prison of prominent ANC members, including Walter Sisulu, presaged a speech to Parliament in February 1990 in which De Klerk announced the unbanning of the ANC, PAC and SACP, the removal of restrictions on the UDF and COSATU, an end to the practice of banning individuals, the lifting of the state of emergency and restrictions on the media, and the suspension of the death penalty. Ten days later, after twenty-seven years in prison, Nelson Mandela was released. In June 1991, the Group Areas Act, Land Acts, Population Registration Act and Reservation of Separate Amenities Act were repealed, ending statutory apartheid. The NP set about recruiting black members and almost half the Coloured MPs in the House of Representatives joined the party. The pace of the changes even took members of the party caucus by surprise (Morris, 1991: 55–6).

Explanations for these changes have ranged between two extremes. On one side are the analysts who claim that De Klerk's government had no option but to engage in negotiations with the ANC, due to South Africa's dire economic position and the failure of all preceding attempts to restore political stability and order (Price, 1991; Wolpe, 1988; Lodge, 1992). The reification of the geographical concept of white space had also obviously failed, with squatter communities bridging the gaps between most metropolitan areas and the homelands which served them with labour. The influence of this evident spatial contradiction has often been underestimated by political commentators who are wont to see political struggles being enacted in some kind of ethereal vacuum. The fact that 'on the ground', in front of the observer's very eyes, space supposedly reserved for white use was blatantly inhabited by blacks, must have been significant in the general loss of apartheid morale. On the other side are those who perceive South Africa's economic situation to have been at least sustainable, and continued political repression to have been possible in the medium term, although they have little to say about the contested occupation of space. According to this perception, De Klerk's moves towards negotiation were more contingent on particular domestic and international developments, making negotiations propitious in 1990. An entry into negotiations at this point, rather than later, would render them far more likely to progress in the government's favour (Schlemmer, 1990, 1991b; Schrire, 1992b). Nevertheless, it is unlikely that the government would have seized the opportunity to negotiate, however propitious, unless previous initiatives to maintain white political, spatial and economic superiority and stability had failed.

If negotiations were taken up merely as one of a range of options, that range had narrowed considerably by the time that De Klerk

assumed the presidency. Friedman (1991) points out that for negotiations to have been entered into while the government was still able to
remain in power without them, the government must have concluded
that the costs of maintaining the *status quo* were not worth paying, and
that it had a reasonable prospect of defending its core interests in a
new system. Conversely, those excluded from power must have
concluded that they could not overthrow the state in the foreseeable
future, but that it was possible to achieve through negotiation an order
qualitatively different from the prevailing one.

If negotiations were begun partially as a positive step due to propitious timing, they were also partially the negative result of the closing
off of other options for maintaining white minority rule in the long
term. Apartheid, even Botha's 'reformist' brand, had remained viable
only as long as certain conditions persisted: '1. the South African
economy continued to be dynamic and growth oriented; 2. black South
Africans acquiesced in white rule; 3. the international community was
prepared to trade with and invest in South Africa; and 4. white South
Africans remained broadly united and cohesive' (Schrire, 1992b: 8).
To these, I would add a fifth: apartheid's conceptual separation between
white and black space was manifest. Each of these conditions was
patently unsustainable by 1990.

Narrowing political options

The adaptations made to apartheid structures since the 1960s had all
failed to accommodate its political, spatial and economic contradictions.
The NP's Separate Development or 'multinationalism' of the 1960s
and 1970s and Botha's 'selective incorporation' of a black urban middle
class in the 1980s, had been ineffective in the face of continued internal
political resistance, economic constraints and international hostility.
By the late 1980s there was little momentum remaining in Botha's
securocrat strategy. It had been rendered impotent largely by the
insurrection. The NP government had run out of options for further
adapting white minority rule to changing internal and external political
and economic environments:

> Herein lies the dilemma facing [Botha's] regime: Shut off from the
> possibility of a coercive solution it can only hope to stabilize the political
> situation through reforms which will win support from important con-
> stituencies among black people. However, given the configuration of
> white interests, notwithstanding the reformist postures of corporate
> capital and others, it can offer only extremely limited reforms. Since
> those reforms are concerned with black representation and not merely
> with redistribution by way of education, wages, housing and so forth,

they necessarily provide the political conditions for a [continuing] resurgence of the mass democratic movement. (Wolpe, 1988: 109)

The reforms themselves then, generated further political and economic
instability.

In order to transcend this unsustainable situation, negotiations
leading to concessions beyond those heretofore acceptable to the 'configuration of white interests' (Wolpe, 1988: 109) would be necessary.
And the resurgence of resistance which occurred in 1989 helped usher
in this realization. The MDM's new defiance campaign was launched
in the context of the resegregation of public amenities by Conservative
Party councils. White hospitals became the first target and black
protesters were admitted for treatment. The protests remained peaceful
until police killed at least twelve protesters in Cape Town, precipitating
a stayaway by three million workers in September 1989 and a march
by 35,000 (the largest ever) through Cape Town, with similar pro-
cessions in other cities. The choice of segregated hospitals as a target
for demonstration, and of schools as the subject of verbal protestation,
was shrewd. As the costs of maintaining their segregation mounted,
many whites were coming to favour integration within these institutions. The closure, through under-use, of white hospitals and schools,
contrasted sharply and evidently with the continuing overcrowding of
corresponding black facilities. The government's response to the
decision by some white schools to admit black pupils was muted, since
it was already considering integration if the majority of parents voted
for it. This policy was subsequently effected.

In contrast to the mid-1980s, when 'the insurrectionary movement
was being pulled into uncharted courses by cadres of youth in the
streets of the townships, the popular protest in the late 1980s was
choreographed and coordinated and seemed much more under the
command of its leaders' in the MDM (Lodge, 1992: 114). The revival
of organic resistance soon after the state felt relatively secure of its
suppression of the mid-1980s uprising, emphasized the continuing
instability that could be expected in the absence of significant political
change. Further, as Price (1991) points out, each successive peak episode
of resistance – Sharpeville, Soweto, the 1984–86 insurrection – had a
larger mass base, was more politically radical, lasted for a longer period
and produced more costly international isolation. After each peak, the
level of domestic political militancy did not return to the *status quo ante*,
but remained higher. There was therefore a kind of cumulative effect of
the main episodes of unrest on South Africa's international standing.
The time lag between periods of major unrest was also diminishing, and
the organizational capacity growing during each successive period,

contributing to a gradual, but perceptible decline in the quality of life for whites, both materially and psychologically (Price, 1991).

The state had not only lost the political initiative that Botha had been confident of in dealing with internal resistance on a national scale, it had also lost the control of local black administration that it had exercised through surrogate structures. By March 1991, about forty informal civic associations were already involved in negotiations with provincial authorities, stepping into the local vacuum left by the insurrectionary rejection of the BLAs (*Anti-Apartheid News*, March 1991). An agreement in January 1991 to establish a Metropolitan Chamber for the central Witwatersrand area, covering both Johannesburg and Soweto, was the outcome of the lifting of the township rent boycott in return for the writing off of arrears and the resumption of services at locally negotiated tariffs. It set a precedent for local government negotiations with civic structures across the country, accompanying central government moves towards negotiations with the ANC. The local developments represented a profound shift in the balance of political power towards black organizations, further restricting the range of options available to the government at the centre.

That range of options was also effectively constrained by shifts in political attitude within the government's white constituency. The 1989 white election made it clear that a continuation of Botha's policies would lead to further erosion of NP support to both the left and the right. On the left, a larger, relatively wealthy Afrikaans class, some elements of which formed an intelligentsia, had emerged. It was both socially and economically upwardly mobile, and a creature of the big cities (Schlemmer, 1991b: 20). This class, an extension of the 1970s verligte tendency, now showed a greater propensity than ever to vote towards the liberal left wing in white elections. The NP could only encompass these voters by itself shifting further towards this extreme, so as to occupy ground held formerly by the Progressive Federal Party, and now, by the DP. Yet, on the right were more reactionary white voters, to whom the Conservative Party was becoming increasingly attractive. To escape this 'pincer threat' (Schlemmer, 1991b) to its dominance over the white electorate, De Klerk's NP had to move relatively quickly in the direction of reform, so as both to retain the reformist white vote and, through speed, minimize the coherence and level of organization of the Conservative Party's opposition.

Narrowing economic options

Just as, if not more pressing than the challenges from black and white political traits, were the economic problems that De Klerk's administration inherited. If political difficulties alone could not influence his government to negotiate, when combined with economic considerations, the range of alternatives was even more restricted. By 1989, the government was in a 'Catch 22' situation: 'On the one hand the state's ability to successfully pursue its counterrevolutionary strategy required resources. These resources could only come from an expanding economy ... on the other hand continuing with the repressive strategy threatened future economic growth' (Price, 1991: 273).

By 1988, the brief economic optimism of the preceding year had been reversed. During the 1987 'miniboom', Pretoria had attempted to raise the volume of exports and thus earn more foreign exchange. However, South Africa's dependence on imports meant that economic expansion soon brought an increasing volume of imports and thus, greater claims on foreign-exchange reserves. From 1986 to 1988, the import bill increased by 60 per cent, while additional costs could not be met by borrowing due to sanctions (Price, 1991). In 1988, the impact of sanctions was fully recognized for the first time in the annual reports of key South African economic concerns – for example, Trust Bank of South Africa, First National Bank, Rand Mines Ltd, and Standard Bank Investment Corporation (Price, 1991).

The 1988 Commonwealth proposals, accepted by all members but the UK, would begin a three-stage 'ratcheting up' of particular sanctions, which were designed to make it very difficult indeed for the South African government to reject demands for the effective dismantling of apartheid. Aside from such formal measures, by April 1988, one-fifth of the British firms in South Africa had pulled out under mounting domestic anti-apartheid pressure and British investment had fallen from £6 billion in 1980 to under £3 billion in 1986. From January 1984 to April 1989, 184 US companies left, driven out by the threat of further Congress penalties like the double taxation of Mobil (Davenport, 1991: 464). However, formal government trade restrictions were not as damaging to the South African economy as informal financial reticence, since they merely resulted in a shift of trading partners from West to East. Financial constraints imposed by private banks, acting according to their own perception of economic risk, led to a fall of the rand on the international money market from $1.36 in 1981 to $0.41 in 1989. South Africa's foreign debt increased to $20 billion by 1990, resulting, in 1989, in rescheduling arrangements to avoid reneging (Davenport, 1991: 465).

The most serious impact of South Africa's balance-of-payments deterioration was that it precluded capital growth (see Kahn, 1991). Growth had been below 2 per cent throughout the 1980s, while population had been increasing at the rate of 2.5 per cent (Davenport, 1991:

465). With a soaring defence budget reaching 9 billion rand in 1989, the administrative costs of apartheid 'were – it seems – more damaging than contrived economic measures to the national economy' (Davenport, 1991: 465). But sanctions augmented the effect, particularly by forcing out foreign companies with important access to international markets and technology.

The government needed an injection of new capital that would not just be exported again to pay off debt and buy imports, but the chief economist of SANLAM made it clear that 'unless we get certain reforms here we won't get foreign capital again. We have to at least show the outside world that we are moving in the right direction' (quoted in Price, 1991: 275). When relative political calm returned after the mid-1980s insurrection, analysts realized that new investment still was not coming in to restore the balance of payments. Only a guaranteed long-term political solution would give South Africa the perceived stability required for investor confidence (Schlemmer, 1991b).

The failure of Botha's economic policies and of political repression to restore structural stability contributed to a political division in the ruling elite. Securocrats saw further reform as too risky since black 'radicals' were too powerful. On the other side of the growing divide were those associated with economic and foreign relations policy, who stressed the risk to economic survival of continued repression, and emphasized the role of reform in ending international economic isolation. It was this wing of the government that was increasingly backed by business and finance.

For the reformist group, another of Botha's significant failures was his professed aim of rationalizing and reducing the costs of government. Instead, the Tricameral Parliament, continuing duplication of administrative departments and increasing security and regional destabilization costs, had led to an increase in government expenditure as a percentage of GNP from 21 per cent in 1980 to 32 per cent in 1989 (Schrire, 1992b). 'It was ironic that Botha, the efficient hardheaded administrator, who came to power determined to rationalize government, created a massive government structure that helped to undermine the South African economy on which it depended' (Schrire, 1992b: 121). The blame for this malignant growth was placed on the restriction, after 1986, of the sources of government advice to the security establishment.

On his election as party leader, De Klerk came to represent the critical, reformist wing of the party. On his accession to the presidency, with a continuing high degree of centralized power (Morris, 1991), he set about establishing control over the enlarged security establishment, especially the NSMS. In adopting the reformist line, De Klerk also chose to further the interests of business where, despite Botha's initial courting of capital, they had conflicted, especially after the Rubicon speech, with those of the previous government. The sector in general urged further reform on the government during the second half of the 1980s for several reasons (Lee et al., 1991). The business sector's concern was voiced most clearly in 1989, over the impact of black consumer boycotts and the implementation of separate amenities. Carletonville and Boksburg town centres were both subject to an almost complete black boycott due to their Conservative councils' decision to uphold the Separate Amenities Act. Business representatives across the country called for the complete removal of the Act, rather than its selective imposition according to the dictates of particular councils, while the Carletonville Chamber of Commerce lobbied Parliament and took legal action against the town council, which resulted in the removal of 'Whites Only' signs. The episode demonstrated both the political impact that a coherent business lobby could have and the power of united black consumers.

A second area of business concern was more general. Discontent was being expressed in 1989 at economic policy, particularly at excessive government expenditure, which prompted calls for rationalization. The criticism of many business leaders was expressed by Aubrey Dickman, Chief Economist of the Anglo American Corporation: 'ideological concerns have taken precedence over economic exigencies' (Lee et al., 1991: 103).

Sanctions were a third cause for concern. In 1989, Chris Van Wyk of Bankorp updated an earlier report and estimated that sanctions had reduced the potential growth rate by 10 per cent, leading to the loss of 500,000 employment opportunities (cited in Lee et al., 1991: 104). A professed concern over gross societal inequalities, particularly in education, contributed to the desire for significant change. Finally, an immediate demonstration of the necessity of structural change was provided by industrial relations with black workers. A tentative alliance emerged between employers and black unions, against the government's 1989 Labour Relations Amendment Act. The alliance represented a recognition by employers of the inextricable link between the shopfloor and the wider political concerns of the union members. It was appreciated by employers that stayaways and industrial disruption would not end until political satisfaction had been achieved by the workforce.

Even under Botha, the concerns of business had overlapped significantly with those of reformists within the government. Their first triumph over the securocrats came in August 1988, with the signing of the Angola–Namibia accord. 'From Pretoria's vantage point the accord represented both a pragmatic adjustment to a gloomy economic reality and an effort to alter that reality' (Price, 1991: 276). The administrative cost of occupying Namibia had assumed greater significance as the shortage of resources within South Africa became more evident. The costs of military involvement against the SWAPO independence movement were raised even higher when Cuban troops and equipment moved into the besieged town of Cuito Cuanavale, in southern Angola, to repel South African forces. The battle served to highlight the failures of securocrat policies which had proved unable to guarantee either peace or economic security. By urging South Africa's extrication from an unwinnable war, the reformers in the government had achieved something of a coup and within two months, as a sign of renewed favour, South African diplomats were again visiting European countries (Price, 1991).

Having attained this success, the government reformist bloc focused on South Africa's internal situation. The question expressed by De Klerk – 'do we want them [our children] to inherit new sanctions and boycotts?' (cited in Price, 1991: 278) – led reformers within the party to the conclusion that negotiations with black organizations seen as legitimate by much of the black population were necessary to resolve South Africa's endemic crisis. The black 'moderates' with whom Botha had contemplated negotiations – mostly homeland leaders and councillors – were now rendered largely irrelevant by the general 'culture of liberation' that had developed with the insurrection. Given its ascension to a position of widespread internal and international political legitimacy, the ANC's participation would be required for a restoration of stability. The fact that it would command the support of many of the black trade unions also made its role in a future settlement crucial, since the trade unions' success had 'brought home to government the magnitude of the confrontation they faced if they forced the black community into "illegality"' (*Guardian*, 20 April 1992). The election of Cyril Ramaphosa, leader of the miners' union, as ANC Secretary General in 1991 was 'a recognition of the role the trade union movement had played in bringing about the dramatic government reforms of 1990' (*Guardian*, 20 April 1992). Once negotiations with the ANC were accepted as the way out of structural crisis, De Klerk's initial, drastic reforms were inescapable.

Thus, a lack of further options for the preservation of white minority rule and, particularly, a lack of alternative ways out of structural economic crisis can be seen as the prime influences on De Klerk's decision to negotiate. However, Moll (1989) argues that it is easy to overemphasize the role of economic deterioration. De Klerk's government would be aware that South Africa still had certain dependable economic securities. There was a strong food-producing sector, huge mineral resources, only a limited dependence on oil, a highly developed manufacturing sector, significant technological know-how and a fair level of local savings. If negotiations with the ANC were seen as too dangerous, they need not have been entered into yet, even as a last resort. Despite poor economic performance, the state could probably have held on to power in an unstable and conflict-prone political environment for some years to come (Brewer, 1989c). The decision to negotiate could well have been the only option for restoring long-term stability, but it could have been delayed. The reason it was taken in 1990, then, was not just because alternatives had failed for the government, but also because the timing was propitious.

Negotiations as choice

While the 1990 announcements were dramatic, the political environment into which they were introduced had already been partially prepared for them by a series of prior adjustments.

> The legalisation of the African trades unions in 1980; the abolition of influx control in 1986; the granting of full property rights to Africans in the common area of South Africa; the opening of Central Business Districts (CBDs) to occupational pursuits by all races; and the law providing for certain 'white' areas to become areas of 'free settlement' had the unintended combined effect that [by the late 1980s] government itself [had] destroyed the central purposes and principles of apartheid. (Schlemmer, 1991b: 22)

A number of positive developments led De Klerk to identify 1990 as the right time for the completion of apartheid's legal demise. De Klerk embarked on 'an attempt to secure a settlement under conditions which would enhance his chances of preserving the crucial political interests of his constituency'. In this light, in 1990, 'his strategic position was more favourable than it could be calculated to be ever again' (Schlemmer, 1990: 258). By negotiating now rather than later, the ANC would be more likely to accept the government's 'bottom line'. It was the government's perception of internal, regional and international developments in the late 1980s and early 1990s that encouraged this understanding.

Domestically, the 1989 election result was interpreted by De Klerk as a mandate for further reform from the 70 per cent of white voters backing the NP and DP, and this conclusion was actively diffused through the media. De Klerk was also emboldened by the failure of the Conservative Party to do as well in the election as was expected. The domestic security situation had improved and, importantly,

Western intelligence had suggested to De Klerk that the ANC was not as powerful as Botha had feared (Schrire, 1992b: 133).

Internationally, in the light of the traditional South African communist bogeyman, the crisis of the USSR in 1990 was reassuring for De Klerk. For many whites, the elimination of the Soviet threat, manifest in the ANC, was a consideration in favour of *rapprochement*. Within the region, South Africa and the USSR were even involved in a 'working relationship' in the Namibian and Angolan negotiations. The fact that the USA, USSR and Western powers had displayed an 'even handed approach' (Schlemmer, 1991b) in these negotiations (extending even to a favourable lack of reaction when South African troops killed hundreds of SWAPO guerrillas moving outside their peace-brokered containment zones) raised expectations for a similarly benign attitude to internal negotiations with the ANC. The Namibian settlement had also won the government a degree of international respect, extending beyond the countries directly involved in the 'solution', and De Klerk could rely on widespread moral support for internal negotiations.

The Namibia settlement had had the additional effect of pushing the ANC towards a more compromising position. It meant the loss of Angolan bases, with no prospect of re-establishment elsewhere in southern Africa, given Mozambique's recent compliance with Pretoria. 'Armed liberation became an absolutely remote ideal' (Schlemmer, 1991b: 17). But De Klerk was aware that there was possibly no need to make fundamental socio-economic concessions in negotiations with the ANC anyway:

> The 'reasonableness' of Pretoria in abolishing legal apartheid has put great pressure on the opposition to respond in kind. International opinion wants South Africa saved from another failed socialist experiment, and the prolonged recession further pressures the ANC to accept far-reaching concessions. It appears as if the ANC cannot but accept the democratic and constitutional clamps around its options. If the ANC were again to withdraw from negotiations, as it did in May 1992, it would have to return sooner or later in order to avoid a descent into barbarism. (Adam and Moodley, 1993: 35)

Within South Africa, even as the main party in government, it was appreciated that the ANC's capacity to redistribute and equalize material wealth between white and black would be constrained. The NP leadership under De Klerk was only too aware of the limitations: the fixed rate of investment had fallen from 32 per cent of GDP in 1975 to 17 per cent in 1991 and in order to redistribute the ANC would need a growing economy; the organization could not nationalize or deficit finance to such a degree as was anticipated by many of its followers, for fear of deterring investors; and the facts that white taxes were already high and that many blacks paid no taxes, would preclude much redistribution by way of taxation (Adam and Moodley, 1993). The cumulative impact of these developments and realizations was to make it

> abundantly clear that the strategic balance had shifted in favour of the South African government by 1990. The major price had been the relinquishing of Namibia ... in early 1990 the government could view the possible outcomes of compromise with the ANC far more positively than at any time since it came to power. (Schlemmer, 1991b: 17–18)

Even in this context though, the ANC would not be that easily co-opted. In 1990, as a result of the insurrection, the ANC itself had far more coherent internal support than it had ever had before. While, in 1990, the timing of negotiations was propitious for the government, the trend in black politics made them inevitable sooner or later.

The transition to democracy

The following account of the four years of transition which marked the interregnum between apartheid and democracy is necessarily brief: this book is concerned more with the structural and spatial configuration of apartheid and post-apartheid society than with the specifics of the transition 'moment'. For a more comprehensive treatment of the politics of the interregnum, see Johnson (1994) and Sparks (1995).

Although the 'main players' in the transition process – the ANC and NP leaderships – disputed, often vehemently, the extent of the transfer of power that was to occur and its timing, they shared the imperative that the transition itself be relatively smooth and economically benign. In December 1991, the Convention for a Democratic South Africa (CODESA) was established to hammer out the terms of the transition to democracy. Represented within CODESA were the South African government, the NP itself, the ANC, South African Communist Party (SACP), DP, Inkatha (now known as the Inkatha Freedom Party, IFP), the Tricameral Parliament parties and the homeland government parties.

While CODESA was still addressing preliminaries, a NP defeat by the Conservative Party in a local by-election prompted De Klerk to put the idea of continued negotiation to the white electorate. In a referendum in March 1992, the NP secured a favourable vote of 69 per cent. However, even with the electorate's realization that the abandonment of apartheid was now irreversible without heightened economic and political crisis, the NP negotiators within CODESA still held out for a small minority veto on future legislation under the new constitution. Deadlock over this issue had already stalled the transition process when the killing of forty-two residents of Boipatong by IFP followers, who had apparently been in collusion with the police, made the breakdown of negotiations decisive.

The Boipatong massacre, as it became known, was one particularly vicious manifestation of a more general escalation of violence in the townships. While Mangope and Gqozo, the 'independent' homeland leaders of Bophuthatswana and Ciskei respectively, would, in the course of the transition, be either overthrown or effectively by-passed, the former following an abortive Afrikaner Weerstandbeweging (AWB) rescue attempt, and the latter after the shooting of demonstrators by homeland security forces, Buthelezi remained determined not only to retain political control in KwaZulu, but to secure a national leadership role. Although he seemed to lack enough political support for his ambitions, the IFP found willing assistance from within the state security forces. During 1991, the ongoing 'Inkathagate' scandal revealed the extent of covert state intervention on the IFP's behalf. Many of the 7,000 deaths which occurred in the almost continuous violence which racked the townships between 1989 and 1992 were linked to the security forces' logistical support for, and even training of, Inkatha attackers. Buthelezi was able to develop a strategy based upon an implicit threat of civil war in the event of his ambitions being thwarted. A further nuance was added to this tactic when Inkatha joined forces with white right-wingers, similarly determined to wreck the transition process if their minority goals were not secured.

The worrying drift towards perpetual violent instability, combined with the resumption of ANC-led 'mass action', contributed towards an NP concession over the size of the prospective veto and the resumption of negotiations in early 1993. It was agreed that a new government, to be elected in April 1994, would serve a five-year term under the negotiated constitution, during which time a finalized new constitution could be legislated.

Buthelezi, threatened by marginalization if the elections went ahead without him, and facing the potential fragmentation of the IFP (perhaps prompted by the Zulu King Zwelithini who, although manipulated by Buthelezi thus far, may have seen an outlet for more independent ambition), agreed to participate in the elections at the last minute. From 26–29 April 1994, South Africans, in the first democratic elections in their history, voted President Mandela into office. De Klerk became one of two Vice-Presidents and Buthelezi, with his IFP securing a dubious victory in the regional KwaZulu/Natal elections, became Minister for Home Affairs.

The shape of the 'new South Africa'

With growing familiarity between negotiators from the ANC and the NP, the relative moderation and economic realism of the ANC leadership must have struck many members of the NP establishment. The ANC's early attempts to placate business interests and its shedding of the perception of nationalization as panacea would have enhanced NP peace of mind at the prospect of less restricted ANC power. But of equal importance in the tendency to concede more than was first envisaged was the impact of extraneous events. The sheer scale of a strike against more extensive VAT, the countrywide protestation at the Boipatong and Bisho shootings, and the genuine grief at the murder of the former MK Chief of Staff and SACP leader, Chris Hani, all contributed to the realization that vehement and nationwide support for an unhampered ANC government precluded economic or political stability under any substantially different order.

But political and economic stability is by no means assured for South Africa. First, the political credibility of the new ANC administration is not unchallenged. Questions over members' past behaviour are likely to fade as the party exercises power, but they have none the less vexed some political observers. Despite the suppression of an internal report, in 1993 it was revealed that there were incidents of routine torture at an external ANC training camp; there have been allegations of financial mismanagement and corruption in the ANC's financial arm, Thebe, and within the party's Social Welfare Department and Women's League under Winnie Mandela; Nelson Mandela's personal intervention to prevent a police search of ANC headquarters after a March 1994 shooting on an Inkatha march raised some suspicions, and there is annoyance within black townships at the 'yuppification' of ANC leaders, extending even to friendships with the likes of Sol Kerzner, the millionaire who made his fortune out of homeland casinos. Yet, in comparison with the known illegitimate actions of the NP and Inkatha, the ANC is on relatively secure ground.

Political instability in the 'new South Africa' is more likely to come from an inability to meet material expectations raised by the transition process than from the discrediting of leaders. The death throes of apartheid sent South Africa into economic trauma and the legacies of racial domination in land, health, education, transport and employment are all biting more evidently now that their most obvious source has been removed. Secondly, according to the World Bank, South Africa has the greatest recorded inequality of any country in the world, with two-thirds of the black population surviving below a defined 'minimum living level' (Ramphele, 1991). The Development Bank of South Africa has estimated that nine million are now completely destitute. Apart from the misery associated with such poverty, it has wider, long-term political implications. The ANC has been supported by impoverished black South Africans not just for its historic opposition to apartheid, but because of its promise to deliver material salvation, in much the same way that the NP did for the volk. With competition for the resources now at the ANC's disposal, scenarios disturbing for the prospect of future political stability can be posited. If high expectations are not fulfilled, brutalized, conflict-accustomed black youth could well turn out once more in opposition to the authorities. But perhaps of even more political importance than their absolute poverty is its obvious contrast with relative white wealth.

In 1992, the 76 per cent of the population defined as African held only 33 per cent of personal income. The 8.6 per cent defined as Coloured held 9 per cent of income, the 2.5 per cent defined as Indian held 4 per cent and the 13 per cent defined as White still accounted for 54 per cent of personal income. Racial variations are accompanied by geographical differences in living standards. Of the nine Development Regions, Gross Geographical Product *per capita* was 1.89 times the national average in the PWV area and only 0.32 times the national average in the region containing the homelands of Venda, Lebowa and KwaNdebele (figures from Smith, 1994: 228). Within these regions, in turn, there are gross variations, for instance, between urban and rural areas and between areas of formal housing and shacks. Somehow, the new state structures have to initiate moves towards greater social justice 'in a society where some 60% of the population live below the bread-line, 55% are illiterate, 40% are unemployed ... 25 people a day die of TB and 300 a day become HIV positive. This litany of misery could be much longer' (Sonn, *Race Relations News*, February 1993).

The new government needs to diminish inequality, both in the interests of social justice and of political survival. Both goals also require some kind of restitution to those who suffered under apartheid. Particularly meaningful, and therefore, particularly high on the agenda, is land reform. 'Land has been, and continues to be, an important source of power which some people can wield over others, from the traditional chiefly prerogative of allocating land, through the privatiza-tion of ownership introduced by the colonizers, to the racialized control of the apartheid era' (Smith, 1994: 231), and now there are four main groups within South African society with extensive claims on the land that was once part of the construct of white space. The first is com-posed of established black farmers, still residing in 'black spots'. The second is of white owners who feel entitled to the land by birthright, inheritance and occupation. The third consists of business owners who have invested in the land, and the fourth of blacks whose ancestors, or who themselves were forced off the land under policies of segregation and apartheid. This is perhaps the largest group (Sachs, 1990). The state has 1.25 million hectares (about 1 per cent of the land area) to redistribute to the last group, but it must be able both to obtain more and to resolve conflicting claims to the same land. Each involves opportunity costs. For instance, according to Moore (1992) the purchasing of one-tenth of white farms at market value would cost 7 billion rand – a sum which could build 200,000 houses or 3,000 primary schools.

There is a desperate need for each of these alternatives. The shortage of low-cost housing is well established, but after the repeal of the pass laws in 1986, over 1,000 people a day entered the urban areas (Ramphele, 1991). It is estimated that seven million now live in informal settlements. This is about one-quarter of the African population, and about a half of those living in the major cities (Smith, 1994). Their location, predominantly on the urban periphery, imposes the extra burden of high transport costs and limited access to central services. Even the advantages of the proliferating minibus services – low cost, convenience and, at least during the political transition, less likelihood of attack than on public transport – are partly counteracted by the dangerous driving of unlicensed operators and the possibility of being caught up in taxi wars between rival outfits. A widely proposed solution to the problems of urban informal sprawl is the infilling of land closer to the city centres. Vacant land in Johannesburg, for instance, is owned by mining houses. Such 'inward urbanization' would certainly make more efficient use of existing urban infrastructure (Smith, 1994).

Improvement in education and health care, too, is a requirement not only of morality, but also of stability and productivity. Democratic structures like the civics must be incorporated in political decision-making in order not to exclude those who are already highly politically mobilized at the 'grassroots'. But if their participation is to be constructive, their members must be given the opportunity to engage in informed debate, aware of macro-scale alternatives. The greater contribution of well-educated and healthy workers to the economy is obvious, and Cole (1994) stresses the long-term environmental implications of continued poor sanitation and service provision in growing squatter communities.

Yet Van der Berg (1991) demonstrates that general equalization with white levels of government spending on education, health and pensions would require three times the current level of government expenditure. If spending is held constant, broad racial equalization would result in a reduction of white expenditure to one-third its current level and cuts also for Coloureds and Indians. Apart from a widespread transfer of resources from whites and other wealthy groups (already subject to high personal, if not business taxation) to the poorest, the resources for attempted equalization could come from two other sources: re-allocation from elsewhere within the state budget and overall economic growth. Government borrowing already accounts for 6 per cent of GNP (*Independent on Sunday*, 24 April 1994), so there is little hope for an expanding overall budget without such economic growth. There is leeway for the reallocation of existing state funds, now that expend-iture amounting to about 1 per cent of GDP on the apparatuses and defences of apartheid has been saved (Van der Berg, 1991). Moll (1991b) estimates that a reduction in defence expenditure by 2 per cent of GDP, the abolition of apartheid and of the industrial decentralization strategy, plus modest tax increases and 'prudent' borrowing, could yield the equivalent of 6.4 per cent of GDP. To equalize social spending at white levels 21.3 per cent would be needed. (Smith, 1994: 244).

If it is to redistribute with economic growth, the new government will require a dramatic turnaround in current economic fortunes. Over the last decade, the annual growth of GDP has been less than 1 per cent, and with population growth at 2.5 per cent, there have been generally negative rates of GNP per capita (Smith, 1994: 243). The formal economy absorbs only 10 per cent of the economically active population, while 30 per cent work in the informal sector (Development Bank of South Asia, cited in Smith, 1994). No immediate prospect of a rise in formal employment, very low rates of domestic savings and the long-term difficulties faced by a primary product exporter (*Financial Times*, 22 April 1994) all increase the dependence on investment from outside. It was the growing realization of these difficulties, not all brought about solely by apartheid, that edged the ANC into an economic rapport with the NP during negotiations and led to its relinquishing the prospect of nationalization.

No matter how comprehensive their rendering, no statistics of poverty or economic performance can address the more intangible experiences of deprivation with which the new South Africa has to deal. While Said was describing the psychological impact of colonialism in general, his remarks are well attuned to the victim of twentieth-century apartheid, who is 'tired of the logic that reduces him [*sic*], the geography that segregates him, the ontology that dehumanizes him, the epistemology that strips him down to an unregenerate essence' (Said, 1993: 323). Apart from such demoralization, which itself has been resisted in the mobilization to overcome apartheid, statistics similarly cannot reveal 'poverty's texture: the dull ache of deprivation, the acute tension generated by violence and insecurity, the intricacies of survival and all its emotions – despair, hope, resentment, apathy, futility and fury' (Bundy, 1992: 25).

Perhaps some of apartheid's most pernicious and subtle damage was inflicted through the severing of people from the places which were their homes. As Smith (1994) writes, 'the depths of attachment people form with territory and place have long been recognised in humanistic geography. ... But geographers [and historians] have devoted much less attention to the loss of place' (1994: 275). For those removed from their farms, for instance, 'farming [was] more than just a productive activity, it [was] an act of culture, the centre of social existence and the place where personal identity [was] forged' (Sachs, 1990, quoted in Smith, 1994: 232). For many more, in both rural and urban areas,

> [e]viction from the neighbourhood in which one was at home [was] almost as disruptive of the meaning of life as the loss of a crucial relationship. Dispossession threatens the whole structure of attachments through which purposes are embodied, because these attachments cannot readily be re-established in an alien setting ... in all such situations, the ambivalence of grieving has to work itself out. (Marris, 1986: 57)

The legacies of segregation and apartheid, both psychological and material, will remain embedded in South African life for many years. In general terms, 'at present, the most likely scenario is that South Africa will steadily come more closely to resemble a normal capitalist society, its inherited racial inequalities interpenetrated and blurred by class cleavages' (Smith, 1994: 247), but the spatial cleavages of apartheid, particularly those associated with the attempt to maintain white urban space, present particular barriers to be overcome.

As under apartheid, it is the established urban interests that are most likely to be successful in competition for the new state's resources. While COSATU and the new urban government structures, which largely represent formal township residents, will be extremely powerful constituencies within the new body politic, less organized and less economically significant urban squatters may find the pace of material improvement too slow. Traditional rural societies in the impoverished former homelands could be even further neglected in the implementation of the ANC's economic reconstruction plan.

Conclusion: conceptualizing South African social and spatial formation

Some of the more recent theoretical work on the construction of South African society (see Norval, 1990, 1994) has been primarily concerned with the fabrication of antagonistic identities. The political structures within which social formation has occurred are, implicitly, direct products of these intangibly shaped identities. Thus, for Norval, apartheid's political phases were commensurate with shifting boundaries of white identity: 'I would ... argue that it is possible to trace out the most significant changes in South African society, from the stages of resistance to changes in the form of the state, by carefully following the various discourses in their interaction, and the associated construction of identities over the years' (1990: 142). Norval proceeds by describing the changing bases of insider group identity under apartheid. She begins with the exclusivist Afrikaner volk which appropriated the state in 1948. Under Verwoerd, the criteria for inclusion within the dominant identity were broadened, with the incorporation of English-speakers as part of a hegemonic white bloc. The process of a more general white inclusion continued under Vorster, with blacks remaining the excluded, homogeneous 'other'. With the further pursuit of Separate Development, the excluded group was differentiated ethnically, but remained 'other'. In the 1980s though, with Botha's Total Strategy, the boundaries of insider group definition were extended (at least in government strategy), so as to incorporate urban, 'middle-class' blacks, and the conceptual 'other' mutated into a communist (but still largely black) threat.

While these were, broadly, the shifting parameters of the dominant political identity, the account overlooks the grounding of these discourses in material conditions. In this sense, perhaps Norval's conception has moved *too* far from Marxism. Many of the twentieth-century shifts of insider group definition can be directly linked not only to changing conditions of resistance (something for which Norval does account), but also to changing economic circumstances. This is not to be economically reductionist, but it is to link discussion of political identity more firmly to the socio-economic conditions which were more traditionally the concern of apartheid's analysts. Thus, while Norval sees the NP's late 1980s crisis as the result of 'increasing disintegration of the attempts of the NP discourse to create stable systems of purely differential identities' (Norval, 1990: 18), the material roots of this crisis of political identity remain unacknowledged. Despite concession to the 'social and political dimensions' (Norval, 1990: 18) of shifts in group identity, political discourse is generally seen as taking place at an abstracted level, floating above the material conditions of political, social and economic life.

Pratt hints at a stronger bond between the cultural and the material:

> In the midst of current scholarly critique of colonialist discourses, con-
> temporary readers can scarcely fail to link [the] creation of a speechless,

denuded, biological body [in the eighteenth- and early nineteenth-century European conceptualization of Africans] with the deracinated, dispossessed, disposable workforce European colonists so ruthlessly and tirelessly sought to create in their footholds abroad. (1992: 53)

The creation of white South Africans' African 'other', was from the early days of colonization grounded partly in the possibility, and hence the requirement, of servitude. In the late nineteenth century, the presence of black migrant labourers in white space played a crucial role in reflexively defining urban white self-perception. Wade shows how, for urban English-speakers in particular, migrant labourers 'created an emotional crisis which smoulders to this day' (1993: 2). The reaction was a discourse which legitimated the maintenance of influx control to prevent further black urbanization, and the rustication of those migrants in the city once their work was done: 'The white insistence on the inevitability of black social collapse in the urban situation [was] a vital ingredient of white self-perception, of the white group's idea of itself as possessing complete autonomy and unlimited power' (Wade, 1993: 47).

The white construction of an 'othered' black identity remained integral to their own sense of identity, and to their own material position, well into the twentieth century:

> For the apartheid system to continue to exist and provide the surplus needs of the white minority, that minority has to exercise political power in a manner based on a wide-ranging denial of reality. In practice, this means a mechanism that enables the whites to deny the existence of blacks as autonomous individuals. ... They [most whites] seem locked in a furious attempt to reject a group which has no desire to be accepted by them but which has long since become internalised, a part of the total social fact ... whites inhabit a psychotic perceptual world as the price they pay for power. (Wade, 1993: 48, 106)

Whites' spatial sense is crucial to this psychosis. The need for whites to possess white space *exclusively*, and the implicit threat of culturally shared space, lay at the core of segregation and apartheid. The denial of historical and geographical reality were inextricable.

While these insights into the links between identitative formation, materialism and space are enormously valuable in conceptualizing South African social formation, a further step is needed to link that social formation in turn to the evolution of South Africa's distinctive political structures. That is an analysis of the interaction between the social groups formed from the shifting parameters of identity on the one hand, and the highly interventionist South African state on the other.

Given the perhaps unique importance of the state in shaping South Africa's human geography and social interaction, state theory should comprise a part of any general survey. The absence of such a component in many analyses led Mitchell and Russell (1989b) to emphasize the need for 'bringing the state back in'.

Early Marxist notions of the state tended to be ranged along a narrow spectrum, from functionalist (the state acts in the interests of the economic system as a whole) to instrumentalist (the state is the agent of whichever are the 'ruling classes'). An example of the former position is that of Lea (1982: 198, quoting Davis, 1981) who argues that the post-Soweto attempt by government to address partially the black housing shortage was entirely intended to 'guarantee the conditions for continued capital accumulation'. The work of Poulantzas was intended to escape such confining Marxist notions. Instead of the pliant agent of capital, for Poulantzas, the state is the site of struggle between different fractions of the dominant classes. The dominant fractions of the bourgeoisie, according to 'fractionalists' who based their work on Poulantzas, form a power bloc and contend for hegemony within it, sometimes, when deadlocks occur, seeking support from non-bourgeois classes. The resulting alliances can produce state policies which appear to contradict the interests of capital; but such ostensibly anti-business policies are 'ultimately in the real interest of capital' (Yudelman, 1987: 252).

Fractionalist periodization of the South African state was 'littered with "turning points" where the balance of power shifted between fractions' (Yudelman, 1987: 252), particularly 1924 and 1948. Davis, Kaplan, Morris and O'Meara (1976) provide illustration with an account of the struggles between mining capital and 'national' manufacturing and agricultural capital to dominate state policy on foreign trade. The implementation of protectionist policies indicated that national capital was hegemonic at a given time, while a shift towards free trade manifested the usurping of that hegemony by foreign (largely mining) capital. Despite Poulantzas's original aim of widening the state's agenda, fractionalist studies of the South African state have still tended to portray its role as limited to that of political agent to whichever fraction of capital was dominant.

While a Poulantzian analysis can be seen as 'neo-Marxist', Yudelman points out that its divergence from liberal analyses is not that great. Liberals have portrayed the state as trying to ensure a stable environment for competing groups in capitalist society. Such a framework has been adopted to its fullest extent in a liberal work by Lipton (1985). Lipton argues that, overall this century, white labour and agricultural capital were the dominant influences on the state, despite the 1920–24 dominance of foreign-owned mining capital and that of mining, manufacturing and commercial capital from 1939 to 1948. Her analysis departs from that of the fractionalists, though, in her emphasis on the nationalist or ethnic formation of the dominant groups, rather than their economic nature. In this sense, she approaches closer to recent concern with the identitative formation of the groups comprising society. White, and particularly Afrikaner, workers' and farmers' interests could not be served by the operation of 'free market' forces. The institutionalized racism of apartheid was largely an attempt by the state to intervene on behalf of these politically powerful groups, by effecting unskilled black labour controls and the suppression of black producers and skilled classes.

Lipton's emphasis on the political and ideological rather than the economic nature of the 'dominant classes' leads to the conclusion that 'South Africa's development since Union does not support the thesis that the state was the instrument of capital' (Lipton, 1985: 370). The mining companies and other key economic interests, although economically dominant, were, at times when they were in conflict with white labour, the bureaucracy or weaker agricultural interests, overridden. The 'foreign' nature of many of the economically dominant fractions of capital rendered them politically unsuitable for a close alliance with Afrikaner-led government, particularly under the NP.

Although the stress on the political or ethnic nature of the most influential groups distinguishes Lipton's liberal analysis from the fractionalists (who did recognize national and foreign capital differentiation, but put the onus on their economic role), her conception of the state shares the limitation of an implied pliability, a non-autonomous reaction to demands placed upon it, which has been criticized by observers such as Yudelman (1984, 1987) and Greenberg (1987). Yudelman's main point is that liberal and Marxist theories of the state all see it as representational, regardless of whether they see it as representing the general interest, a particular class or a particular social group. His own feeling is that the state should be seen in some senses as an actor in its own right, although not entirely autonomous, due to the limited range of choices it has in seeking to satisfy its major constituencies.

Before elaborating on Yudelman's perception of the South African state, it is necessary to introduce more universal approaches to the role of the state in capitalist society, developed by theorists such as Miliband and Habermas. Their ideas provide the framework for much of the more recent work specifically on the South African state.

Miliband was concerned to accord the state more autonomy than that allowed by traditional accounts. For him 'an accurate and realistic "model" of the relationship between the dominant class [for which we might substitute 'identity'] in advanced capitalist societies and the state is one of the partnership between two different, separate forces, linked to each other by many threads, yet each having its own separate spheres of concern' (quoted in Graaff, 1990: 58). Greenberg's analysis goes further, as he 'portrays the state as relatively disconnected from social group interests and, instead of carrying out the dictates of social groups, it imposes its own project on a quiescent and pliant manufacturing sector', while 'Glaser and Posel came to similar conclusions though they attribute more weight to demands of capitalists in altering and shaping these policies' (Nattrass, 1991: 675). Following Miliband, then, the state can be seen to possess more autonomy than fractionalists or some liberal analysts have granted it.

While neo-Marxist accounts tended to emphasize the economic role of whichever group most swayed the state, and liberals defined it by its political role, according to Habermas,

> the independence of economy and politics in 'early' capitalism has been replaced by their intersection in 'late' or 'advanced' capitalism so that a new system of concepts is required which is capable of clarifying the role of the state in managing the various economic, political and sociocultural crises of advanced capitalism. (Habermas, 1975, quoted in Johnston, et al., 1990: 83)

The duality of the state's political and economic concerns renders it susceptible to crises, both of legitimation in the eyes of its political constituents and of economic accumulation. Its position is influenced both by political ideas and by material economic reality.

In the light of South Africa's mid-1980s insurrection, by the late 1980s, 'analysis of South African conflict [was] now focusing on the state's legitimation crisis, its lack of accepted authority ... and increasing inability to perform its everyday functions without the exercise of naked force'. But the late apartheid state's legitimation crisis was accompanied by an accumulation crisis. With 'the growing inability of the economy to generate the revenue or jobs necessary to underpin social or political programmes ... there [was] structural crisis in the economy itself' (Yudelman, 1987: 250–1).

Due to the state's concern with legitimation as well as accumulation, Yudelman sees it as not so much the instrument of capital, more a relatively autonomous agent which enters into a relationship of symbiosis with capital (or, we can add, with other, wider dominant social identities). The state's concern to satisfy non-materially defined constituencies in society, as well as the conditions for capital accumulation, means that it does not submit itself pliantly to the caprice of whichever fraction of capital is dominant.

Yudelman suggests that the South African state was 'exposed earlier than most modern states to the necessity of resolving the tension between legitimation and accumulation' (1987: 253). The long-term relationship of symbiosis between the state and capital in South Africa developed in the post-Anglo-Boer War reconstruction period, under pressure of demands from the gold-mining industry and because of the concentration and homogeneity of capital in this early period, and it persevered despite changes in government. That the state did not entirely submit itself to the whim of dominant fractions of capital was due to the similarly early need for legitimation: the concentration of political power in the hands of culturally defined Afrikaners, disproportionately found in the agricultural and working classes, led to large-scale state intervention on their behalf. The state needed to legitimate itself within the white population, and Afrikaners in particular, through ideology and by broadening representation. At the same time, it needed to protect the accumulation process in order to ensure continued economic growth. 'Because the state needed private enterprise to optimize the accumulation function, and because capital needed the state to perform the legitimation function, a relationship of mutual dependence was the natural outcome' (Yudelman, 1987: 253).

Applying Yudelman's concept, we can see that, at certain times, the tension between the accumulation function and the legitimation function becomes manifest – for instance, during the 1922 miners' strike, when mining capital's imperative to erode the job colour bar conflicted with Afrikaans miners' desire to retain it. In this instance, Smuts's government of the day, by enforcing the demands of capital, lost out politically in the 1924 election, but the long-term relationship of symbiosis between state and capital, by and large, remained intact.

For Botha's government, Yudelman believes that the symbiosis was strengthened by the entrenchment of a legitimation crisis stemming from both black resistance and a loss of Afrikaner working- and middle-class support for ineffective reformism. 'Business has always had a large voice in determining policy, but the current mutually reinforcing economic and political crises and the government's weakness have enabled business increasingly to influence fundamental policy changes instead of confining itself, in public at least, simply to reacting to government's initiatives' (Yudelman, 1987: 251). However, the general thrust of Botha's political strategy after 1986 was security rather than economically oriented, and business, unable or unwilling, due to a short-termist approach, to drive the government to radical reform, generally remained discontented with government policy formulation. De Klerk's government, to a greater extent than Botha's, concerned itself with the real, long-term concerns of business (see Lee et al., 1991).

Although more sophisticated than early Marxist or Poulantzian theories of the state, the conception of long-term symbiosis as a whole can still be seen as simplistic in some regards. Despite Yudelman's stress on the distinction between state and government, his portrayal glosses over the contradictory relations existing within the body of the state's components. For example, the conflict in the late 1980s between the pro-Botha security establishment and the reformist foreign affairs and Constitutional Development departments over the leadership of the NP government, took place within state structures while reflecting wider divisions in Afrikaner society. Yudelman also seems preoccupied with the narrow relations between state and capital, overlooking relations which are just as significant, between the state and other identitative groups within society.

Apart from contradictory relations within the state, there can also be contradictory relations between different sets of state policies pursued in the interests of different social groups. A neglected aspect of the state's autonomy is its attempts to cope with the unintended social effects of its own agenda – for instance, the strong reaction from blacks against the new constitution of 1983–84, which undermined state capital accumulation strategies (and this from a government which was ostensibly more concerned than any other with developing a coherent Total Strategy). Realistic theories of the state, then, must also account for the historical inertia of 'accidental' changes in the relationship between state and society. They must additionally concern themselves with the wider geographical context within which states are active. Generally, most theories of the South African state address only its domestic parameters, overlooking the often crucial influence of other states and the geopolitical international system. For a recent overview of South African state theory as well as a localized study of local–central state relations, see Robinson, 1996.

But perhaps a more significant neglected dimension of state activity brings us back to the question with which this concluding section began – the formation of identity. State theorization helps us to conceive how social group demands have been filtered or redirected by the state in the construction and adaptation of the segregationist and apartheid political systems, but the state's role went further than this. The state itself has been an ambiguous and ambivalent participant in *shaping* the identities of those wider social groups. It has both reacted to and helped to draw the shifting boundaries of dominant groups. For example, the perceived widening of dominant group identity in the 1980s so as to include urban insider blacks, identified by Norval

(1990), was an attempt by the state itself to intervene in the shaping of identity (in this case, the inclusion was a futile attempt, but the changing definition of the excluded 'other' as communist succeeded only too well in most white minds). Earlier in the century, Botha and Smuts were able to convince many (though not all) Afrikaners to secure a broader South African identity through collaboration with English-speakers.

Since VOC colonization, the state has both empowered whites' own representations of blacks and reinforced, or even helped initiate, those representations – as, to a greater extent than was argued in Chapter 1, Elphick and Giliomee (1989b) believed was the case with the VOC itself. See also Crais: 'In its intervention in rural social relations the [colonial] state contributed to the rise of a colonialist discourse in daily social practice' (1992: 173). State theory, if it is to become more attuned to contemporary concerns, must pay more attention to the ways in which the state is both reactive and proactive in the shaping of identity and social group formation.

The extent to which white representations of blacks, empowered in the past by the state, have remained steadfast is remarkable. Pratt (1992) noted a tendency in late eighteenth-century travel-writing to treat *all* blacks as an iconic 'he' (that is, the standard adult male specimen).

> This abstracted *he/they* is the subject of verbs in a timeless present tense. These characterise anything 'he' is or does not as a particular event in time, but as an instance of a pregiven custom or trait (as a particular plant is an instance of a genus or species). Particular encounters between people get textualised, then, as enumerations of such traits. (Pratt, 1992: 64)

Through the intervening centuries, the same tendency remained within white writing about blacks. Although it finally disappeared from academic discourse in the post-war period, in the late 1980s the more deep-rooted ability to fix a timeless 'other' and to behave according to that construction, continued to characterize white South African discourse (itself obviously a generalization, but an acknowledged one) as a whole.

If there is to be greater social justice and stability in the new South Africa, most South Africans (and not only whites) have to extend the boundaries of their identity so as to incorporate former 'others', but crucially, *on their own terms*; to overcome the 'denial of coevalness' (Fabian, 1983: 35). Accordingly, spatial conceptions, too, must become more inclusive. As Wade puts it, 'the South African landscape in English-language documents [and as Coetzee (1988) shows, in Afrikaans documents too] has always been white-created, white perceived' (1993: 126). Consequently, both Coetzee (*Dusklands*) and Brink (*An Instant in the Wind*) 'present the Afrikaner as an incomplete person, raging or suffering for completion. This seems impossible to achieve unless or until he manages to incorporate the black into his sense of self' (Wade, 1993: 148). The mutual integration of blacks and whites into 'perceptual apparatus as a human being and not as a composite fiction of all the historical fears and fantasies which have their origins in the long struggle for land and power in South Africa' (Wade, 1993: 153) must be accompanied by the rejection of the need for white space or any other culturally exclusive sense of place.

Bibliography

Adam, H. 1987, 'Black Unions and Reformist Politics', in Butler, J. et al., Eds, Middletown, Connecticut.

Adam, H. 1990, 'Cohesion and Coercion', in Giliomee, H. and Gaganio, J., Eds, Oxford and Cape Town.

Adam, H. and Giliomee, H. 1979, *Ethnic Power Mobilized: Can South Africa Change?*, Yale University Press, New Haven, Connecticut and London.

Adam, H. and Moodley, K. 1986, *South Africa without Apartheid: Dismantling Racial Domination*, University of California Press, Berkeley, California.

Adam, H. and Moodley, K. 1993, *The Opening of the Apartheid Mind*, University of California Press, Berkeley, California.

Anderson, B. 1991, *Immagined Communities: Reflections on the Origin and Spread of Nationalism* (revised edition), Verso, New York and London. An influential treatment of the general formation of national identity.

Anthias, F. and Yuval-Davis, N. in association with Cain, H. 1993, *Racialized Boundaries: Race, Nation, Gender, Colour and Class and the Anti-Racist Struggle*, Routledge, London.

Armstrong, J. and Worden, N. 1989, 'The Slaves, 1652 to 1834', in Elphick, R. and Giliomee, H. Eds, Middletown, Connecticut.

Ashforth, A. 1990, *The Politics of Official Discourse in Twentieth Century South Africa*, Oxford University Press, Oxford.

Atkins, K.E. 1993, *The Moon is Dead! Give Us Our Money! The Cultural Origins of an African Work Ethic, Natal, South Africa, 1843–1900*, Heinemann, James Currey, London.

Barber, J. and Barratt, J. 1990, *South Africa's Foreign Policy: The Search for Status and Security, 1945–1988*, Cambridge University Press, Cambridge.

Barrow, B. Ed. 1976, *Tony Grogan's Vanishing Cape Town*, Don Nelson, Cape Town.

Beavon, K.S.O. and Rogerson, C.M. 1982, 'The Informal Sector of the Apartheid City: The Pavement People of Johannesburg', in Smith, D. Ed., London.

Beinart, W. 1982, *The Political Economy of Pondoland, 1860 to 1930*, Cambridge University Press, Cambridge.

Beinart, W. 1987, 'Worker Consciousness, Ethnic Pluralism and Nationalism: The Experiences of a South African Migrant, 1930 to 1960', in Marks, S. and Trapido, S. Eds, Harlow.

Beinart, W. 1988, 'Agrarian Historiography and Agrarian Reconstruction', in Lonsdale, J. Ed., Cambridge.

Beinart, W. 1994, *Twentieth Century South Africa*, Oxford University Press, Oxford.

Beinart, W. and Bundy, C. Eds 1987, *Hidden Struggles in Rural South Africa: Politics and Popular Movements in the Transkei and Eastern Cape, 1890–1930*, Ravan, Johannesburg.

Beinart, W., Delius, P. and Trapido, S. Eds 1986, *Putting a Plough to the Ground: Accumulation and Dispossession in Rural South Africa, 1850–1930*, Ravan, Johannesburg.

Bell, P. 1988, 'A Place Apart', *Leadership*, 7, 6.

Berger, I. 1987, 'Solidarity Fragmented: Garment Workers of the Transvaal, 1930–1960', in Marks, S. and Trapido, S. Eds, Harlow.

Blackwell, L. and May, H.J. 1947, *This is South Africa*, Shuter and Shooter, Pietermaritzburg.

Bloomberg, C. 1990, *Christian Nationalism and the Rise of the Afrikaner Broederbond in South Africa, 1918–1948*, Ed. Dubow, S., Macmillan, Basingstoke.

Blumer, H. 1965, 'Industrialisation and Race Relations', in Hunter, G. Ed. *Industrialisation and Race Relations*, Oxford University Press, London and Oxford.

Bonner, P., Hofmeyr, I., James, D. and Lodge, T. Eds 1989, *Holding Their Ground: Class, Locality and Culture in 19th and 20th Century South Africa*, Wiwatersrand University Press and Ravan, Johannesburg.

Bozzoli, B. 1978, 'Capital and the State in South Africa', *Review of African Political Economy*, 11.

Brain, J. 1989, 'Natal's Indians, 1860–1910: From Co-operation Through Competition to Conflict', in Duminy, A. and Guest, B. Eds, Pietermaritzburg.

Brain, J. 1994, 'An Economic Transformation: The Indian Community in Natal', in Guest, B. and Sellers, J. Eds, Pietermaritzburg.

Brewer, J. Ed. 1989a, *Can South Africa Survive?*, Macmillan, Basingstoke.

Brewer, J. 1989b, 'Internal Black Protest', in Brewer, J. Ed., Basingstoke.

Brewer, J. 1989c, 'Five Minutes to Midnight', in Brewer, J. Ed., Basingstoke.

Brookes, A. and Brickhill, J. 1980, *Whirlwind Before the Storm*, IDAF, London.

Brookes, E.H. and Webb, C. de B. 1987, *A History of Natal*, 2nd edition, University of Natal Press, Pietermaritzburg.

Browett, J.G. 1976, 'The Application of a Spatial Model to South Africa's Development Regions', *South African Geographical Journal*, 58, 2.

Browett, J.G. and Fair, T.J.D. 1974, 'South Africa 1870–1970: A View of the Spatial System', *South African Geographical Journal*, 56, 2.

Bundy, C. 1972, 'The Emergence and Decline of a South African Peasantry', *African Affairs*, 71, 285.

Bundy, C. 1979, *The Rise and Fall of the South African Peasantry*, Heinemann, London.

Bundy, C. 1980, 'Peasants in Herschel: A Case Study of a South African Frontier District', in Marks, S. and Atmore, A. Eds, Harlow.

Bundy, C. 1992, 'Development and Inequality in Historical Perspective', in Schrire, R. Ed., Cape Town.

Bunting, B. 1969, *The Rise of the South African Reich*, reprint, 1986, IDAF, London.

Butler, J. 1987, 'Interwar Liberalism and Local Activism', in Butler, J. et al., Eds, Middletown, Connecticut.

Butler, J. Elphick, R. and Welsh, D. Eds 1987, *Democratic Liberalism in South Africa*, Wesleyan University Press, Middletown, Connecticut.

Carter, P. 1987, *The Road to Botany Bay: An Essay in Spatial History*, Faber, London.

Chaskalson, M. 1991, 'The Road to Sharpeville', in Clingman, S. Ed., Johannesburg.

Christopher, A.J. 1983, 'From Flint to Soweto: Reflections on the Colonial Origins of the Apartheid City', *Area*, 15, 2.

Christopher, A.J. 1984, *South Africa: The Impact of Past Geographies*, Juta, Cape Town.

Christopher, A.J. 1989, 'Spatial Variations in the Application of Residential Segregation in South African Cities', *Geoforum*, 253.

Christopher, A.J. 1990, 'Apartheid and Urban Segregation Levels in South Africa', *Urban Studies*, 417.

Christopher, A.J. 1991, 'Port Elizabeth', in Lemon, A. Ed., Indiana and Cape Town.

Clifford, J. and Marcus, G.E. Eds, 1986, *Writing Culture: The Poetics and Politics of Ethnography*, University of California Press, Berkeley, California.

Clingman, S. Ed. 1991, *Regions and Repertoires: Topics in South African Politics and Culture*, Ravan, Johannesburg.

Cobbett, W. and Cohen, R. 1988, *Popular Struggles in South Africa*, James Currey, London.

Cobbing, J. 1988, 'The Mfecane as Alibi: Thoughts on Dithakong and Mbolompo', *Journal of African History*, 29.

Coetzee, J.M. 1983, *Life and Times of Michael K*, Penguin, London.

Coetzee, J.M. 1988, *White Writing: On the Culture of Letters in South Africa*, Yale University Press, New Haven, Connecticut and London. Reflects novel approaches in its treatment of landscape as a cultural 'text'.

Coetzee, J.M. 1990, *Age of Iron*, Secker and Warburg, London.

Cohen, R. 1986, *Endgame in South Africa?*, UNESCO, London and Paris.

Cohen, W.B. 1980, *The French Encounter with Africans*, Indiana University Press, Bloomington, Indiana and London.

Cole, K. Ed. 1994, *Sustainable Development for a Democratic South Africa*, Earthscan, London.

Colenbrander, P. 1979, 'The Zulu Political Economy on the Eve of War', in Duminy, A. and Ballard, C. Eds, Pietermaritzburg.

Comaroff, J. and Comaroff, J. 1991, *Of Revelation and Revolution: Christianity, Colonialism and Consciousness in South Africa*, vol.1, The University of Chicago Press, Chicago, Illinois. Well regarded beyond its subject area as an insightful account of pre- and early colonial interaction across cultural boundaries.

Cook, G.P. 1991, 'Cape Town', in Lemon, A. Ed. Bloomington, Indiana and Cape Town.

Crais, C. 1992, *White Supremacy and Black Resistance in Pre-Industrial South Africa: The Making of the Colonial Order in the Eastern Cape, 1770–1865*, Cambridge University Press, Cambridge. An account informed by recent emphases on identity formation and cultural interaction.

Crankshaw, O. and Hart, T. 1990, 'The Roots of Homelessness: Causes of Squatting in the Vlakfontien Settlement South of Johannesburg', *South African Geographical Journal*, 72, 2.

Crush, J. 1992, 'Beyond the Frontier: The New South African Historical Geography', in Rogerson, C. and McCarthy, J. Eds, Oxford and Cape Town.

Curtin, P.D. 1964, *The Image of Africa: British Ideas and Action, 1780–1850*, University of Wisconsin Press, Madison, Wisconsin and London.

Dauskaardt, R. 1990, 'The Changing Geography of Traditional Medicine: Urban Herbalism on the Witwatersrand, South Africa', *Geojournal*, 22–3.

Davenport, T.R.H. 1991, *South Africa: A Modern History*, Macmillan, Basingstoke. Comprehensive history textbook.

Davies, R.J. 1991, 'Durban', in Lemon, A. Ed., Bloomington, Indiana and Cape Town.

Davies R., Kaplan D., Morris M. and O'Meara D. 1976, 'Class Struggle and the Periodisation of the State in South Africa', *Review of African Political Economy*, 7.

De Kiewiet, C.W. 1957, *A History of South Africa, Social and Economic*, Oxford University Press, Oxford. 'Classic' liberal account.

Delius, P. 1983, *The Land Belongs to Us: The Pedi Polity, the Boers and the British in the Nineteenth Century Transvaal*, Ravan Press, California.

De Villiers, M. 1988, *White Tribe Dreaming*, Penguin, London.

Dewar, D. and Watson, V. 1982, 'Urbanization, Unemployment and Petty Commodity Production and Trading: Comparative Cases in Cape Town', in Smith, D. Ed., London.

Dubow, S. 1987, 'Race, Civilisation and Culture: The Elaboration of Segregationist Discourse in the Inter-war Years', in Marks, S. and Trapido, S. Eds, Harlow.

Dubow, S. 1989, *Racial Segregation and the Origins of Apartheid in South Africa, 1919–1936*, Macmillan, Basingstoke.

Dubow, S. 1995, *Scientific Racism in Modern South Africa*, Cambridge University Press, Cambridge.

Duminy, A. and Ballard, C. Eds 1979, *The Anglo-Zulu War: New Perspectives*, Shuter and Shooter, Pietermaritzburg.

Duminy, A. and Guest, W. Eds 1989, *Natal and Zululand from Earliest Times to 1910: A New History*, University of Natal Press, Shuter and Shooter, Pietermaritzburg.

Du Toit, A. 1983, 'No Chosen People: The Myth of the Calvinist Origins of Afrikaner Nationalism and Racial Ideology', *American Historical Review*, 88.

Eldredge, E. and Morton, F. Eds 1994, *Slavery in South Africa: Captive Labour on the Dutch Frontier*, Westview and University of Natal Press, Oxford and Pietermaritzburg.

Elphick, R. 1987, 'Historiography and the Future of Liberal Values in South Africa', in Butler, J. et al., Eds, Middletown, Connecticut.

Elphick, R. and Giliomee, H. Eds 1989a, *The Shaping of South African Society, 1652 to 1840*, Wesleyan University Press, Middletown, Connecticut. Together with Crais, 1992, the fullest treatment of early colonization and its repercussions for indigenous peoples.

Elphick, R. and Giliomee, H. 1989b, 'The Origins and Entrenchment of European Domination at the Cape, 1652 to c.1840', in Elphick, R. and Giliomee, H. Eds, Middletown, Connecticut.

Elphick, R. and Malherbe, V.C. 1989, 'The Khoisan to 1828', in Elphick, R. and Giliomee, H. Eds, Middletown, Connecticut.

Elphick, R. and Shell, R. 1989, 'Intergroup Relations: Khoikhoi, Settlers, Slaves and Free Blacks, 1652–1795', in Elphick, R. and Giliomee, H. Eds, Middletown, Connecticut.

Eyles, J. and Smith, D.M. Eds 1988, *Qualitative Methods in Human Geography*, Polity Press, Cambridge.

Fabian, J. 1983, *Time and the Other: How Anthropology Makes Its Object*, Columbia University Press, New York.

Fanon, F. 1963, *The Wretched of the Earth*, Penguin, Harmondsworth. Extremely influential account of colonial and anti-colonial psychology.

Feit, E. 1965, 'Conflict and Communication: An Analysis of the "Western Areas" and "Bantu Education" Campaigns', unpublished PhD, Michigan.

Fisher, F., Schlemmer, L. and Webster, E. 1978, 'Economic Growth and Its Relationship to Social and Political Change', in Schlemmer, L. and Webster, E. Eds, Johannesburg.

Fox, R., Nel, E. and Reintges, C. 1991, 'East London', in Lemon, A. Ed., Bloomington, Indiana and Cape Town.

Freund, W. 1989, 'The Cape Under the Transitional Governments, 1795–1814', in Elphick, R. and Giliomee, H. Eds, Middletown, Connecticut.

Freund, W. 1991, 'South African Gold Mining in Transformation', in Gelb, S. Ed., Cape Town and London.

Friedman, S. 1991, 'The National Party and the South African Transition', in Lee, R. and Schlemmer, L. Eds, Cape Town and Oxford.

Gelb, S. Ed. 1991, *South Africa's Economic Crisis*, David Philip, Zed Books, Cape Town and London.

Gellner, E. 1994, *Encounters with Nationalism*, Blackwell, Oxford.

Giliomee, H. 1987, 'Apartheid, Verligtheid, and Liberalism', in Butler, J. et al. Eds, Middletown, Connecticut.

Giliomee, H. 1989a, 'The Eastern Frontier, 1770–1812', in Elphick, R. and Giliomee, H. Eds, Middletown, Connecticut.

Giliomee, H. 1989b, 'The Beginnings of Afrikaner Ethnic Consciousness, 1850–1915', in Vail, L. Ed., Berkeley, California.

Giliomee, H. and Gaganio, J. Eds 1990, *The Elusive Search for Peace: South Africa, Israel and Northern Ireland*, Oxford University Press, Oxford and Cape Town.

Giliomee, H. and Schlemmer, L. 1989, *From Apartheid to Nation Building*, Oxford University Press, Oxford.

Goldin, I. 1989, 'Coloured Identity and Coloured Politics in the Western Cape Region of South Africa', in Vail, L. Ed., Berkeley, California.

Graaff, J. 1990, 'Towards an Understanding of Bantustan Politics', in Nattrass, N. and Ardington, E. Eds, Oxford.

Greenberg, S. 1987, *Legitimating the Illegitimate: State, Markets and Resistance in South Africa*, University of California Press, Berkeley, California.

Greenfeld, L. 1992, *Nationalism: Five Roads to Modernity*, Harvard University Press, Cambridge, Mass.

Gregory, D. 1994, *Geographical Imaginations*, Blackwell, Oxford. Sets the agenda for new approaches to geography informed by insights from the wider social sciences and literary analysis.

Gregory, D. and Urry, J. 1985, *Social Relations and Spatial Structures*, Macmillan, Basingstoke.

Grieg, R. 1980, 'An Approach to Afrikaans Film', *Critical Arts: A Journal for Media Studies*, 1, 14–24.

Grundy, K. 1991, *South Africa: Domestic Crisis and Global Challenge*, Westview, Boulder, Colorado, San Francisco and Oxford.

Guelke, L. 1989, 'Freehold Farmers and Frontier Settlers, 1657–1780', in Elphick, R. and Giliomee, H. Eds, Middletown, Connecticut.

Guest, B. and Sellers, J. Eds 1994, *Receded Tides of Empire: Aspects of the Economic and Social History of Natal and Zululand Since 1910*, University of Natal Press, Pietermaritzburg.

Gunner, E. 1988, 'Literature and Apartheid', in Lonsdale, J. Ed., Cambridge.

Guy, J. 1980, 'Ecological Factors in the Rise of Shaka and the Zulu Kingdom', in Marks, S. and Atmore, A. Eds, Harlow.

Guy, J. 1982, *The Destruction of the Zulu Kingdom*, Ravan, Johannesburg.

Habermas, J. 1975, *Legitimation Crisis*, Heinemann, London.

Halbach, A. 1988, 'The South African Homeland Policy and Its Consequences: An Evaluation of Separate Development', *Development Southern Africa*, 508.

Hanlon, J. 1986, *Beggar Your Neighbours: Apartheid Power in Southern Africa*, CIIR, London.

Harries, P. 1982, 'Kinship, Ideology and the Nature of Pre-Colonial Labour Migration', in Marks and Rathbone Eds, London.

Hart, D.M. 1988, 'Political Manipulation of Urban Space: The Razing of District Six, Cape Town', *Urban Geography*, 9.

Hart, D.M. and Pirie, G.H. 1984, 'The Sight and Soul of Sophiatown', *Geographical Review*, 74, 1.

Hart, G. 1989, 'On Grey Areas', *South African Geographical Journal*, 81.

Harvey, D. 1982, *The Limits to Capital*, Blackwell, Oxford.

Hedges, D. 1978, 'Trade and Politics in Southern Mozambique and Zululand in the 18th and Early 19th Centuries', unpublished PhD thesis, London.

Hirson, B. 1979, *Year of Fire, Year of Ash*, Zed, London.

Hobsbawn, E.J. 1987, *The Age of Empire*, Weidenfeld and Nicolson, London.

Hobsbawm, E.J. 1990, *Nations and Nationalism Since 1780: Programme, Myth, Reality*, Cambridge University Press, Cambridge.

Hofmeyr, I. 1991, 'Popularising History: The Case of Gustav Preller', in Clingman, S. Ed., Johannesburg.

Hope, C. 1986, *The Hottentot Room*, Heinemann, London.

Horowitz, D. 1991, *A Democratic South Africa? Constitutional Engineering in a Divided Society*, University of California Press, Berkeley, California.

Huddleston, T. 1956, *Naught for Your Comfort*, Collins, London.

Humphries, R. and Shubane, K. 1991, 'Homelands and Provinces: Dynamics of Change and Transition', in Lee, R. and Schlemmer, L. Eds, Cape Town and Oxford.

Hyam, R. 1972, *The Failure of South African Expansion, 1908–48*, Macmillan, Basingstoke.

Hyslop, J. 1991, 'Food, Authority and Politics: Student Riots in South African Schools, 1945–1976', in Clingman, S. Ed., Johannesburg.

Ingham, K. 1988, *Jan Christian Smuts: The Conscience of a South African*, Weidenfeld and Nicolson, London.

James, W.G. and Simons, M. Eds 1989, *The Angry Divide: Social and Economic History of the Western Cape*, David Philip, Claremont.

Johnson, P. and Martin D. Eds 1989, *Aparthied Terrorism: The Destabilization Report*, Indiana University Press, Bloomington, Indiana.

Johnson, R.W. 1977, *How Long Will South Africa Survive?*, Macmillan, Basingstoke.

Johnson, S. 1994, *Strange Days Indeed: South Africa from Insurrection to Post-Election*, Bantam Books, London.

Johnston, R.J. 1991, *A Question of Place*, Blackwell, Oxford.

Johnston, R.J., Gregory, D. and Smith, D.M. Eds 1990, *The Dictionary of Human Geography*, 2nd edition, Blackwell, Oxford.

Kahn, B. 1991, 'The Crisis and South Africa's Balance of Payments', in Gelb, S. Ed., Cape Town and London.

Kane Berman, J. 1978, *Soweto: Black Revolt, White Reaction*, Ravan, Johannesburg.

Kane Berman, J. 1979, *South Africa: A Method in the Madness*, Pluto, London. British edition of the above.

Katzen, M.F. 1982, 'White Settlers and the Origin of a New Society, 1652–1778', in Wilson, M. and Thompson, L. Eds, London and Cape Town.

Keegan, T. 1986, *Rural Transformations in Industrializing South Africa: The Southern Highveld to 1914*, Macmillan, Basingstoke.

Kennedy, P.A. 1981, 'Mpande and the Zulu Kingship', *Journal of Natal and Zulu History*, 4.

Kentridge, M. 1991, *An Unofficial War: Inside the Conflict in Pietermaritzburg*, David Philip, Cape Town and Johannesburg. Vividly written, this gives a taste of the terrible conflict in Natal in the 1980s.

Khosa, M. 1990, 'The Black Taxi Revolution', in Nattrass, N., and Ardington, E. Eds, Oxford.

Krige, D.S. 1991, 'Bloemfontein', in Lemon, A. Ed., Bloomington, Indiana and Cape Town.

Kuhn, T. 1970, *The Structure of Scientific Revolutions*, University of Chicago Press, Chicago, Illinois.

Kuper, A. 1988, 'Anthropology and Apartheid', in Lonsdale, J. Ed., Cambridge.

Kuper, L. 1971, Review of 'Class and Colour in South Africa, 1850–1950', in Kuper, L., London.

Kuper, L. 1974, *Race, Class and Power*, Duckworth, London.

Kuper, L., Watts, H. and Davies R. 1958, *Durban: A Study in Racial Ecology*, Jonathan Cape, London.

Laclau, E. Ed. 1990, *New Reflections on the Revolution of Our Time*, Verso, London.

Laclau, E. Ed. 1994, *The Making of Political Identities*, Verso, London.

Lambert, R. and Webster, E. 1988, 'The Re-Emergence of Political Unionism in Contemporary South Africa?', in Cobbett, W. and Cohen, R. Eds, London.

Lea, J.P. 1982, 'Government Dispensation, Capitalist Imperative or Liberal Philanthropy? Responses to the Black Housing Crisis in South Africa', in Smith, D. Ed., London.

Lee, R. and Schlemmer, L. Eds 1991, *Transition to Democracy, Policy Perspectives 1991*, Oxford University Press, Cape Town and Oxford.

Lee, R., Sutherland, M., Phillips, M. and McLennan, A. 1991, 'Speaking or Listening? Observers or Agents of Change? Business and Public Policy, 1989–90', in Lee, R. and Schlemmer, L. Eds, Cape Town and Oxford.

Leftwich, A. Ed. 1974, *Economic Growth and Political Change*, Allison and Busby, London.

Legassick, M. 1980, 'The Frontier Tradition in South African Historiography', in Marks, S. and Atmore, A. Eds, Harlow.

Legassick, M. 1989, 'The Northern Frontier to c.1840: The Rise and Decline of the Griqua People', in Elphick, R. and Giliomee, H. Eds, Middletown, Connecticut.

Legassick, M. and Hemson, D. 1976, *Foreign Investment and the Reproduction of Racial Capitalism in South Africa*, Anti-Apartheid Movement, London.

Lelyveld, J. 1987, *Move Your Shadow*, Abacus, London. One of the better journalistic accounts of the absurdity of apartheid.

Le May, G.H. 1971, *Black and White in South Africa*, MacDonald, London.

Lemon, A. 1982, 'Migrant Labour and Frontier Commuters: Reorganizing South Africa's Black Labour Supply', in Smith, D. Ed., London.

Lemon, A. 1987, *Apartheid in Transition*, Gower, London.

Lemon, A. Ed. 1991a, *Homes Apart: South Africa's Segregated Cities*, Paul Chapman, London; Indiana University Press, Bloomington, Indiana and David Philip, Claremont, South Africa. Excellent collection of case studies of the evolution of spatial urban structures.

Lemon, A. 1991b, 'The Apartheid City', in Lemon, A. Ed., Bloomington, Indiana and Cape Town.

Lester, A. Forthcoming, 'Cultural Construction and Spatial Strategy on the Eastern Cape Frontier, 1806–1838', *The South African Geographical Journal*.

Lewsen, P. 1987, 'Liberals in Politics and Administration, 1936–1948', in Butler, J. et al., Eds, Middletown, Connecticut.

Lipton, M. 1985, *Capitalism and Apartheid: South Africa, 1910–1986*, Gower and Wildwood House, London. Ground-breaking analysis which challenged Marxist interpretations of the relationship between apartheid and capitalism.

Lipton, M. 1988, 'Capitalism and Apartheid', in Lonsdale, J. Ed., Cambridge.

Lodge, T. 1983, *Black Politics in South Africa Since 1945*, Longman, Harlow. The most comprehensive single-volume account of resistance to apartheid.

Lodge, T. 1989, 'The United Democratic Front: Leadership and Ideology', in Brewer, J. Ed., Basingstoke.

Lodge, T. 1992, 'Rebellion: The Turning of the Tide', in Lodge, T. and Nasson, B. Eds, London.

Lodge, T. and Nasson, B. Eds 1992, *All Here and Now: Black Politics in South Africa in the 1980s*, Hurst, London.

Lonsdale, J. Ed. 1988a, *South Africa in Question*, Cambridge University Press, Cambridge.

Lonsdale, J. 1988b, 'Introduction', in Lonsdale, J. Ed., Cambridge.

Luckhardt, K. and Wall, B. 1980, *Organize ... Or Starve! The History of the South African Congress of Trade Unions*, Lawrence and Wishart, London.

Lupton, M. 1992, 'Class Struggle Over the Built Environment in Johannesburg's Coloured Areas', in Smith, D. Ed., London.

MacCrone, I.A.D. 1937, *Race Attitudes in South Africa: Historical, Experimental and Psychological Studies*, Oxford University Press, Cape Town.

McGrath, M. 1990, 'Economic Growth, Income Distribution and Social Change', in Nattrass, N. and Ardington, E. Eds, Oxford.

Mclennan, B. 1986, *A Proper Degree of Terror: John Graham and the Cape's Eastern Frontier*, Ravan, Johannesburg.

Macmillan, W.M. 1929, *Bantu, Boer and Britain: The Making of the South African Native Policy*, London; 2nd edition, Clarendon Press, Oxford, 1963.

Macmillan, W.M. 1930, *The Cape Colour Question*, Faber and Gwyer, London.

Macmillan, W.M. 1931, *Complex South Africa*, Faber and Faber, London. All three Macmillan books are classic, concerned early liberal accounts.

Mabin, A. 1989, 'Does Geography Matter?', *The South African Geographical Review*, 71, 2.

Mabin, A. and Parnell, S. 1983, 'Recommodification and Working Class Home Ownership: New Directions for South African Cities?', *South African Geographical Journal*, 65.

Magubane, B. 1989, *South Africa from Soweto to Uitenhage: The Political Economy of the South African Revolution*, Africa World Press, New Jersey.

Maharaj, B. 1992, 'The "Spatial Impress" of the Central and Local States: The Group Areas Act in Durban', in Smith, D. Ed., London.

Malan, R. 1990, *My Traitor's Heart*, Vintage, London. Gripping rendering of apartheid's peculiar psychoses.

Marcus, T. 1989, *Modernising Super-Exploitation: Restructuring South African Agriculture*, Zed Books, London and New Jersey.

Maré, G. 1992, *Ethnicity and Politics in South Africa*, Zed Books, London and New Jersey.

Maré, G. and Hamilton, G. 1987, *An Appetite for Power: Buthelezi's Inkatha and South Africa*, Ravan, Johannesburg and Indiana University Press, Bloomington and Indianapolis, Indiana.

Marks, S. 1970, *Reluctant Rebellion: The 1906–8 Disturbances in Natal*, Clarendon Press, Oxford.

Marks, S. 1986, *The Ambiguities of Dependence in South Africa: Class, Nationalism and the State in Twentieth Century Natal*, Ravan, Johannesburg.

Marks, S. and Anderson, N. 1988, 'Diseases of Apartheid', in Lonsdale, J. Ed., Cambridge.

Marks, S. and Atmore, A. Eds 1980a, *Economy and Society in Pre-Industrial South Africa*, Longman, Harlow.

Marks, S. and Atmore, A. 1980b, 'Introduction', in Marks, S. and Atmore, A. Eds, Harlow.

Marks, S. and Rathbone, B. Eds 1982, *Industrialisation and Social Change in South Africa: African Class Formation, Culture and Consciousness, 1870 to 1930*, Longman, London.

Marks, S. and Trapido, S. Eds 1987a, *The Politics of Race, Class and Nationalism in Twentieth Century South Africa*, Longman, Harlow. Each of these books co-edited by Marks pushed Marxist analyses into new, less deterministic realms.

Marks, S. and Trapido, S. 1987b, 'The Politics of Race, Class and Nationalism', in Marks, S. and Trapido, S. Eds, Harlow.

Marris, P. 1986, *Loss and Change*, revised edition, Routledge and Kegan Paul, London.

Marx, C. 1994, 'The Ossewabrandwag as a Mass Movement, 1939–1941', *Journal of Southern African Studies*, 20, 2.

Massey, D. 1984, *Spatial Divisions of Labour: Social Structures and the Geography of Production*, Macmillan, London.

Maylam, P. 1990, 'The Rise and Decline of Urban Apartheid in South Africa', *African Affairs*, 89.

Miliband, R. 1969, *The State in Capitalist Society*, Quartet, London.

Mitchell, M. and Russell, D. 1989a, 'Black Unions and Political Change in South Africa', in Brewer, J. Ed., Basingstoke.

Mitchell, M. and Russell, D. 1989b, 'Political Impasse in South Africa: State Capacities and Crisis Management', in Brewer, J. Ed., Basingstoke.

Modisane, B. 1963, *Blame Me on History*, Penguin, Harmondsworth.

Moll, T. 1989, '"Probably the Best Laager in the World": The Record and Prospects of the South African Economy', in Brewer, J. Ed., Basingstoke.

Moll, T. 1990, 'From Booster to Brake? Apartheid and Economic Growth in Comparitive Perspective', in Nattrass, N. and Ardington, E. Eds, Oxford.

Moll, T. 1991a, 'Did the Apartheid Economy Fail?', *Journal of Southern African Studies*, 17, 2.

Moll, T. 1991b, 'Conclusion: What Redistributes and What Doesn't', in Moll, T. et al., Eds, Cape Town.

Moll, T., Nattrass, N. and Loots, L. Eds 1991, *Redistribution: How Can It Work in South Africa?*, David Philip, Cape Town.

Moodie, T.D. 1975, *The Rise of Afrikanerdom: Power, Apartheid and the Afrikaner Civil Religion*, University of California Press, Berkeley, California.

Moore, B. 1992, 'The Case for Land Tax: From Entitlement to Restitution', *Indicator South Africa*, 9, 2.

Morris, M. 1991, 'State, Capital and Growth: The Political Economy of the National Question', in Gelb, S. Ed., Cape Town and London.

Mostert, N. 1992, *Frontiers: The Epic of South Africa's Creation and the Tragedy of the Xhosa People*, Jonathan Cape, London. Gives a vivid impression of conflict and co-operation between settlers, administrators, missionaries, Khoisan and Xhosa in the Cape eastern frontier region.

Nattrass, N. 1990, 'Economic Power and Profits in Post-War Manufacturing', in Nattrass, N. and Ardington, E. Eds.

Nattrass, N. 1991, 'Controversies About Capitalism and Apartheid in South Africa: An Economic Perspective', *Journal of Southern African Studies*, 17, 4.

Nattrass, N. and Ardington, E. Eds 1990, *The Political Economy of South Africa*, Oxford University Press, Cape Town.

Newton-King, S. 1980, 'The Labour Market in the Cape Colony, 1807–1828', in Marks, S. and Atmore, A. Eds, Harlow.

Nolutshungu, S. 1982, *Changing South Africa, Political Considerations*, Manchester University Press, Manchester.

Norton, C. 1948, *Opportunity in South Africa*, Rockliff, London.

Norval, A.J. 1990, 'Letter to Ernesto', in Laclau, E. Ed., London.

Norval, A.J. 1994, 'Social Ambiguity and the Crisis of Apartheid', in Laclau, E. Ed., London.

O'Dowd, M.C. 1974, 'South Africa in the Light of the Stages of Economic Growth', in Leftwich, A. Ed., London.

O'Dowd, M.C. 1978, 'The Stages of Economic Growth and the Future of South Africa', in Schlemmer, L. and Webster, E. Eds, Johannesburg.

O'Meara, D. 1983, *Volkskapitalisme: Class, Capital and Ideology in the Development of Afrikaner Nationalism, 1934 to 1948*, Cambridge University Press, Cambridge. Important Marxist analysis of Afrikaner nationalism.

Parnell, S. 1988, 'Land Requisition and the Changing Residential Face of Johannesburg, 1930 to 1955', *Area*, 20.

Parry, R. 1983, ' "In a Sense Citizens, But Not Altogether Citizens... ": Rhodes, Race and the Ideology of Segregation at the Cape in the Late 19th Century', *Canadian Journal of African Studies*, 17, 3.

Peires, J.B. 1981, *The House of Phalo: A History of the Xhosa People in the Days of Their Independence*, Ravan, Johannesburg.

Peires, J.B. 1989a, 'The British at the Cape, 1814–1834', in Elphick, R. and Giliomee, H. Eds, Middletown, Connecticut.

Peires, J.B. 1989b, *The Dead Will Arise: Nongqawuse and the Great Xhosa Cattle-Killing Movement of 1856–7*, James Currey, London. Well-researched account of the Xhosa cattle-killing movement.

Pickles, J. 1988, 'Recent Changes in Regional Policy in South Africa', *Geography*, 73, 3.

Pirie, G.H. 1982, 'The Decivilizing Rails: Railways and Underdevelopment in Southern Africa', *Tijdschrift voor Economische en Sociale Geografie*, 73, 4.

Pirie, G.H. 1992 'Travelling Under Apartheid', in Smith, D. Ed., London.

Plaatje, S. 1915, *Native Life in South Africa*, 1982 reprint, Ravan Writers Series, Johannesburg.

Posel, D. 1991, *The Making of Apartheid, 1948–1961: Conflict and Compromise*, Oxford University Press, Oxford.

Poulantzas, N. 1973, *Political Power and Social Class*, New Left Review, London.

Pratt, M.L. 1986, 'Fieldwork in Common Places', in Clifford, J. and Marcus, G.E. Eds, Los Angeles, California.

Pratt, M.L. 1992, *Imperial Eyes: Travel Writing and Transculturation*, Routledge, London. Section on cultural perceptions of late eighteenth- and early nineteenth-century travellers to South Africa likely to become very influential.

Price, R. 1991, *The Apartheid State in Crisis: Political Transformation in South Africa, 1975–1990*, Oxford University Press, Oxford. The best political analysis of apartheid's later years.

Ramphele, M. Ed. 1991, *Restoring the Land*, Panos, London.

Rantete, J. and Swilling, M. 1991, 'Organization and Strategies of the Major Resistance Movements in the Negotiation Era', in Lee, R. and Schlemmer, L. Eds, Cape Town and Oxford.

Reintges, C. 1992, 'Urban (Mis)Management? A Case Study of the Effects of Orderly Urbanisation on Duncan Village', in Smith, D. Ed., London.

Rich, P. 1981, 'Segregation and the Cape Liberal Tradition', in *The Societies of Southern Africa in the 19th and 20th Centuries*, 10, Institute of Commonwealth Studies, London.

Rich, P. 1984, *White Power and the Liberal Conscience: Racial Segregation and South African Liberalism*, Ravan, Johannesburg.

Rich, P. 1989, 'Doctrines of "Change" in South Africa', in Brewer, J. Ed., Basingstoke.

Richardson, P. 1986, 'The Natal Sugar Industry in the 19th Century', in Beinart, W. et al., Eds, Johannesburg.

Robeson, E.G. 1946, *An African Journey*, Gollancz, London.

Robinson, J. 1996, *The Power of Apartheid: State, Power and Space in South African Cities*, Butterworth-Heinemann, Oxford.

Rogerson, C.M. 1982, 'Apartheid, Decentralization and Spatial Industrial Change', in Smith, D. Ed., London.

Rogerson, C.M., Bernstein, A., Beavon, K.S.O. and Hart, D.M. 1989, 'Urbanization in the Third World: Policy Papers for South Africa', *The South African Geographical Journal*, special issue, 71, 3.

Rogerson, C.M. and McCarthy, J. Eds 1992, *Geography in a Changing South Africa, Progress and Prospects*, Oxford University Press, Oxford and Cape Town.

Ross, R. 1989, 'The Cape of Good Hope and the World Economy, 1652 to 1835', in Elphick, R. and Giliomee, H. Eds, Middletown, Connecticut.

Sachs, A. 1990, 'Rights to Land: A Fresh Look at the Property Question', *Societies of Southern Africa in the 19th and 20th Centuries*, Institute of Commonwealth Studies, London.

Said, E. 1978, *Orientalism*, Routledge and Kegan Paul, London. Highly influential account of the cultural representation of 'others', and its consequences.

Said, E. 1989, 'Representing the Colonized: Anthropology's Interlocutors', *Critical Inquiry*, 15.

Said, E. 1993, *Culture and Imperialism*, Chatto and Windus, London.

Said, E. 1995, 'East isn't East: The Impending End of the Age of Orientalism', *Times Literary Supplement*, 3 February.

Saunders, C. 1988a, *The Making of the South African Past: Major Historians on Race and Class*, David Philip, Cape Town. Useful interpretation of shifting views of South African history.

Saunders, C. 1988b, 'Historians and Apartheid', in Lonsdale, J. Ed., Cambridge.

Schlemmer, L. 1990, 'Strategies for the Future', in Giliomee, H. and Gagano, J. Eds, Oxford and Cape Town.

Schlemmer, L. 1991a, 'Negotiation Dilemmas After the Sound and Fury', *Indicator South Africa*, 8, 3.

Schlemmer, L. 1991b, 'The Turn in the Road: Emerging Conditions in 1990', in Lee, R. and Schlemmer, L. Eds, Cape Town and Oxford.

Schlemmer, L., Stack, L. and Berkow, C. 1991, 'Transition and the White Grass Roots', in Lee, R. and Schlemmer, L. Eds, Cape Town and Oxford.

Schlemmer, L. and Webster, E. Eds 1978, *Change, Reform and Economic Growth in South Africa*, Ravan, Johannesburg.

Schrire, R. 1992a, *Adapt or Die: The End of White Politics in South Africa*, Hurst Update Series, London.

Schrire, R. Ed. 1992b, *Wealth or Poverty: Critical Choices for South Africa*, Oxford University Press, Cape Town.

Scott, D. 1992, 'The Destruction of Clairwood: A Case Study on the Transformation of Communal Living Space', in Smith, D. Ed., London.

Seekings, J. 1988, 'The Origins of Political Mobilisation in the PWV Townships, 1980–1984', in Cobbett, W. and Cohen, R. Eds, London.

Shell, R. 1989, 'The Family and Slavery at the Cape, 1680–1808', in James, W.G. and Simons, M. Eds, Claremont.

Shell, R. 1994, *Children of Bondage: A Social History of the Slave Society at the Cape of Good Hope, 1652–1838*, Wiwatersrand University Press, Johannesburg.

Simons, J. and Simons, R. 1969, *Class and Colour in South Africa, 1850–1950*, International Defence and Aid Fund for Southern Africa (IDAF) reprint, London, 1983. Early attempt to set South African social formation within a Marxist framework.

Skinner, Q. 1985, *The Return of Grand Theory in the Human Sciences*, Cambridge University Press, Cambridge.

Smit, P. 1979, 'Urbanization in Africa: Lessons for Urbanization in the Homelands', *South African Geographical Journal*, 61, 1.

Smit, P., Olivier, J.J. and Booysen, J.J. 1982, 'Urbanization in the Homelands', in Smith, D. Ed., London.

Smith, A.D. 1986, *The Ethnic Origins of Nations*, Basil Blackwell, Oxford.

Smith, A.D. 1991, *National Identity*, Penguin, Harmondsworth.

Smith, D. Ed. 1982a, *Living Under Apartheid*, Allen and Unwin, London.

Smith, D. 1982b, 'Urbanization and Social Change Under Apartheid: Some Recent Developments', in Smith, D. Ed., London.

Smith, D. 1987, *Apartheid in South Africa*, 3rd edition, 1990, Update Series, Cambridge University Press, Cambridge. Clear student-orientated account of apartheid's geographical implications.

Smith, D. Ed. 1992a, *The Apartheid City and Beyond*, Routledge, London. Geographical collection on near-contemporary urban South Africa.

Smith, D. 1992b, 'Introduction', in Smith, D. Ed., London.

Smith, D. 1994, *Geography and Social Justice*, Blackwell, Oxford,

Snowden, F.M. Jr, 1983, *Before Color Prejudice: The Ancient View of Blacks*, Harvard University Press, Cambridge, Massachusetts.

Soja, E. 1989, *Postmodern Geographies: The Reassertion of Space in Critical Social Theory*, Verso, London and New York.

Sole, K. 1991, 'Authorship, Authenticity and the Black Community: The Novels of Soweto 1976', in Clingman, S. Ed., Johannesburg.

Soni, D. 1992, 'The Apartheid State and Black Housing Struggles', in Smith, D. Ed., London.

Sparks, A. 1990, *The Mind of South Africa: The Story of the Rise and Fall of Apartheid*, Heinemann, London.

Sparks, A. 1995, *Tomorrow is Another Country: The Inside Story of South Africa's Negotiated Revolution*, Heinemann, London.

Spies, S.B. 1986, 'The Concentration Camps' (insert), in Cameron, T. and Spies, S.B. Eds, *An Illustrated History of South Africa*, Jonathan Ball, Johannesburg.

Spivak, G.C. 1988, *In Other Worlds: Essays in Cultural Politics*, Routledge, London.

Stadler, A. 1987, *The Political Economy of Modern South Africa*, David Philip, Cape Town, Johannesburg and London.

Swan, M. 1987, 'Ideology in Organised Indian Politics, 1891–1948', in Marks, S. and Trapido, S. Eds, Harlow.

Swanson, M.W. 1977, 'The Sanitary Syndrome: Bubonic Plague and Urban Native Policy in the Cape Colony, 1900–1910', *Journal of African History*, 18, 3.

Swanson, M.W. 1983, '"The Asiatic Menace": Creating Segregation in Durban, 1870–1900', *International Journal of African Historical Studies*, 16.

Swilling, M., Humphries, R. and Shubane, K. Eds 1992, *The Apartheid City in Transition*, Oxford University Press, Oxford.

Swilling, M. and Shubane, K. 1991, 'Negotiating Urban Transition: The Soweto Experience', in Lee, R. and Schlemmer, L. Eds, Cape Town and Oxford.

Terreblanche, S. and Nattrass, N. 1990, 'A Periodization of the Political Economy from 1910', in Nattrass, N. and Ardington, E. Eds, Oxford.

Thompson, L. 1985, *The Political Mythology of Apartheid*, Yale University Press, New Haven, Connecticut and London. Under-read and well-written identification of the myths at the heart of Afrikaner nationalist identity.

Tomaselli, K.G. 1988, 'The Geography of Popular Memory in Post-Colonial South Africa: A Study of Afrikaans Cinema', in Eyles, J. and Smith, D.M. Eds, Cambridge.

Tomlinson, R. 1990, *Urbanization in Post-Apartheid South Africa*, Unwin Hyman, London.

Trapido, S. 1971, 'South Africa in a Comparative Study of Industrialisation', *Journal of Development Studies*, 7, 3.

Trapido, S. 1980, '"The Friends of the Natives": Merchants, Peasants and the Political and Ideological Structure of Liberalism in the Cape, 1854–1910', in Marks, S. and Atmore, A. Eds, Harlow.

Turrell, R. 1984, 'Kimberley's Model Compounds', *Journal of African History*, 25.

Turrell, R. 1987, *Capital and Labour on the Kimberley Diamond Fields, 1871–1890*, Cambridge University Press, Cambridge.

Vail, L. Ed. 1989, *The Creation of Tribalism in Southern Africa*, James Currey, London, University of California Press, Berkeley, California. Case studies in the contingent construction of identities within the region.

Van der Berg, S. 1991, 'Redirecting Government Expenditure', in Moll, T. et al. Eds, Cape Town.

Van Onselen, C. 1982, *Studies in the Social and Economic History of the Witwatersrand, 1886–1914*, (2 vols) Longman, London.

Wade, M. 1993, *White on Black in South Africa: A Study of English-Language Inscriptions of Skin Colour*, Macmillan, Basingstoke.

Walker, O. 1948, *Kaffirs are Lively*, Johannesburg.

Wellings, P. and Black, A. 1986, 'Industrial Decentralisation in South Africa: Tool of Apartheid or Spontaneous Restructuring?', *GeoJournal*, 12.

Welsh, D. 1987, 'Democratic Liberalism and Theories of Racial Stratification', in Butler, J. et al. Eds, Middletown, Connecticut.

Western, J. 1981, *Outcast Cape Town*, Allen and Unwin, London. Moving rendition of apartheid in Cape Town.

Western, J. 1982, 'The Geography of Urban Social Control: Group Areas and the 1976 and 1980 Civil Unrest in Cape Town', in Smith, D. Ed., London.

Western, J. 1985, 'Undoing the Colonial City?', *Geographical Review*, 75, 3.

Wills, T.M. 1991, 'Pietermaritzburg', in Lemon, A. Ed., Bloomington, Indiana and Cape Town.

Wilson, F. and Ramphele, M. 1989, *Uprooting Poverty: The South African Challenge*, Norton, New York and London.

Wilson, M. 1982a, 'Co-operation and Conflict: The Eastern Cape Frontier', in Wilson, M. and Thompson, L. Eds, London and Cape Town.

Wilson, M. 1982b, 'The Nguni People' and 'The Sotho, Venda and Tsonga', in Wilson, M. and Thompson, L. Eds, London and Cape Town.

Wilson, M. and Thompson, L. Eds 1982, *A History of South Africa to 1870*, Croom Helm, London and Cape Town.

Wolpe, H. 1972, 'Capitalism and Cheap Labour Power in South Africa: From Segregation to Apartheid', *Economy and Society*, 1, 4. Oft-cited attempt to interpret the transition from segregation to apartheid within a Marxist framework.

Wolpe, H. 1988, *Race, Class and the Apartheid State*, UNESCO, London.

Worden, N. 1994, *The Making of Modern South Africa: Conquest, Segregation and Apartheid*, Blackwell, Oxford. Usefully summarizes recent historical revisionism, but overlooks more recent wider currents of thought in the social sciences.

Worden, N. and Crais, C. Eds 1994, *Breaking the Chains: Slavery and its Legacy in the 19th Century Cape Colony*, Witwatersrand University Press, Johannesburg.

Wright, H.M. 1977, *The Burden of the Present: Liberal Radical Controversy Over Southern African History*, David Philip, Cape Town.

Wright, J. and Hamilton, C. 1989, 'Traditions and Transformations: The Phongolo-Mzimkhulu Region in the Late 18th Century and Early 19th Century', in Duminy, A. and Guest, W. Eds, Pietermaritzburg.

Young, R. 1990, *White Mythologies: Writing History and the West*, Routledge, London. Addresses itself to recent theorization about the role of the subject in history.

Young, T. 1989, 'Restructuring the State in South Africa: New Strategies of Incorporation and Control', *Political Studies*, 62.

Yudelman, D. 1984, *The Emergence of Modern South Africa: State, Capital and the Incorporation of Organized Labour on the South African Gold Fields, 1902–39*, David Philip, Cape Town and Johannesburg.

Yudelman, D. 1987, 'State and Capital in Contemporary South Africa', in Butler, J. et al. Eds, Middletown, Connecticut.

Yuvan-Davis, N. 1993, 'Whose Nation? Whose State?Racial/Ethnic Divisions and "the Nation" in Anthias, F. and Yuval-Davis, N. in association with Cain, H. *Racialized Boundaries: Race, Nation, Gender, Colour and Class in the Anti-Racist Struggle*, Routledge, London.

Index